BAD FAITH,
GOOD FAITH,
AND
AUTHENTICITY
IN SARTRE'S
EARLY
PHILOSOPHY

Bad Faith, Good Faith, and Authenticity in Sartre's Early Philosophy

Ronald E. Santoni

Temple University Press

Philadelphia

Temple University Press,
Philadelphia 19122
Copyright © 1995 by Temple University
All rights reserved
Published 1995
Printed in the United States of America

**Library of Congress
Cataloging-in-Publication Data**

Santoni, Ronald E.
    Bad faith, good faith, and authenticity in
Sartre's early philosophy / Ronald E.
Santoni.
        p.   cm.
    Includes bibliographical references
and index.
        ISBN 1–56639–319–1 (case). —
        ISBN 1–56639–320–5 (pbk.)
    1.   Sartre, Jean Paul, 1905–
2. Authenticity (Philosophy)
3. Self-deception.   I. Title.
B2430.S34S314   1995
128—dc20   94–44692

Dedicated
to
MOM and DAD,
and
MARGO and our SIX:
  CHRISTINA
  MARCIA
  ANDREA
  JUANITA
  JONATHAN
  SONDRA
with
LOVE,
GRATITUDE,
and
THANKSGIVING

Contents

Preface

Although normally attributed to one author—who customarily and courteously accepts full responsibility for the work she or he has written—any book is the product of a community of cooperation and support. The luxury of scholarship and authorship, though requiring self-discipline, resolve, perseverance, and periods of lonely isolation, would not be possible without the shared concern, assistance, friendship, love, and often sacrifice of others. An author can assume responsibility for his or her work without asking others to share it, but an author cannot fairly take credit for a work without giving credit to others. The publication of a book is renewed testimony in support of Sartre's developed recognition that, far from simply threatening "being for-itself" or individual freedom, the Other may enhance or nurture it.

I realize that the number of people or groups to whom I want to give credit is relatively large and that, by mentioning their names, I run the risk of overlooking or slighting others who also have given help or support. But life cannot be lived creatively without risk, and to me it is more important to acknowledge some people personally, at the price of forgetting a few, than to give only lump or anonymous credit. My unmentioned helpers may at least note the generosity of my intent.

Because of history and recent circumstances, I wish first, and again, to acknowledge my debt to my parents, Fred and Phyllis Santoni, who, deprived of a university education themselves, demonstrated the foresight, industry, determination, and sacrifice to enable their children to have what they did not have by way of early opportunity. Without their commitment and encouragement, my present career and opportunities would have likely remained only dreams and awkwardly formulated aspirations. It is my deep regret that my father, who suffered the torment of terminal cancer while I was writing the last chapter of this book, is not alive to view its completion. But I shall cherish the more important completion of having spent a number of long weekends in conversation with him and my mother during his final painful and restless months. In part, at least, I offer this book in his memory.

Next, I express my profound gratitude to my wife, Margo, and our six children—Christina, Marcia, Andrea, Juanita, Jonathan, and Sondra. Subjected to both the beauties and the trials of academic existence, they have together responded with scarcely credible love and support—even criticism when deserved! Although our meal table has not always been a model of organization, it has been a vital center for lively discussion and vehement exchange of ideas among family members alone or among family members with students and colleagues, present or past. It is hard to imagine how anyone could contribute more patiently and selflessly to the sustenance of an academic home, with all its erratic and unpredictable demands, than has my wife, Margo. She has done this with "amazing grace" and an uplifting spirit, while knowing who she is and preserving her autonomy. Without her I could not have done what I have done to this point, however inadequate or humble that may turn out to be. As a mother, life-partner, friend, fellow activist, and human being, she merits sainthood as much as anyone I know. Her moral spirit and penetrating intellect have kept me in place. And our children have gladly joined in testing my inclinations to endorse Sartre's emphasis on autonomy and an ethics of "no excuses." With and through them I have matured.

I wish also to express my indebtedness to fellow scholars who nurtured my developing interest in Sartre (in spite of my dominant training in Analytic philosophy) and encouraged my continuing probes into the ontological roots of some of Sartre's perplexing views, through dialogue and critical exchange in professional colloquia and published discussion. In particular, I thank Phyllis Morris, Maurice Natanson, Joe Catalano, and Karsten Harries, who were not only among the first to engage me concerning my early writings on Sartre but, in one fashion or another, have continued that creative dialectic with me since then. In the same vein, I express appreciation to members of the Sartre Circle, the Sartre Society of North America, and the Society for Phenomenology, who either at specific group meetings or at meetings of the American Philosophical Association, listened to what I had to say and confirmed that disagreement still flourishes in Sartrean scholarship. For the inspiration and encouragement of Hazel Barnes, at these meetings and elsewhere, I am grateful, as I am for continuing conversation with Tom Rockmore, Bill McBride, Tom Flynn, and Ron Aronson, to name only a few. Having been party in the early 1980s to discussions culminating in the formation of the Sartre Circle and the Sartre Society, it has been heartwarming for me to watch these groups grow from small, overlapping bands of committed inquirers to full-fledged fellowships of Sartrean scholars, whose "proceedings" have taken on international significance with respect to Sartre.

There are other associates whose direct or indirect assistance I wish to acknowledge: my long-time friends David Sprintzen and Quentin Kraft, who, though focused on the works of other writers, have had the knack of asking the right Sartrean questions and of insisting on straightforward answers to straightforward queries; my philosophy colleagues at Denison University, especially my long-term colleagues, Anthony Lisska, David Goldblatt, Philip Glotzbach, Steven Vogel, and the late Maylon Hepp, who have put up with my idiosyncrasies and sometimes impatience and raised pertinent questions about earlier versions of some of these chapters (it would be hard to find a more genial and dynamic group of divergent philosophers with whom to work); Benny Lévy, Sartre's closest collaborator during Sartre's last ten years, who, though he did not always see eye to eye with some of my approaches to Sartre, was more than willing, on three occasions, to share with me his own perceptive insights on Sartre and Sartre's philosophy; Michel Contat and Michel Rybalka, whose bibliographical work on Sartre is monumental and to whom any serious writer or researcher on Sartre owes information, insight, the saving of time, and gratitude; and all students of mine who took seriously my admonition to resist discipleship and pressed me to make sense of some of Sartre's most obscure and controversial allegations. It is for my students, perhaps as much as for my colleagues, that I have written this book, and to them I offer thanks for the richness, challenge, and growth that the academic life affords.

Next, I wish to give credit to those persons and institutions who provided the means and environments that allowed my preparation of this book and related writing: the Robert C. Good Faculty Fellowship Committee, which on two occasions supported me with prized awards that kept my family and me nourished while I focused on writing new words rather than orally expressing old ones; the Committee on Professional Development of Denison University and the Denison University Research Foundation, for funding various projects related to this book or my testing of some of its ideas at professional meetings; the Governing Body of Clare Hall, Cambridge University, and the Faculty of Philosophy at Cambridge, for appointments—as Visiting Fellow, Visiting Scholar, Life Member, and Invited Lecturer—which, on three occasions during the past eight years, have allowed me to write and work (and, during one stay, even to teach) in the culturally rich and optimal conditions of Cambridge; the Philosophy Department of Yale University and its administrative assistant Pat Slatter, who provided the appointments, resources, setting, and friendship that were important for my finishing the substance of this book during the academic year 1993–1994 and for my completing other writing projects during earlier stays there; Pat Davis, departmental secretary and keeper of order for philosophers at Denison, who had the unenviable and exasperating responsibility of converting the many drafts of my illegible and rather chaotic handwritten pages into stately printed sheets from the word processor; Angie Harder and (again) Pat Slatter of the Yale staff, who, with generosity of spirit and amazing cheerfulness, assumed the task of retyping yet another of my revisions of the two earliest chapters; Michael Jung, an artist colleague at Denison, who, with little notice but much Sartrean commitment, readily prepared the drawing of Sartre that appears on the cover of this book; the current administration of Denison University—in particular, President Michele Myers and Provost Charlie Morris—who, while acknowledging that I can be a thorn in their sides, have given tangible evidence of supporting my work and scholarly needs and even of appreciating my watchful presence; and, finally, the late Robert C. Good, a former president of Denison University after whom the Faculty Fellowships are named, who left at Denison a standard of academic and moral expectation that other university administrations might properly emulate.

In conclusion, I express my appreciation to the staff of Temple University Press: to former Senior Acquisitions Editor Jane Cullen, a strikingly decent, conscientious, and pleasant person who first exhibited to me the distinctively human dimension which (in my view) differentiates Temple University Press from other presses with which I have worked (I am glad to be part of a noteworthy list which she so caringly cultivated); to David Bartlett, director of the press, and Doris Braendel, the present senior acquisitions editor, for their parallel encouragement and guidance (I have been struck by the humaneness of their concerns in and out of publishing and for their eagerness to engage in genuine discussion on diverse topics); and to all other unnamed people at the press who have helped to guide this book through production. Together they represent additional testimony to my opening statement that the publication of a book signals the work of a community of cooperation and support, not simply the acknowledged labor of one author.

Acknowledgments

The author gratefully acknowledges permission to use significant portions of previously published articles from the editors of the following journals:

International Philosophical Quarterly, for "The Cynicism of Sartre's 'Bad Faith,'" published in *International Philosophical Quarterly*, vol. 30, no. 1 (March 1990), pp. 3–15.

Pacific Philosophical Quarterly, for "Sartre on 'Sincerity': Bad Faith? or Equivocation?, from *Pacific Philosophical Quarterly*, vol. 53, no. 2 (Spring 1972), pp. 150–160.

Philosophy Today, for "Sartre on Sincerity—A Reconsideration," from *Philosophy Today*, vol. 29, no. 2/4 (Summer 1985), pp. 142–147.

Philosophy and Phenomenological Research, for "Bad Faith and 'Lying to Oneself,'" from *Philosophy and Phenomenological Research*, vol. 38, no. 3 (March 1978), pp. 384–398.

R. E. S.
Cambridge, England
July 1994

Introduction

The philosophy of Jean-Paul Sartre is one to which too many philosophers, academics, and laypersons allude, but too few read—at least seriously. I believe that, if one attempts to penetrate even part of Sartre's vast and complex philosophical system, one is confronted not only with some important insights into our human condition but also with existentially disturbing challenges and gnawing difficulties.

One such challenge and difficulty relates to Sartre's views concerning "bad faith" (mauvaise foi), a concept and phenomenon with which, directly or indirectly, Sartre seems to have been concerned from the beginning to the end of his philosophizing. A careful student of Sartre might justifiably argue that bad faith and the possibility of overcoming it form the pervasive interest of his philosophy: the one that, for example, generates his existential inquiry and dominates his psychoanalysis, his biographies, his social and political philosophy, and—perhaps most significantly—his autobiography. To be sure, Sartre's discussion in *The Words* of his own youthful fakery and bad faith is not even subtle. In plain terms it not only suggests the ubiquity of bad faith in Sartre's worldview but also shows that, for Sartre, bad faith is a deeply existential, not simply an academic, concern.

Scores of articles and chapters of books have either cited, commented sketchily on, or, less often, attempted to explicate

Jean-Paul Sartre's views on bad faith. Virtually no aspect of his monumental philosophical corpus (with the possible exception of his position on freedom) has generated more widespread, though not always informed, attention and discussion. It is as if Sartre's pervasive concern with bad faith (or "self-deception," as some writers have insisted) struck a human nerve in philosophers and nonphilosophers alike and, whether comprehended intellectually or not, elicited a response of familiarity, sometimes passion, and often resistance. To both the casual reader and the meticulous student of Sartre's works, Sartre's views on bad faith represented, for the most part, a challenge rather than comfort, grounds for a kind of Tolstoyan self-reexamination rather than existential security or self-complacency. Moreover, though they bring diverging interests and assumptions to Sartre's analysis, continental and analytic philosophers, psychologists and psychiatrists, and scholars of literature and sociology have all raised questions about the very possibility of bad faith and the possibility of overcoming it, given Sartre's ontological assumptions and his outright rejection of the Freudian unconscious in *Being and Nothingness* and elsewhere.

One could not come close to saying the same about Sartre's concept of "good faith," a concept that one might reasonably expect to be unambiguously antithetical to bad faith. For one thing, Sartre himself devotes only two or three analytic pages to it and does so in the context of a detailed discussion of bad faith. For another, scholars of Sartre, limited initially—and mainly—to Sartre's clipped and dense comparative statements on those few pages of *Being and Nothingness (L'être et le néant)*,[1] often pass over this brief and perplexing technical analysis by either resting content with an assumed ordinary-language meaning of good faith or by turning to more readily accessible discussions in Sartre. Few appear willing to try to process, for example, Sartre's baffling counterintuitive claim that good faith (or "sincerity," for that matter) shares the project and goal of bad faith. To date, among commentators writing in English, only Joseph Catalano, I believe, has given sustained and detailed consideration to Sartre's view of good faith (see his "On the Possibility of Good Faith"). And, when writers on Sartre have referred to good faith only in passing, they have, more often than not, shown little sensitivity to what I believe is a much-needed distinction between good faith and authenticity in Sartre. They frequently use the term *good faith* as if it were interchangeable with *authenticity* and constituted the constructive antithesis to, and way out of, bad faith.

To make matters worse, the meaning of authenticity, too, is not immediately evident to readers of Sartre. In early publications—and, more surprisingly, in later ones also—Sartre himself sometimes uses the two expressions synonymously. And, if one were to rely on *Being and Nothingness*, his pivotal ontological work, for an elucidation of Sartrean authenticity, one would encounter disappointment and frustration, for one finds here but cryptic footnote mention of it, combined with some skeletal references to it here and there in the body of the text. Though Sartre declares his intent, in this work, to give the name "authenticity" to "self-recovery" (from the corruption of being), he deliberately abstains from describing it. It is only in the posthumously published *The War Diaries (Carnets de la drôle de guerre)*—in fact written a few years (1939–1940) before the publication of *Being and Nothingness* (1943)—that a searching reader of Sartre sees him unfolding the formative details of his ontological analysis of authenticity and the passage from (presumably) bad faith to authenticity. And, as we shall see, when focused on later writings, this posthumous publication is used to clarify, for example, *Anti-Semite and Jew (Réflexions sur la question juive)* and anticipate what Sartre will say in another, just recently translated (1992) (and long-awaited) posthumous publication, *Notebook for an Ethics (Cahiers pour une morale)*.

In short, although Sartre's notion of bad faith has engaged the interest of academics and laypersons alike—and has even become a kind of watchword for many seeking to understand Existentialist thought—it has hardly been free of conceptual confusion, controversy, and lack of detailed understanding. And bad faith's correlative concepts of good faith and authenticity have suffered not only neglect or belated attention, in that order, but also misunderstanding or obscurity through interchangeable use and plain misspeaking, sometimes by Sartre himself. Moreover, readers of Sartre, struck by the pervasiveness of his concern about bad faith, or worried about the accuracy of his analysis, have had legitimate grounds for asking whether Sartre's ontology allows for an overcoming of bad faith and whether, given Sartre's diverging texts, he intends good faith or authenticity to designate that transcending "possibility," or transformed mode of existing. In a word, questions of clarity and interpretation persist regarding both Sartre's views on bad faith as a driving existential/philosophical concern and his views on good faith and authenticity as possible alternate existential attitudes. (I take the word *attitude* from Sartre's own reference to bad faith and good faith, in *Being and Nothingness*, as "two immediate attitudes."[2]) So, in spite of all that has been written (much of it too general) about Sartre's early philosophy, Sartrean scholarship distinctly invites—nay, needs—a rigorous, detailed analysis and differentiation of these basic existential attitudes and, in the light of such clarification, a carefully argued response to some basic questions generated by previous scholarship and repeated by more cursory readers of Sartre. To the best of my knowledge, no previous study of Sartre has attempted such a differentiation or focused exclusively on bad faith in relation to its correlative existential attitudes of good faith and authenticity. So the time for such disentanglement is ripe; and, given the pessimism too often associated with Sartre's philosophy, especially his early philosophy, it is also time to trace the development and progressive clarity in Sartre's early writings of existential attitudes or ways of existing that suggest a deliverance from the bad faith that, in Sartre's view, congenitally and perennially threatens us.

In this book, I attempt to take on that task and challenge. Specifically, I propose to offer a detailed analytic examination, reconstruction, and differentiation of Sartre's categories of bad faith, good faith, and authenticity as they develop in Sartre's early philosophy (1937–1947). Although I shall focus mainly on *The War Diaries, Being and Nothingness,* "Existentialism Is a Humanism," and *Anti-Semite and Jew,* for my analysis and building of my case, I shall have recourse to other of his works (such as *The Transcendence of the Ego*) and shall, in the end, test my analysis and contentions against his expansive notes in that goldmine of his posthumous publications, *Notebooks for an Ethics.* And, although I shall try rather meticulously to clarify and distinguish each concept in this triad of interconnected categories, it will become clear that it is the challenge posed by Sartre's analysis of bad faith, and my wish to clear the muddle related to conceptual overlap (for example, of "sincerity," "good faith," and "inauthenticity") and Sartre's intended way out of bad faith, that will drive my inquiry here. The reader is entitled to know at the outset that it was Sartre's controversial ontological account of bad faith, coupled with his persevering concern for the nature of authentic existing—both of which happen to coincide with some of my own existential concerns—that steered me away from many of the "regulative" issues of my analytic training and early writing to the concerns of human existence that engaged Sartre and other continental philosophers of his generation. So it is not an overstatement to say that the concept of bad faith, which teased my earliest encounters with Sartre, is at the core of this book; and, further, that the progression of the book's chapters reflects the progression of my related philosophical worries about the soundness and implications of Sartre's analysis, as well as my interest in determining the overall coherence and feasibility of both Sartre's correlative attitudes and his creative alternative to the "hell" of bad faith. The logic of my book's development and argument will become increasingly evident as the book unfolds. And I expect it to move in the direction of showing how a detailed and lucid differentiation of these three basic attitudes can provide the framework for an unambiguously affirmative prospect for overcoming the "immediate attitude"[3] of bad faith in Sartre's philosophy.

In my opening chapter, "Bad Faith and Sincerity: Does Sartre's Analysis Rest on a Mistake?" I do not begin, as a reader might understandably expect, with a full-scale, focused examination of Sartre's systematic analysis of bad faith. I begin, rather, with a methodical discussion of a problem that disturbed my initial readings of Sartre's treatment of bad faith and virtually transformed my passing interest in Sartre's philosophy into a scholarly resolve to understand, critically assess, reconstruct, and reformulate certain central aspects of it. Consistent with my philosophical autobiography, but not controlled by it, this procedure allows me, as I suggested above, to develop Sartre's analysis and challenge of bad faith in the increasing light, detail, and counterchallenge of the problems that I experienced with Sartre's position as I progressively studied and engaged it. Continuing questions prompted continuing reconsideration and refinement of my response to it.

My initial acquaintance with Sartre's "bad faith" left me baffled by his contention that "sincerity" is a "phenomenon of bad faith" and that the "project" of sincerity shares the phenomenological structure and goal of bad faith. My opening chapter expresses that bafflement and attempts to show Sartre's alleged grounds for turning a cherished notion into an illustration of a category and project of bad faith. But, just as importantly, I try here to show that this surprising move takes place through Sartre's *misuse* of the core ontological system that he had developed by 1943 and formulated in his Introduction (entitled "The Pursuit of Being") to *Being and Nothingness*. In short, I contend, as part of my earliest response to Sartre's entanglements with bad faith, that Sartre's thesis about the bad faith of sincerity is rooted in and riddled with an equivocal application of his idiomatic ontological meaning of "to be what one is" to the ordinary-language use of the phrase.

My argument requires both a skeletal account of the Sartrean framework out of which the problem emerges and my initial, though incomplete, formulation of Sartre's analysis of bad faith. Each will run through the book but will be developed and honed in subsequent chapters to form my cumulative response to the issues that my study generates. Yet, even before the conclusion of this chapter, I suggest an alternative to Sartre's approach to sincerity which, while remaining consistent with the terms of his ontological system, anticipates in an embryonic form what Sartre will subsequently offer as his conception of "authenticity" or authentic existence. This sketchy connection is retrospective: I neither saw it nor tried to explore it during my writing of the initial version of this chapter. Nonetheless, my very outline of a more optimistic Sartrean account of sincerity already suggests a way of overcoming our ontological disposition to bad faith and thus calls for a more intense confrontation with more of the details of Sartre's understanding of bad faith. To precisely this task I turn in the next chapter, but not before I consider closely some criticisms raised against the first published version of my "equivocation" argument. Although my reply is intended to give added clarity and substance to my charge, it also presses for a consideration of whether Sartre's analysis of bad faith is viable or tenable.

In Chapter 2, I elaborate the details of Sartre's analysis of bad faith through the notion of "lying to oneself." Chapter I made clear that Sartre initially views bad faith as a kind of "lying to oneself." Chapter 2 is driven by the problem of trying to reconcile bad faith as lying to oneself with Sartre's view of consciousness. If, in fact, consciousness is translucent *(translucide)*, as Sartre insists, and if lying involves hiding or masking the truth, then how can one hide a truth from oneself or deceive oneself, in the inevitable openness and unity of consciousness; in short, how then is bad faith possible? It is Sartre himself who first acknowledges and formulates the problem. But, armed with concrete examples of bad faith and convinced that self-deception is part of our everyday experience, he sets out to show *how* bad faith is possible. I in turn, bothered by the tension within Sartre's position, pursue the question of the feasibility of lying to oneself on Sartre's anti-Freudian terms. If there is no "unconscious," how can Sartre's view of bad faith as lying to oneself be salvaged?

In the "strict" sense of lying (as in lying to the Other), I argue that it cannot. But, by attending more closely to the details of Sartre's analysis, in particular to his concept of *non-persuasive* evidence, I attempt to show the psychological mechanism by which a translucent consciousness can lie to itself in a qualified or modified sense of "lying." To be sure, bad faith for Sartre depends on the ambivalent and mercurial "double-property" of "facticity-transcendence," which he attributes to consciousness. But I contend that his view of bad faith as lying to oneself holds, or can be salvaged, only if one recognizes with Sartre (1) that bad faith, viewed epistemologically, is faith and belief, *not* certainty; and (2) that the primitive project of bad faith, by setting weak requirements for evidence, structures itself in ad-

vance to accept selective and non-persuasive evidence as persuasive, and to consider itself persuaded even when it is only
partially or half persuaded. In this manner, bad faith as a distinctly qualified form of lying to oneself does not collapse before
the translucency of consciousness. But, in surviving, it resembles, I contend, what Sartre views as common lies of "half-persuasion" and refers to as "degenerate aspects" or forms of the
lie. It is hardly a thoroughly successful hiding of truth from
consciousness, and it is a far cry from what Sartre calls the
"ideal lie."

I conclude Chapter 2 with my initial suggestion that, in spite
of Sartre's denial, Sartre's bad faith phenomenon involves a
"cynical consciousness" in which one prepares for one's self-
deceit. This is precisely the worry that generates my continued
probing into Sartre's analysis of bad faith and leads readily to
my analysis and argument of the next chapter.

Hence, in Chapter 3, I propose to elucidate, develop, and
argue for the contention that I only suggest at the conclusion of
the preceding chapter. Although, in my judgment, my reconstruction of Sartrean bad faith to this point has already exhibited a cynical element—at least in the common-usage sense of
"cynical"—I recognize that, in the light of Sartre's sharp dis-
avowal, I need a more careful understanding of Sartre's view of
cynicism in relation to the details of his mechanism of the bad
faith project. I can hardly rely on an ordinary-language sense
of cynicism alone. So, on the basis of Sartre's parsimonious references, I attempt to disentangle what Sartre means by the
"doubly negative attitude" by which he characterizes the "cynical consciousness" of the "ideal lie" (or "strict" lie) to the Other.
Because lying to the Other is, for Sartre, a "phenomenon of
transcendence," its cynicism—its double feature of denying or
negating to itself the falsity (the negation of truth) it is conveying
to the Other—is entirely conceivable. But (I contend), because

of the translucency and unitary structure of consciousness, Sartre disallows the possibility of the cynical consciousness for bad faith. Against Sartre, I argue that the unity and translucency of consciousness rule out for bad faith *only* the "ideal" cynicism that marks the completely successful concealment of truth from the Other, as in the strict lie. Then, relating each aspect of Sartre's cynical lie to the machinations of bad faith as lying to oneself, I attempt to show that a modified form of the cynical lie does take place in lying to oneself or self-deception and how it does so. I contend that even the reassurances that, in bad faith, I give to myself, meet one of Sartre's essential conditions for cynicism; and that, through Sartre's mechanism of half-persuasion, I am able, in lying to myself, to offer my intended reassurances from the perspective of a feigned or false character which—as in the strict, cynical lie to the Other—I take on and adopt *as mine.* In short, I conclude that the structure of bad faith as conceived by Sartre bears, though sometimes in a qualified way, most of the marks by which Sartre has characterized the cynical consciousness.

Although my two preceding chapters focus on bad faith and bring out in detail the manner and mechanism by which bad faith takes place, they hardly complete the story on bad faith, or indicate beyond mere mention or suggestion what Sartre would regard as either the antithesis or the overcoming of bad faith. Indeed, one way of understanding a concept or category better is by coming to terms with its opposite or correlative concept(s). But in the case of Sartre's philosophy, as I have already pointed out, this project becomes problematic because of his appearing to view both sincerity and good faith as sharing bad faith's ideal of being in-itself. If one is to understand bad faith and alternate existential attitudes in Sartre, I am persuaded that one must make sense out of and try to reconstruct Sartre's puzzling account of good faith. One cannot consistently regard good faith both as the opposite or antithesis of bad faith and as an example or instance of the project of bad faith.

Thus, in Chapter 4, I set out to clarify and then, if possible, to rescue "good faith" in Sartre from the conflicting and negative connotations that Sartre's skeletal account sometimes implies. I attempt to do so within the broader aim and context of beginning to explore the relation, in Sartre's formative writings, between good faith and authenticity. Both are "attitudes" or "modes of existing" which Sartre variously offers as contrasting alternatives to bad faith and which interpreters of Sartre (sometimes even Sartre himself) tend to confound and use interchangeably. My attempt to reconstruct good faith as a salvageable and constructive alternative to bad faith becomes the first stage of my overall effort, in the next chapters, to differentiate the "immediate attitude" of good faith from authenticity, and to determine whether, in the end, it is a redeemed sense of good faith, or authenticity, that spells the possibility of genuine self-recovery (from bad faith) in Sartre.

Observing closely the lines of Sartre's limited text on good faith, and following the pioneering lead of Sartre commentator Joe Catalano, I not only emphasize the contrasting attitudes that good and bad faith have toward the ideal of faith (that is, "the unwavering firmness of belief"), but also distance myself from Catalano's view that the ideal of good faith must be seen solely in terms of bad faith's projection of what good faith ought to be. Although I acknowledge that initially the ideal of good faith may, like the "*a priori* ideal of all consciousness," be an ideal of self-consciousness and Being, I argue that good faith, though predisposed to faith's (and human reality's) desire for completeness, for "unwavering firmness of belief," refuses either to pursue this ideal as a goal, or—as does bad faith—to exploit the impossibility of "perfect belief" in order to bypass critical evidence and put unpleasant beliefs and truths out of reach.

Far from using the instability and evanescence of consciousness as an excuse for running away from the freedom of consciousness, or for trying to tie down selected and unjustified
belief, good faith accepts the ambiguity, elusiveness, interrogation, and noncoincidence that are at the heart of *all* consciousness and belief. Put another way, in accepting its freedom, the
good faith consciousness refuses to adopt any project of giving
up its freedom.

I bring to a head my attempt to redeem good faith by making
evident what my inquiry has already shown indirectly; namely,
that good faith in Sartre can, after analysis, be seen from two
clear perspectives: epistemological and ontological. In contrast
to bad faith, good faith, viewed *epistemologically*, retains an
open and critical attitude toward evidence and refuses to allow
the impossibility of self-coincidence of consciousness to become a rationale for bypassing rigorous criteria of evidence and
persuasion. And, unlike bad faith, it refuses to invoke "two-
faced" or ambiguous concepts in order to persuade itself or
self-deceptive beliefs. Yet, more basically, good faith must also
be viewed *ontologically*, in terms of how consciousness responds to its troubled ontological freedom. The good faith consciousness (and "attitude"), in contrast to bad faith, accepts its
abandonment to freedom and responsibility and the anguish
connected with it; that is to say, it (pre-reflectively) accepts
(rather than flees) human reality. In short, it is self-acceptance
as freedom.

To this chapter's topical question, "Can good faith be salvaged?" my answer, then, is strongly affirmative, though with
one qualification: I acknowledge that if, as Sartre suggests, the
project of good faith has been distorted by bad faith's goal of
pursuing and attaining identity and self-coincidence, then good
faith would be condemned to bad faith. But, I conclude, Sartre's
ontology and text do *not* require it.

Yet, as I have already repeated, any readiness to accept good faith as the antithesis of bad faith or as the *only* way out of bad faith leaves one with the question, "Well, what about 'authenticity'?"—a notion that, before analysis, seems strikingly similar to my reconstruction of good faith, and that many passing commentators often fail to distinguish from good faith. It is to this question that I move in Chapter 5. And although, as I have already said, *Being and Nothingness* refers, mainly in footnotes, to authenticity as representing "self-recovery" and "deliverance," it offers little to elucidate the concept. For this reason, as well as to trace the development of Sartre's view of authenticity, I turn to Sartre's lesser works, in particular to his posthumously published *The War Diaries*, in which he proclaims his struggle for authenticity in the "situation" of a "phony war." Here, I contend, we find details of authenticity that are not only seminal but also directive with respect to his maturing conception of authenticity. "Assumptive conversion," "realizing fully one's being-in-situation," willing the "adoption of reality as one's own," "claiming responsibility," "refusing excuses," affirming "true fidelity to ourselves," and "self-recovery," are all marks of Sartre's earliest thinking about authenticity. And, in these *War Diaries*, Sartre even anticipates his worry that the project of authenticity might, by trying to tie down authenticity, become a project of bad faith.

Passing to *Anti-Semite and Jew* (written six or seven years after *The War Diaries*), in which Sartre focuses on the issue of authenticity, I attempt to show that, although Sartre here situates the issue of authenticity in a clear *social*, rather than ontological, context, he does not part from his dominant emphasis on a lucid recognition of who one is in the human condition, or on "living" one's unjustifiable freedom and taking responsibility for it, whatever the situation may be. To be sure, Sartre attributes greater power here to the "situation"—a tendency that progresses in the course of his philosophical development but comes to complement and extend, not to dislocate, his main line of ontological analysis in *The War Diaries*. The confrontation with and acceptance (or rejection) of one's freedom in relation to given social or historical circumstances or structures is inseparably bound up, I contend, with the "attitude" one adopts in relation to human reality, that is, to ontological freedom. And although, in *Anti-Semite and Jew*, Sartre does not take note of or discuss the "willed conversion" and "self-recovery" that figure so prominently in *The War Diaries*, it seems to me clear that, while applying his earlier ontological account of authenticity to the specific social situation of anti-Semitism and racism, he simply takes for granted—for example, in his references to the authentic Jew—the "self-recovery" or "deliverance" that is possible and effected through a willed "assumptive conversion." The "authentic" person rejects "flight" and society's "petrified values" by *reflectively* choosing to value and live the "unsettledness" and "dis-ease" of one's elusive "metastable" and nonsubstantial consciousness or freedom.

I conclude this exploratory chapter on Sartre's "authenticity" by offering a brief account of the relevant views of Francis Jeanson, who eventually became one of Sartre's closest intellectual collaborators. Because of Sartre's glowing assessment of Jeanson's "reading" of the early Sartre in *Le problème moral et la pensée de Sartre*, I use Jeanson's interpretation not only to further my inquiry and offer additional clarification, but also to test the latter against what scholars of Sartre often regard as the "approved" reading or interpretation. And it becomes clear that, though presumably written without access to *The War Diaries*, Jeanson's account strongly corroborates the formative view of authenticity that I have found in *The War Diaries*. With non-coincidence or, in Jeanson's terms, "ambiguity" at its core, human reality or freedom is continuously "susceptible to bad faith," is continuously inclined to fill its nothingness. But human freedom can radically convert, can deliver itself from this bad faith disposition and attitude by resolving—through a reflective, willed choice—to maintain its ambiguity, spontaneity, and gratuity—whatever the situation—and accept responsibility for all of its initiatives. This passage from a "natural bad faith" to a willed self-affirmation of one's freedom and responsibility constitutes, in Jeanson's interpretation, the passage to authenticity and self-recovery. But, for Jeanson, much more pronouncedly than for my own initial reading of Sartre's early works, this existential move is from an awareness of one's ontological freedom (what he calls "factual freedom") to the *valuing* (or "valorization") of that freedom (hence, "freedom-as-valued"). For Jeanson, this conversion to authenticity in Sartre is, unequivocally, a "moral" conversion in which the human being, in self-recovery (from what, in *The War Diaries*, he has called its "fall" into the world), takes on "moral agency." This emphasis, certainly consistent with the details of *The War Diaries* and, as I shall show, with Sartre's *Notebooks for an Ethics*, adds definition and further direction to my investigation and argument.

But the clarification I have offered so far through my positive reconstruction of good faith and my attempt to trace the development of Sartre's concept of authenticity in some of his formative works does not, of itself, answer the question that generated the inquiry of Chapter 5. I argued there that, in spite of human reality's natural quest for being, it is possible for human consciousness, *in good faith*, to confront and affirm its freedom without succumbing to the "flight" of bad faith. However, I also found that, for Sartre, the *authentic* consciousness is marked by a conversion from a natural attitude of fleeing one's freedom to an attitude of accepting, affirming, and valorizing the nonsubstantial freedom and the awesome responsibility to which one is abandoned and condemned. So, after analysis and reconstruction of these terms, even more than before we are left with the question: "How, if at all, can we differentiate authenticity from my redeemed sense of good faith in Sartre?"

It is precisely to this issue that I turn in Chapter 6. Having either mentioned or alluded to "marked resemblances" between these two attitudes or modes of consciousness, I now ask whether certain characteristics which I have attributed, with the help of Jeanson and Catalano, to Sartre's concept of authenticity may, in fact, turn out to be the differentiating features. Specifically, I ask (1) whether the "assumptive [and 'radical'] conversion," which figured so prominently in Sartre's earliest account of authenticity, is peculiar to authenticity; (2) whether this conversion, effected by the *will*, requires, for Sartre, a *reflective* consciousness that cannot, on Sartre's terms, be equally assigned to good or bad faith; and (3) whether authenticity alone, and not my "salvaged" senses of good faith, can carry us to the *moral* level or dimension of existence, or be considered a *moral* category. And, underlying all of these questions, in both the present chapter and the next (final) chapter, is the question of whether good faith, in its redeemed sense, or authenticity alone finally qualifies as the mode of existing that is antithetical to bad faith. In other words, for Sartre does authenticity alone provide the "self-recovery" or "deliverance" from bad faith's "corruption of being"?

Any systematic and detailed consideration of each of the first three questions leads me to conclude—though sometimes with qualifications—that, to be sure, *reflection* (in Sartre's sense), *radical conversion*, and *moral agency* are, together, the three characteristics that differentiate authenticity from the (reconceived) "immediate attitude" of good faith and provide the structure for understanding what *Being and Nothingness* failed to afford; namely, Sartre's way of salvation and deliverance. Although we saw good faith as an alternate attitude to bad faith, which did not share bad faith's spontaneous and immediate flight from anguish, we saw no evidence that Sartre allows for a radical conversion (or "alternation of being") to good faith, as he does with respect to authenticity. Rather, we observed that Sartre perceives good faith as one of the two *immediate* attitudes we can adopt in relation to our being as freedom. At most, the reflective awareness of the possibility of good faith "lays the foundation"—as Catalano would say—for the possibility of a radical change in our fundamental project: that is, of conversion to an authentic way of living. But it is clear, on analysis, that conversion, for Sartre, is a function of *will*, and *willing* is part of a *reflective* consciousness—a consciousness directing itself on consciousness—which, in its pure form, is trying to "recover" itself as nothingness, and as a "spontaneous project," rather than continue its pre-reflective project of fleeing freedom in the direction of the in-itself. In other words, reflection, I contend, is the means by which conversion to authenticity, not to good faith, takes place. And, insofar as good faith is a pre-reflective and "immediate attitude," there is no basis in the early Sartre for viewing it—as we must authenticity—as a *reflective* mode of consciousness or existence. This conclusion allows me to infer at this stage in my study that we may correctly view only authenticity, not good faith, as the way of self-recovery from bad faith; and that therefore only authenticity has the proper claim to being the mode of existing that is antithetical to bad faith in Sartre. Moreover, although I maintain that conversion to authenticity for Sartre marks a passage into the *moral* level of existence and constitutes entry into his "ethics of salvation," I am reluctant—in the light of some statements in the texts studied here—to exclude morality entirely from good and bad faith. The acceptance or rejection of freedom and responsibility, even at an alleged pre-reflective level, does not appear devoid of moral content or implication. In fact, Sartre's assessment of the "man of seriousness" in *Being and Nothing-ness* seems to involve a recognition of bad faith "on the moral plane." Yet, though I do not regard the moral or ethical differentiation of these two sets of categories as hard and fast, I remain convinced that the bulk of Sartre's formative writings makes evident Sartre's intent to make the moral dimension or level another of the distinguishing features of the existential attitude of authenticity. And this is in contrast to even a "redeemed" sense of good faith.

I do not conclude this penultimate chapter without viewing, at least briefly, my differentiating features in relation to Sartre's earliest version of his "existentialist theory of consciousness" as formulated in his brilliant *The Transcendence of the Ego* (*La Transcendance de l'ego;* published in 1937). Following the insights of Thomas Busch, I find here not only the core of much of Sartre's thinking about the role of purifying reflection in our conversion from a natural flight from freedom to an assuming of it, but also the fact that Sartre's thinking in this regard runs parallel to Husserl's notion of the *epoché,* or phenomenological "reduction," through which consciousness, by suspending its attachment to the world, can disengage itself from the "natural attitude" in favor of what Husserl calls the "phenomenological attitude." That is to say, even in *The Transcendence of the Ego,* a consciousness "alienated" by its "natural [bad faith] attitude" can be transformed by a purifying reflection that is comparable to Husserl's "bracketing." Moreover, in regard to an ethical or moral dimension, there is limited, but telling, evidence in *The Transcendence of the Ego*—as Busch has pointed out—for concluding that, by following Husserl's lead here, Sartre already regards this transformation as a *moral* passage to the assumption of responsibility for oneself and others. In short, the differentiating marks that I have attributed to post-conversion authenticity are upheld, not frustrated, by what Sartre says in his essay *The Transcendence of the Ego*. And my "backing up" to *The Transcendence of the Ego*, after analyzing subsequent works of Sartre, also provides support for my contention that authenticity is intended by Sartre as the way out of bad faith as a corrupted consciousness. Thus, in its skeletal way, *The Transcendence of the Ego* both clarifies the source of Sartre's thought and substantiates the main line of argument I have developed in this inquiry.

In my original conception of this book, I anticipated concluding my monograph immediately after my inquiry had yielded the differentiation I had brought to a head in this "differentiating" chapter. And, although I had made brief passing (and supporting) references to Sartre's *Notebooks for an Ethics* (written in 1945 but published only in 1983), I had no intention of including any intensive study of the *Notebooks* as part of my inquiry. If anything, I had deliberately intended to do my work of analysis, reconstruction, and differentiation *without* any protracted appeal to this posthumous publication. But, after deferring my in-depth study of these *Notebooks* until after writing Chapter 6, I determined that my book would be incomplete and I should be remiss in my responsibility to my project and reader, were I not to relate details of this important work to my tentative findings—if only to elucidate further and to test my conclusions. For it became clear to me that no work of Sartre focused more directly on the features of his *authentic* consciousness or brought greater clarity to his view of the passage from bad faith to authentic existence, that is, to deliverance from our natural attitude. And, although incomplete, these *Notebooks* clearly appear to be Sartre's detailed outline for his future work on ethics, which he promised at the end of *Being and Nothingness*—the beginning *and* end, I believe of his ontological, "idealist," or "writer's" ethics.

Hence, in my concluding Chapter 7, my purpose is multifold.

In trying to show the contribution of the *Notebooks* to our understanding of the nature of authenticity in Sartre, I first aim to exhibit what is peculiar to the discussion of it there; namely, the project of "unveiling" or "illuminating" (Sartre is clearly influenced by Heidegger in this regard). Second, while disentangling the *Notebooks'* more mature view of the "original structure" of authentic existence, I set out to test my differentiating thesis against this fuller ontological account, and then to show that the latter vindicates the criterial marks by which I have differentiated authenticity in my foregoing inquiry. In addition, I propose to fill gaps in my preceding analysis and to test other cumulative answers I have offered to the emerging questions and issues of this inquiry.

Very early in the *Notebooks*, we learn that authenticity "lies in unveiling being through the modes of non-being." And later we come to find that reflection is an "unveiling of freedom"[4] and that the authentic for-itself "unveils itself to itself" through a reflective "reprise" in "the immediacy of its perpetual calling into question *(Erlebnis)*."[5] The *reflective* assuming of myself as mine constitutes a *conversion* that renounces identity and appropriation and reveals or discloses the "unappropriable aspect" of *Erlebnis*. A ready connection, I submit, appears to be made among unveiling, reflection, conversion, and authenticity. And Sartre's detailed contrast in the *Notebooks* between the project of *Causa Sui* and the project of creative unveiling, coupled with his outline of "unveiling" in *Truth and Existence (Verité et existence)*—a short work written concurrently with the *Notebooks*—makes clear his distinction between the "natural" projection of the bad faith consciousness to be its own foundation, and the authentic consciousness unveiling and accepting itself as an identityless, gratuitous freedom destined "to manifest Being." Sartre's identification of reflection with a "form of willing"; his understanding of the relationship between pure and impure, purifying and accessory reflection; his conception of conversion in terms of pure reflection's willing the project of spontaneity and autonomy (that is, freedom's "recovering" itself by reclaiming itself as "choice" and taking "itself as end") are never unveiled more clearly than in the *Notebooks*. And, in spite of Sartre's attempt to distance himself from Heidegger, I attempt to show that, at least structurally, the role of purifying reflection in Sartre's conversion to an "authentic way of existing" has close affinities to Heidegger's view of the role of "resoluteness" in relation to authenticity.

Regarding the ethical and moral dimension, I contend that, once again, Sartre's *Notebooks* confirm and enlighten my ascription of it to Sartre's concept of authenticity. Not only does Sartre sometimes refer here to conversion as "moral" but he indicates clearly that the transformation brought about by purifying reflection is a purifying value transformation in which, by valuing and living the gratuity and "new tension" of freedom, one can be liberated from one's "primitive alienation." Put another way, by "unveiling" and "assuming" my freedom, by transforming my contingency into autonomy, I take on responsibility for myself, for all my meanings, for others, and for the world. As Simone de Beauvoir has said in *The Ethics of Ambiguity*, no doubt using Sartre's ontology as ground, "Ethics is the triumph of freedom over facticity." Sartre in the *Notebooks*, I suggest, appears content with his claim in "Existentialism Is a Humanism" that, in willing my freedom, I cannot *not* will the freedom of others ("existential consistency" demands it!) and that, in the name of "the will to freedom," I can, "on the plane of morality," "form judgments" on those who try to ground their existence externally or "escape" their freedom (he often indicts these people as *les salauds*). Although he tells us in the *Notebooks* that ethics' "respect for freedom" "leaves undetermined the relation we *ought* to have with the content of [that] freedom,"[6] he makes it evident, I maintain, that in making freedom my only "end"—my "highest" and "primary" value—I *will* a "norm" by which any identification, objectification, or appropriation of freedom—my own or the Other's—can be judged inauthentic and immoral. And the purifying will of conversion, which ushers in a "new attitude" of authenticity, becomes, I submit, a basis in *Notebooks for an Ethics* for an "Ought-to-be," and for a Sartrean "city [or community] of ends" in which, rather than menacing the Other, each for-itself affirms and promotes the freedom of the Other.

Although Sartre's discussion of the meaning of *morale* (whether translated as "morality" or as "ethics") remains parsimonious in the *Notebooks,* there is little question, I conclude, that, in this unfinished work, *morale* is adjectival in respect to conversion and criterial in respect to authenticity. The reflective act by which we take hold of our spontaneity and affirm freedom as value meets what, in *Notebooks for an Ethics,* Sartre calls "the essential characteristic—morality" and, in *The War Diaries,* marks "true fidelity with ourselves" and the "moralization" of human consciousness. That is to say, Sartre's extended notes in his *Notebooks for an Ethics* not only amplify and corroborate the features of *reflection* and *conversion* which I have attributed to Sartrean authenticity but offer clarification and stronger support for the premises on which I—and certainly Jeanson, de Beauvoir, and others—have identified the passage to authenticity with the passage to "moral agency." Put yet another way, the "unveiling" performed by pure reflection in *Notebooks for an Ethics* offers "deliverance" from the "buffeted," "corrupted" consciousness of "flight" in *The War Diaries* and *Being and Nothingness* and provides additional warrant for making the moral and ethical dimension a culminating feature in differentiating good and bad faith from authenticity and inauthenticity. My thesis of the preceding chapters is clearly vindicated by my confrontation in this chapter with Sartre's belatedly published *Notebooks.*

Yet I do not shrink here from admitting some frustrations and problems related to the differentiation and distinctions that I have been urging. In the remainder of this chapter and book, I propose to show not only some of the recalcitrant texts but also some of the terminological issues that challenge the neatness of what I allege to be Sartre's marks of differentiation between my reconstructed good faith and authenticity in the early Sartre. If, for example, Sartre—as I have alleged—clearly intends to make *reflection* a distinguishing feature of the *post-conversion* categories of authenticity and inauthenticity, he clearly misspeaks when, early in *Notebooks for an Ethics*, he says that "pure reflection" is "good faith" and refers to our natural bad faith attitude—and even our "nature"—as inauthenticity. And the confusion is exacerbated by his references to "alienation" alternately as both inauthenticity and bad faith, as if the two could stand interchangeably for the dominant natural attitude from which we can, reflectively, convert. Sartre's own slips or lapses in language (or plain confusions) may help account for the confusion that sometimes afflicts the writing of too many of his interpreters.

In spite of the occasional looseness and unpredictability of Sartre's language, the emphasis of his overall intentions is, as I have argued, quite clear and discernible. Yet, in the interest of making Sartre's position in this regard less problematic and more readily coherent, I submit, before concluding my book, two distinctions. I offer first, with supporting textual references, a distinction between what *is* bad faith (or good faith or authenticity) and what is *in* bad faith (etc.). This distinction between the *is* of *identity* and the *is* of *attribution* in respect to these existential attitudes would permit Sartre to maintain that reflection is *in* good or bad faith—but not itself good or bad faith—even though bad faith and good faith are generally viewed by Sartre as non-reflective categories. One could then justifiably attribute bad faith to the will or reflection that effects an inauthentic mode of existing.

Second, I suggest that Sartre's core writings would read more coherently if a sharper distinction were drawn between human reality's "primitive project" or "immediate attitude" (or "original attitude") of bad faith (the original non-reflective project of trying to attain self-coincidence or in-itself-for-itself) on the one hand, and the bad faith of secondary choices, deeds, beliefs, and situations on the other. Although particular acts or deeds of bad faith (including what I have here called "epistemological bad faith") are manifestations or expressions of our natural bad faith (ontological) attitude of fleeing freedom in pursuit of *being*, it is important to be able to speak of these choices without making them identical to our original project. This distinction would not only afford added clarity to the interpretation of Sartre on bad faith and related existential attitudes, but would also provide an additional basis for allowing Sartre, without inconsistency, to speak of impure reflection, for example, as being *in* bad faith. Neither Sartre nor his interpreters have noted the distinction sufficiently.

I conclude my study with a question that seems to flow naturally for both writer and reader: "After the *Notebooks*, is the differentiation I have offered between authenticity and good faith, in its reconstructed sense, still defensible?" I acknowledge that Sartre, in the *Notebooks*, makes only scant reference to good faith and, when he does, sometimes appears, as I showed earlier, to use it interchangeably and to confound it with authenticity. Although in the *Notebooks* he elucidates and confirms the categories of bad faith, authenticity, and even inauthenticity, he does little to illuminate the "immediate attitude" of good faith. Nonetheless, by referring here to good faith in a constructive and salutary way—virtually collapsing it, at times, into authenticity—and emphasizing beyond equivocation that pure reflection is required in the conversion from the "unreflective plane" to authentic existence, Sartre, for the most part, continues the ontological structure and analysis that make my reconstruction of Sartrean good faith feasible, and my differentiation of it from the conversion-related attitude of authenticity recommendable.

Whether or not, finally, I am right in insisting on a positive sense of good faith in Sartre which can be distinguished markedly from Sartre's more important and challenging concept of authenticity, I hope that my readers will respect my argument as well as my wish to rescue good faith from the controlling tentacles of bad faith. And I hope that, in spite of my reservations about Sartre's pervasive concept and challenge of bad faith, my analysis in these chapters will provide a detailed and persuasive reconstruction not only of bad faith, but also of the contrasting existential attitudes that serve to confirm an available optimism in Sartre's philosophy. My book will have succeeded if it shows that, far from condemning us irreversibly to bad faith, as some interpreters have insisted, Sartre's early philosophy provides a deliverance from bad faith and the tormenting hell of trying to ground ourselves in *being*. If there still linger questions about this, I trust that the present study, culminating in my criterial appeal to his *Notebooks for an Ethics*, will put them to rest. The way out of Sartrean hell is authenticity—that is to say, living "in accord" with oneself as unjustifiable freedom and taking responsibility for it. The *Notebooks for an Ethics* brings that point unambiguously to a head.

BAD FAITH,
GOOD FAITH,
AND
AUTHENTICITY
IN SARTRE'S
EARLY
PHILOSOPHY

1   Bad Faith and Sincerity: Does Sartre's Analysis Rest on a Mistake?

In this opening chapter, I intend to deal with an issue that vexed my earliest confrontation with Sartre's *Being and Nothingness*. Although it may strike the reader as indirect and somewhat off center with regard to my announced topic and project, this issue—I remind the reader— made evident to me the need to study Sartre closely, and generated my intense inquiry into bad faith and its corollary and alternate ways of "existing."

Specifically, I want to focus on Sartre's view of "sincerity" as it is developed in *Being and Nothingness*—in particular, on his contention that sincerity is a "phenomenon of bad faith."[1] Sartre's argument that the phenomenological structure and goals of sincerity parallel those of bad faith is to me problematic and highly misleading. In what follows, I shall attempt to show the equivocation and related difficulties that plague Sartre's analysis in this regard. In addition, before concluding, I shall suggest very briefly an alternative, more constructive account of sincerity that is consistent with, even implied in, Sartre's terms and ontological framework. Finally, I shall attempt to respond to a few of the criticisms leveled against my earlier formulation of my charge of equivocation in Sartre's analysis.

Before proceeding to these tasks, it seems to me imperative
to provide at least a skeletal account of the background and
main points of reference from which the analysis and contentions of this chapter, and this book, must be viewed. The reader
will come to understand that, though somewhat indirect with
respect to my book's main analysis and differentiation, the present chapter begins to provide the necessary foundation and
framework for what is to come. It is a building block for understanding the *challenge* of Sartre's complex concept of bad faith.

General background

A number of central Sartrean contentions and terms must be
born in mind while approaching his analysis of sincerity. Here
I shall give only a brief account of those necessary for a confrontation with the issues of this chapter. I shall provide
greater, more refined, detail regarding all of these as my overall
analysis, reconstruction, and differentiation of key Sartrean
concepts unfold in this book.

First, it must be remembered that Sartre adopts Husserl's
view that all consciousness is consciousness *of* something.[2] This
is an indirect endorsement of Brentanos' earlier contention
that intentionality is an essential feature of consciousness. To
say that consciousness is consciousness *of* something means
for Sartre that "there is no consciousness which is not a *posit-
ing* of a transcendent object," or, in other words, "that consciousness has no 'content'." Consciousness is "positional"; "it
transcends itself in order to reach an object"; it is directed
toward the outside for its "content" (e.g., the table). This means,
as Spiegelberg has pointed out, that "consciousness of" involves "in the first place a reference from the *intending* act to
the *intended* object beyond as a distinct entity."[3] Transcendence
for Sartre is thus the "constitutive structure" of consciousness;

or, to put it another way, consciousness is "congenitally oriented toward" being other than itself.[4] It is precisely this view of the intentionality or transcendence of consciousness that pushes Sartre to make his fundamental distinction between two types of being: on the one hand, being for-itself (l'être pour-soi), or the being of consciousness, and on the other hand, being in-itself (l'être en-soi), or the being that transcends consciousness, the being that consciousness "intends," or, to paraphrase Spiegelberg, the being to which being for-itself refers by virtue of its intentionality.[5] Hence, in its innermost nature, pour-soi, seen in terms of intending consciousness, may be said to relate to and imply a being other than itself (en-soi), which is at once both a transcendent and a transphenomenal being.[6]

Second, for Sartre "human reality" is seen as "a being which is what it is not and which is not what it is."[7] Consciousness[8] and being for-itself[9] (l'être pour-soi), often used by Sartre interchangeably with human reality, are frequently described in an identical manner. In other words, in direct contrast to being in-itself (l'être en-soi), being for-itself, or human reality as for-itself, cannot be said to have identity. Being for-itself must not be said to be purely and simply what it is[10] as is, say, a table. As "for-itself," human reality is rather a lack, "and . . . what it lacks is a certain coincidence with itself."[11] To use other terms of Sartre, the "distinguishing characteristic" of consciousness is that it is "a decompression of being." Unlike en-soi, it is not "full of itself"; it is not a plenitude of being[12]; indeed, it is "total emptiness."[13] We shall see that this characterization of "human reality as for-itself," as well as Sartre's crucial distinction between pour-soi and en-soi, is germane to his view of sincerity.

Third, consciousness is translucent for Sartre. That is, consciousness is aware of itself, consciousness is consciousness (of) consciousness, and it is a non-thetic self-consciousness. The notion of "a consciousness ignorant of itself" is absurd.[14]

To put the matter in another way, for Sartre there is a "pre-reflective cogito," which is the condition not only of the Cartesian cogito[15] but also of all reflection.[16] We shall see later that, because of this pre-reflective cogito and because of the translucency of consciousness, "I am acquainted with the aspect [of my being] which I do not wish to see" and that "I must of necessity perpetually carry within me what I wish to flee."[17] This point is important for understanding Sartre's notion of "bad faith" and his contention that one is never *not* conscious of one's self-deception.

Fourth, Sartre sees the human being distinctively in terms of freedom and maintains that this freedom is revealed to us in anguish. He tells us that "there is no difference between the being of a man and his being-*free*"[18] and that, indeed, "anguish is the reflective apprehension of freedom by itself."[19] In a sense, then, we *are* anguish, yet in the human condition, we wish to flee this anguish. And the way we flee anguish is by trying "to apprehend ourselves from without as an Other or as *a thing*,"[20] in other words, as being in-itself (*l'être en-soi*). So, for Sartre, I can become involved in *bad faith* while in the very process of apprehending myself as anguish. For I attempt to flee anguish in order not to know, but, because of the *pre-reflective cogito*, I am not able to avoid knowing that I am fleeing; that is to say, "the flight from anguish is only a mode of becoming conscious of anguish; . . . anguish can be neither hidden nor avoided."[21] To think that I can hide, or indeed attempt to hide, my anguish is *bad faith*. It is an attempt to turn what I am as a human reality, as a *pour-soi*, as "a being which is what it is not and which is not what it is," into the mode of being of *en-soi*, into an object, into a "thing." But, to use Sartre's words once again, it is at the price of bad faith that "we are anguish-in-order-to-flee-anguish within the unity of a single consciousness."[22]

Clearly, this review of basic background materials leads directly to Sartre's conception of "bad faith" and invites a more detailed and careful examination of the same. This is appropriate for an introductory chapter intending to challenge Sartre's view that sincerity is a "phenomenon of bad faith." And it is even more important in the light of the central role that bad faith will assume in directing my inquiry in this book. Thus, I turn immediately to a preliminary elaboration of Sartre's view of "bad faith"[23] and attempt to show how, in relation to it, Sartre develops what I shall call "the problem of sincerity."

"Bad faith" and "the problem of sincerity"

Sartre comes to grips with the nature of "bad faith" by first contrasting it with "falsehood" or "lying in general." He is quite willing to allow that bad faith is essentially a "lie to oneself," providing one makes the crucial distinction between lying to oneself and "lying in general." "The essence of the lie," says Sartre, "implies in fact that the liar actually is in complete possession of the truth which he is hiding."[24] Through the lie, consciousness affirms its existence as "*hidden from the Other*," and for its own gain exploits the ontological duality between myself and myself as viewed by the Other. Although bad faith may be regarded as a lie to oneself, and although it does share in appearance the structure of falsehood, it cannot maintain the ontological duality of *deceiver* and *deceived*. For bad faith differs essentially from "lying in general" or falsehood in that it involves one's hiding the truth from oneself. This is "what changes everything," says Sartre. Bad faith entails "the unity of a *single* consciousness," for the one who is lying and the one to whom the lie is told are one and the same person. And this means also that bad faith is not thrust upon one; it is not an intruder on human consciousness; an individual is not infected with it. Rather, bad faith is an individual project; consciousness affects itself with it. I am the originator of my lie, and I have a pre-reflective awareness of the deception of which I am attempting to persuade myself. That is to say, because of the "total translucency of consciousness," "that which affects itself with bad faith must be conscious (of) its bad faith since the being of consciousness is consciousness of being."[25]

To elucidate further, all knowing for Sartre involves the consciousness of knowing. The possibility that there is knowing that is "ignorant of itself" makes no sense.[26] How can the censor, for example, do his censoring without being conscious of that which he is censoring or repressing? Yet what kind of self-consciousness can the censor possess? And Sartre's answer to this provides us with another fundamental clue to the nature of bad faith: "It must be the consciousness (of) being conscious of the drive to be repressed, but precisely *in order not to be conscious of it.*"[27] In structure this is not unlike what, above, we saw Sartre calling "anguish-in order-to-flee-anguish within the unity of a single consciousness." What is it but bad faith?

We see then that the first act of bad faith is, indeed, "to flee what it cannot flee, to flee what it is."[28] We observe also that this flight involves a kind of breakdown at the very heart of being; for human reality, in bad faith, refuses to acknowledge itself as what it is (that is, as simultaneously "to be what it is not and not to be what it is"). But this does not yet take us to "the problem of sincerity." To bring this problem to a head we must appeal to still another form of characterizing the human being. The human being for Sartre is both a *facticity* (a "given" or a "what is") and a *transcendence* (the possible projects of its freedom, or the possibilities associated with "what it is not"). What bad faith does is "to affirm their identity while preserving their differences"; it "affirms facticity as *being* transcendence and transcendence as *being* facticity."[29] In bad faith, I am caught up in the ambiguity of affirming my transcendence in the mode of being of *en-soi* or a thing, and vice versa. Maintaining this ambiguity may allow me to feel that I can escape all reproaches, but in fact I can do so only by fleeing my responsibilities as being for-itself *(l'être pour-soi)*, by regarding myself as a thing, and by violating what I am as a human consciousness.[30] In the course of this book, I shall offer concrete illustrations of this pattern of bad faith.

Hence, bad faith as a kind of lying to oneself expresses itself in a number of characteristic ways. Bad faith not only tries to flee the human consciousness of which it is, but it expresses itself in patterns that try both to establish that "I am not what I am"[31] and to "constitute myself as a being what I am not."[32] Moreover, it attempts to turn the human being "which is what it is not and which is not what it is" into a being "what is," into a fixed being, into a being with identity. By so doing it is involved in the self-destroying enterprise of trying to transform the transcendence of *pour-soi* into facticity, of making being for-itself exist in the mode of in-itself. Human consciousness is not simply *what it is*, says Sartre, and the human being is not simply *what he or she is*. Out of this consideration "the problem of sincerity" develops for Sartre.

Although Sartre speaks initially of the "idea of sincerity" as the "antithesis of bad faith,"[33] we readily see that he does not view the two concepts as antithetical. The ideal of sincerity is "that a man be *for himself* only what he *is*."[34] "To be sincere . . . is to be what one is."[35] The problem-question that immediately arises is formulated as follows: "But is man what he is? And more generally how can he *be* what he is when he exists as consciousness of being?" Further, if "sincerity proposes for us an absolute equivalence of being with itself as a prototype of being . . . it is necessary that we *make ourselves* what we are. But what *are we* . . . if our mode of being is having the obligation to be what we are?"[36] Here is the core of Sartre's "problem of sincerity." To it we must now give focal attention.

What Sartre is suggesting, essentially, is that the project of sincerity sets for itself an ideal or task that is impossible to fulfill. The meaning of this ideal "contradicts" the very structure of consciousness. For to aim "to be what one is" is to violate one's consciousness as "being what one is not and not being what one is." As a continued attempt to adhere to oneself, "total, constant sincerity" is by nature "a constant effort to dissociate oneself from oneself." An individual frees himself from his "essential" being (freedom) by that act through which he constitutes himself an object for himself. "Who can not see," asks Sartre, "that the sincere man constitutes himself as a thing in order to escape the condition of a thing by the same act of sincerity?" Consider, for example, the man who confesses that he is evil. Such a confession permits him to exchange his awesome "freedom-for-evil" for a kind of fixed evil character: "he is evil, he clings to himself, he is what he is." But at the same time this confession allows the man to regard himself as somehow beyond evil, as being a freedom with a virgin future. As Sartre puts it, "By the same stroke, he escapes from that thing. . . . He derives a *merit* from his sincerity, and the deserving man is not the deserving man as he is evil but as he is *beyond* his evilness."[37] What is this, he asks, but bad faith?[38]

Sartre is even more emphatic. He contends that the essential structure of sincerity is the same as that of bad faith and that its goal scarcely differs. As we have seen, the goal of bad faith is to flee from oneself, to put oneself out of reach; or, to use another terminology, its end is "to cause me to be what I am, in the mode of 'not being what one is,' or not to be what I am in the mode of 'being what one is.' " Similarly, the goal of sincerity is "to bring me to confess to myself what I am in order that I may finally coincide with my being; in a word, to cause myself to be, in the mode of the in-itself, what I am in the mode of 'not being what I am.' " For Sartre, this is all the same "game of mirrors." Even for me initially to have the intention of being sincere, I must at the same time both be and not be what I am; and then that intention aims at forcing me to move from one mode of being to another. So being sincere is one of the ways of falling into bad faith.[39] And this is not all. Even to be able to conceive an intention in *bad faith* requires that I be such a being that "within my being I escape from my being." For Sartre, this contention carries with it the controversial implication that bad faith is a possibility *"only because* sincerity is conscious of having to miss its goal inevitably" by virtue of its very nature.[40] If it were not possible, for instance, to *determine* myself as cowardly in the sense of my being able simultaneously both to deny courage of myself and to escape the cowardice that I affirm, I could not be in bad faith. In Sartre's words, "if it were not on principle *impossible* for me to coincide with my *not-being-courageous* as well as with my being courageous,[41] then any project of bad faith would be prohibited me."[42] Hence, Sartre asserts unambiguously that, *if bad faith is to be possible at all,* sincerity itself *has to be* in bad faith. "The condition of the possibility for bad faith is that human reality, in its most immediate being, in the intrastructure of the prereflective *cogito,* must be what it is not and not be what it is."[43] Put another way, bad faith is rooted in being for-itself's ontological ambiguity of *facticity and transcendence,* in its "double property" of "thatness" and "becoming," of "what is" and "what is not." And sincerity is not only the same, in "its essential structure" and goal, as bad faith but is also a necessary condition of the very possibility of bad faith.

As I said, I find this contention disturbing and misleading, and I believe it to be based on a faulty analysis. In what follows, I shall attempt to show the core defects of Sartre's arguments and to suggest an alternate interpretation of sincerity which nonetheless accords with Sartre's basic notion of human reality as *pour-soi* and with his early philosophical position in general.

The root defects of Sartre's analysis

I submit that *equivocation* lies at the root of Sartre's analysis of sincerity and of what I take to be his erroneous depiction of sincerity as bad faith. Specifically, I contend that Sartre equivocates on the meaning of "being what one is" and of his key expression "being which is what it is not and which is not what it is," and that these equivocations vitiate the fundamental soundness of Sartre's analysis of sincerity. Let me explain.

As we have seen, there is no question that Sartre identifies being sincere with "being what one is" and that he regards sincerity as an impossible ideal, the very meaning of which contradicts the nature of consciousness. But there is much to question about the way in which, in this context, Sartre reads or interprets "being what one is" or "to be what one is." Upon analysis, Sartre appears to be taking a formulation of the meaning of sincerity as it is employed in ordinary language and relating that nontechnical formulation of an ordinary-language usage to his highly technical and specialized notion of being for-itself *(l'être pour-soi)*. In other words, he seems to be juxtaposing an ordinary-language formulation of sincerity with his own idiosyncratic philosophical view of human reality as consciousness. To be sure, if one ignores the different contexts in which the words are used, as well as the different meanings the words appear to have in the different contexts, Sartre can justifiably say that sincerity's aim "to be what one is" appears to contradict and violate the "nature" of consciousness as "being what it is not and not being what it is." Further, in ordinary language, *"sincere"* is so frequently used to connote the quality of "genuinely meaning what one says" or "truly living

what one professes" that one can readily understand Sartre's
initial characterization of sincerity as "being what one is." But
what is less understandable, and indeed seems unjustified, is
his ready movement from the level of discourse of everyday,
common language to the level of discourse of technical and
systematic philosophy. This kind of maneuver appears to involve a confounding of universes or categories of discourse. For
instance, on what I might call the ordinary-language assumption that being sincere is "being what one is," Sartre proceeds
quickly to say the following about the ideal of sincerity:

> It is necessary that a man be *for himself* only what he *is*. But is
> this not precisely the definition of the in-itself—or if you prefer—
> the principle of identity?[44]

What we must notice about this rather quick but crucial step
is that Sartre immediately endows the "to be what one is" of
everyday discourse with the full power of his own philosophical
meanings (note the introduction of being *for himself* here) and,
on the basis of this, seems prepared to let sincerity suffer the
consequences. Although, as a characterization of sincerity,
"being what one is" emerges from an ordinary-language context, Sartre without hesitation places it in his own ontological
system and allows it to take on the basis of *en-soi* ("in-itself")
and the objectifying characteristic of identity. (As we have seen,
being in-itself "is what it is.") What makes this step so crucial is
that, once placed in the web of Sartre's idiosyncratic system,
sincerity is "made" to admit of "family relations" which, in
common usage, it would not be said to have. If, as Sartre states,
the project and goal of sincerity is "to be what one is," and if
"to be what one is" means what Sartre defines it to mean in his
characterization of being in-itself (or *en-soi*), then it does seem
to follow that consciousness, in seeking "absolute equivalence"
and "self-coincidence," is trying to put itself "out of reach," is

attempting to escape its freedom in order to constitute itself as *thing*, and thus, in bad faith, is violating human reality. In other words, Sartre's system of technical philosophical meanings seems to allow these and other conclusions to follow.

But my contention is precisely that Sartre's crucial step is philosophically illegitimate. It is based on an equivocation. The meaning of "to be what one is" as intended by ordinary language cannot be identified with the meaning of that expression when it is used by Sartre technically either to define the "in-itself" or to characterize human reality's bad-faith goal to tie down or objectify consciousness. But Sartre appears either to ignore or to exploit this ambiguity. And he makes no effort to justify his move from one universe of discourse to another. Left as is, his procedure seems to be arbitrary, unwarranted, and indifferent to the meaning differences of the different language contexts. And any inference he draws about sincerity on the basis of his having inserted "being what one is" (as an ordinary-language expression) into his own distinctive system of ontological meanings, would likewise appear presumptuous, questionable, and philosophically illicit.

I want to elucidate my point by developing yet another illustration. We have already seen that, after locating a common-usage meaning of sincerity as "being what one is," Sartre immediately raises the question of the possibility of a person's being "what one is." It is clear that the difficulty he sees here emerges from his unquestioning acceptance of these words in terms of his own distinctive philosophical vocabulary and system of meanings. This becomes evident in the question that immediately follows: "How can he *be* what he is when he exists as consciousness of being?"[45] The problem arises because of what Sartre assumes about the "nature" of consciousness—namely, its fluidity, its "tension" within itself, its "being what it is not and not being what it is," its non-coincidence. And, given this assumption, it is no wonder that Sartre should affirm that the project of sincerity *proposes* for us a coincidence or "absolute equivalence of being" with itself and that, on the basis of his analysis of bad faith, sincerity's "proposal" is *in* bad faith. From here, Sartre proceeds to argue, as we have seen, that "if it were not on principle *impossible* for me to coincide [for example] with my not being courageous . . . then any project of bad faith would be prohibited me."[46] So it is a relatively easy step for him to conclude this procession of argument with the provocative contention that the bad faith of sincerity is *necessary* if bad faith is to be possible at all.

But again I submit that this disturbing conclusion is rooted in Sartre's failure to distinguish between the meaning of "being what one is" as used in ordinary language and the meaning of the expression when it is read into his philosophical system. Once Sartre's "move" is allowed, once "being what one is" is shifted out of its ordinary-language context into his system of philosophical meanings, Sartre's line of reasoning makes sense, for it is systemic. But I urge that his initial move should not be allowed, for it is built on equivocation. If my argument is sound, this illustration not only unveils the equivocation, but also supports my contention that the important inference under analysis, like some other of Sartre's contentions about sincerity, is not acceptable. An elementary point of logic tells us that one cannot base valid argument on equivocation, explicit or implicit.

Although I believe that I have already reached the core of the basic defect in Sartre's line of argumentation, I wish to add strength to my case by pointing to another instance of equivocation and to an ensuing problem. Specifically, I contend that, in arguing for the bad faith of sincerity, Sartre also equivocates in respect to the meaning of the expression "a being which is what it is not and which is not what it is." Earlier we saw that Sartre uses this expression to differentiate being *for-itself,* free human consciousness, or human reality. What Sartre seems to mean here is that consciousness is the type of being "such that in its being, its being is in question" insofar as it lacks identity and concrete "is-ness" and is evanescent.[47] Also, he appears to mean that, as *distinctively* human reality, consciousness lacks a coincidence with itself, and that, as a being which "is the foundation of itself as a lack of being, . . . it determines its being by means of a being which it is not."[48] To elaborate, Sartre seems to be suggesting that, although consciousness is a being that posits its own essence, it is never just this essence, it is never just the "what it is" of essence, never just its past, for it is also "what it is not" but could be; that is, its possibilities, its future. This seems to be Sartre's phenomenological description of the ontological structure of consciousness. But when Sartre comes to his discussion of bad faith and sincerity, "being what it is not and not being what it is" seems to take on a different and rather baffling connotation. We are now told that it is in *bad faith* that "human reality is constituted as a being which is what it is not and which is not what it is."[49] Sartre says, "With bad faith a truth appears . . . , the ontological characteristic of the world of bad faith with which the subject suddenly surrounds himself is this: that *here* being is what it is not, and is not what it is."[50]

Suddenly, it seems that the very structure of the world of bad faith is revealed to be the ontological structure of being for-itself. This surprising assertion raises a rather serious problem for Sartre. Briefly put, if the ontological characteristic of bad faith is identical with the structure of consciousness or being for-itself, and if "in bad faith human reality is constituted as a being which is what it is not and which is not what it is," how can Sartre possibly assert that sincerity is in bad faith or that sincerity has the same basic structure as bad faith? For if to be sincere is, as Sartre says, *to be what one is,* it obviously does *not* have the structure of *being what it is not and not being what it is*. As we have noted earlier, Sartre sees the goal of sincerity as "contradicting" the very structure of consciousness. But if now bad faith is said to share the fundamental structure of consciousness, sincerity cannot be said to be in bad faith, even though Sartre's fundamental argument has been that sincerity *is* in bad faith and does share its essential structure. Sartre would have fared better here if he had simply stayed with his contention that only a consciousness or a freedom or a for-itself that is *not* what it is and is what it is not is capable of being in bad faith, for only a being that is not something can *attempt* to be something.

One is left to wonder, then, whether Sartre's analysis of sincerity moves logically at this point into a contradiction, and whether the meaning Sartre now ascribes to "being which is what it is not and which is not what it is" has the troublesome consequence of giving consciousness or human reality the structure of bad faith *by definition.* Although the alleged variation and trading of meanings in this instance takes place *within* the network of Sartre's highly idiosyncratic philosophical system and does not seem to involve an illicit move from ordinary-language meaning into a system of sophisticated philosophical meanings, it appears—given its consequences—to add evidence *against* the soundness of Sartre's analysis of sincerity and bad faith. I shall give more detailed attention to Sartre's pervasive notion of bad faith in subsequent chapters.

For the time being, I trust that I have unfolded some of the core difficulties regarding Sartre's basic contentions concerning sincerity. I hope also that my argument may serve to alert readers of Sartre to the ambiguity that sometimes surrounds his use of language, and encourage them to proceed cautiously and reflectively when considering Sartre's unsettling discussion of basic existential attitudes. Given the problems and misgivings

I have tried to express, I wish now, before concluding this chapter, to outline, however briefly, an account of sincerity which, while proposing a constructive alternative to the analysis criticized above, retains Sartre's terminology and the framework of his key concepts.

A suggestion for reconstruction

We have seen, in spite of the ambiguity associated with the preceding problem, that Sartre views the "to be what one is" of sincerity's project as an objectification and falsification of human reality and thus in bad faith. How can man be "what he is," asks Sartre, if he is "consciousness of being"? I have tried to show the equivocation involved in the movement of Sartre's thought here. I now wish to suggest that, if Sartre had been more attentive to the ordinary-language meaning of "to be what one is," he might well have avoided this equivocation and come up with a *translation* of the "being what one is" as used in ordinary language that does not condemn sincerity to bad faith.

I submit that to aim to be what I am or to express myself honestly as the person I am does not necessarily entail, even on Sartre's terms, constituting myself in the mode of *en-soi* or of a kind of fixed "thing." On the contrary, I suggest that a careful listening to the way "sincerity" and "being what [or who] one is" is used in ordinary language indicates a meaning that "intends" *being* the person who I am—*not* hiding from, fleeing from, or thingifying that person. The *who* or what I am, as "human reality," may well be, as Sartre suggests, "a being which is what it is not and which is not what it is." Only an uncritical and equivocal "reading off" of this expression permits Sartre to argue that "being what [or who] one is" distorts human reality by failing to respect the inevitable non-coincidence of human consciousness. If Sartre had paid greater respect to ordinary language, he might have recognized that "being what one is" as employed in common usage may well mean "being what it is not and not being what it is" when translated into the idiosyncratic discourse of his phenomenological ontology. Sartre appears either inattentive to this possibility or so immersed in his own system of philosophical meanings that he is unable to view "what one is" except as a violation of human reality, or as an objectification of free human consciousness. But I submit that "being what one is" ("being sincere") may involve being or living or existing in a mode in which one recognizes and accepts that "one is not what one is and is what one is not." That is to say, sincerity is often intended to mean that one is "what one is" in the mode of being of self-consciousness, not in the mode of the objectification or thingification of consciousness, or of fleeing one's freedom. Following this line of development, I suggest that *to be* or *to live* in such a mode may well be, for Sartre, to live *self-consciously*. To say the least, it is within the range of my possibility to face and recognize myself lucidly and honestly and to live as "freedom," as "consciousness", as the "foundation of my values," as a "being which is what it is not and which is not what it is." Although this possibility may be linguistically problematic for Sartre, there is no a priori basis for ruling it out. In fact, as I shall make evident in subsequent chapters, living in accord with the freedom one is may well be the key to Sartre's conception of "authenticity."

Hence, my suggestion is that, even granting the Sartrean framework and terminology, there is room to interpret sincerity as living self-consciously of the fact that one is a "being which is what it is not and which is not what it is." Put more generally, sincerity then becomes the life of authentic self-consciousness or the life of honest self-awareness. Although this interpretation would continue to recognize that consciousness, by its very nature, carries with it the "permanent risk of bad faith,"[51] it would preclude the view that being sincere entails lying to oneself and shares the goal and essential structure of bad faith. In addition, it would regard as a serious misunderstanding of sincerity the notion that sincerity is a necessary condition for the possibility of bad faith. Granted that, upon expansion and close analysis, my proposed meaning may turn out to be defective, I yet think that it has the provisional advantage over Sartre's own analysis of being in greater accord with both the ordinary-language meaning of sincerity and the humanizing spirit of existentialism.

Although, as one or two critics have pointed out, Sartre's view of authenticity shares part of the meaning I am attributing to sincerity, I shall want, as the reader will see, to differentiate authenticity (in Sartre) from both sincerity and "good faith." In retrospect, I acknowledge, as at least one critic[52] has pointed out, that my suggested reconstruction of sincerity bears some resemblance to the view of authenticity that is later disclosed in Sartre's posthumous literature. But the *Notebooks for an Ethics* will make clear that Sartre would have no time for any identification of the two.

Some criticisms and rejoinders

Since my initial articulation and presentation—in *The Personalist*[53]—of the analysis and argument that I have presented above in revised form, a number of colleagues[54] in Sartrean scholarship have favored me with questions about the adequacy of my thesis and countersuggestion. Of the criticisms and questions raised, I believe that only those of A. D. M. Walker of England have appeared systematically in published form. In "Sartre, Santoni, and Sincerity,"[55] Walker challenges both my critique and my suggested reconstruction of Sartre's analysis of sincerity. Although he concedes that Sartre does appear to commit the fallacy of equivocation, he contends that my analysis fails to "dissolve" *fully* the Sartrean "problem of sincerity." And granting my appeal to ordinary-language or common usage, Walker attempts to discredit my argument further by suggesting a "more compelling argument"—still rooted in ordinary language—to show that the concept of sincerity cannot be accommodated by Sartre's ontological framework and system.

In deference to philosophical criticism (yet parting from the main purpose of this chapter) I wish, in ending, to respond to Walker's challenge. Among other considerations, I want to show that Walker's criticisms do not get to the heart of my critique of Sartre. More specifically, I shall attempt to show that Walker's criticisms are often based on misinterpretation of my argument, and that his version of the common usage argument against the attainability of sincerity within Sartre's ontological system remains arbitrary, questionable, and unconvincing.

I shall proceed by first presenting the particular objection that I wish to meet. I shall then offer a brief response to that specific criticism.

1. In the first of his central objections to my argument, Walker notes (in a deliberate understatement) that in several passages Sartre speaks "in a surprising way for one who wants either to ignore or to exploit the ambiguity in the phrase 'being what one is'."[56] Specifically, he turns to Sartre's discussion of the case of the homosexual and his critic ("the champion of sincerity"). As the reader may recall, Sartre commends the homosexual's refusal to admit that he is a homosexual in the sense that his past mistakes constitute for him a *destiny*. But he also criticizes the homosexual's evasion insofar as he refuses to face up to his past actions and the implications of his past actions, and "lays claim to 'not being a pederast' in the sense in which this table is not an inkwell." That is to say, the pederast under-

stands "not being" in the sense of "not-being-in-itself." According to Sartre, the pederast "plays on the word *being*," "slides surreptitiously" from one connotation of being to another, tries to "put himself beyond reach," and, in this regard, is in bad faith.[57]

Walker makes much of this discussion.[58] He affirms that it not only shows that Sartre is "alive to the general possibility of equivocation in this area," but also that the equivocation committed by the self-deceiving homosexual is precisely the equivocation of which I accuse Sartre. Because Sartre is familiar with the equivocation for which (allegedly) I fault his analysis of sincerity, it follows, Walker seems to infer, that my criticism is defective.

My rejoinder: Walker appears to have misunderstood what I was arguing in my earlier paper and what, in essence, I have rearticulated above in this opening chapter.

My essential argument is that Sartre moves illicitly from an ordinary-language formulation or meaning of sincerity as "being what one is" (genuinely meaning and living what one professes) to his highly technical and idiosyncratic philosophical formulation of "being what one is," and then reads off the peculiar meaning that the term has in his own ontological system. This equivocation allows him to say that sincerity's aim of "being what one is" (in the ordinary-language sense) is in bad faith, for it does violence to the being of consciousness by trying to "glue down" being "which is not what it is and is what it is not," in Sartre's technical idiom.

Walker is wrong in contending that the homosexual's equivocation on the word *being* is the same one that I attribute to Sartre. The root equivocation to which I point (the reader will be quite familiar with it by now) is an equivocation that moves surreptitiously from the ordinary-language meaning of "to be what one is" to the idiomatic meaning of the same expression in Sartre's ontological system. The equivocation that Sartre ascribes to the pederast is an equivocation in which, *given* Sartre's distinction between the two radically disparate types of being, the homosexual disingenuously exploits the ambiguity of being and the double aspect ("facticity-transcendence") of human reality in order to avoid acknowledging his homosexuality. Thus, Walker misinterprets one of the core defects I attribute to Sartre's analysis of sincerity.

2. For Walker, there is a *second* reason for affirming that Sartre's treatment of the case of the homosexual calls into question my critique of his analysis of sincerity.

> Against the background of linguistic awareness outlined [above], Sartre is quite clear that what the "champion of sincerity" demands from his friend is, in effect, an admission that he is, in the mode of the *en-soi,* an homosexual—the denial of *this* is the commendable element in the homosexual's attitude. But plainly if sincerity *is* in this way linked with claims to being in the mode of the *en-soi,* Sartre has a suitable premiss on which to base his assertions about the problematic nature of sincerity.[59]

Walker goes on to argue that Sartre *does* have reasons for believing that sincerity demands "an admission of being in the mode of the *en-soi.*" For example, the homosexual confesses to his friend (the "champion of sincerity") in order to attain peace of mind and relief from his feelings of guilt. But he can obtain that relief and ensuing peace of mind only by acknowledging his homosexuality in the mode of *en-soi,* in which he can escape responsibility for his behavior. Walker acknowledges the defects in this and other of Sartre's arguments in this regard: yet he is willing to disregard their "unsoundness" here. In the present context, his specific purpose is to show that Sartre has *other* arguments, "besides the one *ascribed to him by Santoni,* for believing that the ideal of sincerity is problematic" (italics

mine). These arguments defeat my critique, he alleges, by showing that Sartre's analysis of sincerity "is not the result of mere
muddle or confusion."

My rejoinder: I maintain that Walker's contention here does
not hold. His criticism seems to be grounded in a confusion
between what I call "the problem of sincerity," on the one
hand, and what I contend to be the root equivocation out of
which this problem emerges, on the other.[60] When Walker argues, for example, that Sartre has a premise on which to base
his statements about the problematic nature of sincerity, and
that there are Sartrean reasons for believing that the ideal of
sincerity is problematic (a point, incidentally, with which I do
not disagree!), he is dealing with what I label Sartre's "problem
of sincerity." That problem has to do with sincerity's setting for
itself a task or ideal which is "impossible to fulfill." Far from
being "hidden from consciousness," this impossibility is the
"very stuff of consciousness."[61]

I do not contend, as Walker implies, that Sartre has no suit-
able premise or argument for maintaining that sincerity's structure, ideal, or goal is problematic. Nor do I argue that the core
equivocation to which I point constitutes the problem of sincerity. Rather (and here I am repeating myself) I attempt to show
that Sartre's problem of sincerity, as well as his conclusion that
the project of sincerity is futile and self-deceptive, is a *consequence* of his unwarranted insertion of an ordinary-language
formulation of sincerity into his highly technical system of philosophical meanings. Although this move is one of equivocation,
and this equivocation, I contend, leads Sartre to a defective account of sincerity, I never intend to say that the equivocation
constitutes either Sartre's "problem of sincerity" or the *sole* argument for maintaining sincerity's problematic nature. In fact,
I go out of my way to suggest that, once Sartre makes the equivocal transition from an ordinary-language formulation of "sin-

cerity" to a translation of it in terms of the idiosyncratic vocabulary of his phenomenological ontology, he has a basis for arguing and showing the problematic and futile structure of sincerity.[62] Yet equivocation remains at its root.

3. Walker's *third* criticism is more indirect. He seeks to offer "a further, more compelling argument which Sartre could have used to demonstrate . . . that the idea of sincerity is impossible of attainment." In so doing, Walker's intent is to disparage my argument further by showing that Sartre's treatment of sincerity must not be dismissed as resting on "a trivial slip or equivocation."[63]

Essentially, Walker's argument is that the use of the concept of sincerity presupposes, as background for its use, "an acceptance of some set of values." We would not, for example, call "sincere" the person who said threateningly, "If you do that again, I'll kill you," even if he meant what he said. Nor would we call "sincere" the person who said to another, "I hate you!," even if that were an honest expression of his sentiment. To understand or explain such linguistic facts, Walker contends, we must turn to the etymological roots of the word *sincere.* If we take seriously the Latin, Greek, and English etymologies, we must recognize in *sincerity* the root notion of "freedom from foreign admixture of impurity," or simply "freedom from impurities." But for x (a sentiment) to be "sincere" or "insincere," x must initially be pure, for only that which is uncorrupted is susceptible of corruption. From this Walker concludes that, if we are to use the concept of sincerity, we need, "antecedently to our use," to endorse certain standards and accept certain values. The acceptance of such values or standards is a prerequisite for the evaluation implied in our categorizing certain aspects of human behavior and feelings as "impurities" or as "impure."

On Walker's analysis, it is exactly this part of the concept of sincerity—so often neglected by the "popular view of sincerity"—that Sartre's overall philosophical framework is unable to accommodate. Given Walker's etymological perspective on sincerity, the pursuer of sincerity must be in bad faith, for (on Sartrean terms), in trying to be free from impurities, one is either taking for granted "transcendent givens" independent of human subjectivity ("the spirit of seriousness") or one is trying to live up to fixed values which one has already chosen or created (which also reflects the "spirit of seriousness").

My rejoinder: I wish to point out that, even if one were to grant Walker the premises and basis of his argument, some of his conclusions do not follow. For example, even if Walker's etymological point about value-standards implicit in the use of *sincerity* holds, it does not follow either that Sartre's philosophical framework cannot accommodate the notion of sincerity or necessarily that "the idea of sincerity is impossible of attainment."[64] By relating his own etymological argument to Sartre's repudiation of objectivism and Sartre's own theory of evaluation, Walker shows only, if his argument is valid, that, for Sartre, the person who pursues sincerity as a goal is in bad faith. But to show that the project of sincerity is in bad faith because of Sartre's views on values is *not* to show that it cannot be accommodated or accounted for in Sartre's ontological system, unless Walker means only what Sartre already intends to say; namely, that though the project of sincerity is in bad faith, its *goal* (to be what one is) is "impossible to attain." Because consciousness for Sartre is not what it is and is what it is not, neither sincerity nor any other *fixed* state of consciousness is possible. And to pursue sincerity—or even authenticity (as we shall see)—as though one can *be* it, as though one can say definitively at a certain point, "I am that," is to flee from one's consciousness as freedom and to deceive oneself (bad faith).

Similarly, although Walker's joining of his etymological argument with Sartre's position on values relegates the pursuit of sincerity to bad faith, and shows that the ideal of sincerity becomes problematic, it does not logically entail, as Walker contends, that the project of sincerity is impossible in the everyday sense of *sincere*—in which, for example, the champion of sincerity *may* (against Sartre's reading) be asking the pederast to be sincere.

Finally, I must mention, however briefly, another of my misgivings. I am uncomfortable with Walker's insistence that, even by standards of ordinary-language usage, it would be inappropriate to describe as "sincere" or "as having spoken sincerely" someone who said to another, "You're not welcome!" or "I hate you!"

Walker does not recognize that what he views as the root etymological expression—"freedom from impurity" or "freedom from foreign admixture of impurity"—is itself open to ambiguity. Regarding the cases he offers (of honest but personally hurtful remarks), he seems to be saying that "sincere" is not applied in common usage and cannot appropriately be applied because the sentiments expressed are not free from the foreign "impurities" of personal offense and malice. But it is important to note that, while Webster's *Second Unabridged Dictionary* lists under *sincere* and *sincerity* such meanings as "pure," "unmixed," "unadulterated," and "honest," it goes on, with greater specificity, to characterize that purity in terms of freedom from simulation, hypocrisy, disguise, or false pretense. I submit that ordinary-language usage of *sincerity* and its correlates allows the same differentiation and makes the same specification. What is said to be "sincere" ("unmixed," "unadulterated," "being in reality what it appears to be") does not, in ordinary language, connote "unmixed" and "unadulterated" in *all* respects—including, for example, freedom from anger, malice, jealousy, or meanness. Thus, given the context of sincerity, both etymological background and ordinary usage specify and limit the bounds of "purity." And although Walker may have come up with some supportive ground for continuing Sartre's case against sincerity, he has certainly not shown that Sartre's ontological system is incapable of giving an account of it. In specific ways, Sartre's ontology *does* account for it by providing the framework for exhibiting both the *bad faith* of it as a project and the impossibility of attaining it as a state with which consciousness can coincide. But, as I have tried to show, at the foundation of Sartre's argument is an illicit attribution of the technical meanings of his ontological system to an ordinary-language formulation of sincerity (namely, "to be what one is").

In short, Walker's promise of a "more compelling argument" in behalf of Sartre via an appeal to the etymological roots of *sincerity* does not appear to have been fulfilled. And his overall argument against my principal argument above does not seem to have salvaged Sartre's analysis or touched mine significantly. Moreover, for the record, my readers may note that I never contend—as Walker claims—that Sartre's analysis of sincerity is the result of "mere muddle" or a "trivial slip." Sartre's equivocation is not "mere" and his misstep is hardly "trivial." But, I repeat, this does not imply that Sartre is without grounds, within his own system, for questioning the ideal or goal of sincerity.

IN SPITE of inevitable inadequacies in the present chapter, I hope that my confrontation with Sartre here—as well as in the subsequent chapters of this book—will lead more students and scholars to Sartre's demanding philosophical work—a work which, whether one likes it or not, constitutes a wealth of important philosophical and existential challenges. We must resist the easy temptation, often offered by those who haven't read Sartre closely, to dismiss him as outmoded or too philosophically temperamental. I suspect that the core challenges presented by his overall philosophical position to our cultural assumptions are just as relevant (and perhaps annoying) today as when they were initially written. And that hardly represents grounds for ignoring him.

2

Bad Faith and "Lying to Oneself"

In Chapter 1, I attempted to show some equivocations related to Sartre's claim that sincerity is a "phenomenon of bad faith" and shares its fundamental structure and goal. Although I do not retract the thrust of my argument, I now believe that I either ignored or overlooked some of the complexities and problems involved in Sartre's views on bad faith. In the present chapter, I wish to attend to a few of these issues. While attempting to offer a close, integrative analysis of Sartre's views on bad faith, I intend to raise some questions concerning the adequacy of his position, as it develops. In particular, in the light of his initial characterization of bad faith, I shall raise the question of whether, given his ontological premises and system of meanings, it is possible to lie to oneself. On Sartre's terms, of course, this question entails the question of the possibility of bad faith. Despite my persistent misgivings, I shall concede that there is, finally, a highly modified sense of "lying to oneself" in which bad faith as lying to oneself becomes a possibility for Sartre. But even this qualified sense, I shall show, is not without its problems.

Let us begin by reviewing Sartre's preliminary characterization of bad faith and elucidating the initial and gnawing question to which it gives rise.

Lying in general and lying to oneself

Sartre's discussion of bad faith follows both his discussion of the origin of negation and his introductory definition of human consciousness as "a being such that in its being, its being is in question in so far as this being implies a being other than itself."[1] The human being is not only the being through whom concrete negations *(négatités)* come into the world; he is also the being who can take negative attitudes toward himself. In order to illustrate this possibility of self-negation, he chooses to examine "one determined attitude . . . *essential to human reality* . . . which is such that consciousness instead of directing its negation outward turns it towards itself."[2] For Sartre this attitude is *bad faith.*

Sartre, in a preliminary move which remains to tantalize the rest of his discussion, allows that bad faith is a "lie to oneself."[3] He does this with one proviso; namely, that lying to oneself be distinguished from "lying in general," or falsehood. The essence of the lie, as we have seen, entails that the liar is actually and completely in "possession of the truth which he is hiding": "a man does not lie about what he is ignorant of."[4] Moreover, the liar *intends* to deceive and does not try either to hide this intention from himself or to disguise the translucency *(translucidité)* of consciousness.[5] Through the lie, consciousness affirms its existence as hidden from the Other and exploits for its own ends the ontological duality between myself and myself viewed from the eyes of the Other.[6]

But the situation cannot be the same for bad faith. As lying to oneself, bad faith, of course, hides or misrepresents truth. As we saw in the preceding chapter, "what changes everything is that in bad faith it is from myself that I conceal the truth."[7] Here there is no ontological duality between deceiver and deceived. On the contrary, bad faith entails "the *unity* of a single consciousness." The one who lies and the one to whom the lie is told are one and the same. Consciousness "affects itself" with bad faith. Hence, it must have both an intention and a project of bad faith. Moreover, given the complete translucency of consciousness, "that which affects itself with bad faith must be conscious (of) its bad faith."[8] Otherwise, we would have a consciousness ignorant of itself, which, for Sartre, is patently absurd.[9] Early in *Being and Nothingness*, we learn that, because of the self-referential and pre-reflective nature of consciousness,[10] we can wish "not to see" a specific aspect of our being only if we are acquainted with the aspect that we do not wish to see. Accordingly, our flight from anguish, for instance, "in order not to know" is in *bad faith* because, given "the unity of the same consciousness", we "cannot avoid knowing" from what we are fleeing. The flight from anguish is necessarily "a mode of becoming conscious of anguish."[11]

But at this point we need no further details. If bad faith, in contrast to falsehood, is originally viewed as a lie to oneself, if it unites in a single consciousness both the deceiver and deceived, if it is pre-reflectively aware of the deceit with which it is trying to afflict its own consciousness, then a question must arise as to its possibility. Given the translucent nature of consciousness, is it possible for me to hide the truth from myself? Or, to put the issue more pointedly, is it possible, in the light of Sartre's characterization both of the lie and of human consciousness, to lie to oneself? We must give concentrated attention to this question.

Is lying to oneself possible?

At the end of his preliminary characterization of bad faith, Sartre himself seems troubled by this issue. Concealing the truth from myself implies knowing it, but "How then," he asks, "can the lie subsist if the duality which conditions it is suppressed?"[12]

If the "being of consciousness" is the "consciousness of being," he ponders, perhaps then my consciousness of bad faith is in good faith. But then this "whole psychic system," is done away with. He quickly avows, "If I deliberately and cynically attempt to lie to myself, I fail completely in this undertaking; the lie falls back and collapses beneath my look; it is ruined *from behind* by the very consciousness of lying to myself which pitilessly constitutes itself well within my project as its very condition."[13]

To be sure, Sartre acknowledges the problem and appears to have a clear awareness of it. It seems obvious that he is right in inferring that, if the would-be liar "knows" (or "is in possession of") the truth she is trying to disguise, then any conscious effort to hide that truth from herself would be in vain. Yet this acknowledgment, even of the failure or inevitable self-destructiveness of any deliberate attempt to lie to oneself, does not lead Sartre to abrogate his preliminary conception of bad faith. What we discover here, Sartre tells us, is the "evanescence" of bad faith. This is a phenomenon that fluctuates between good faith and cynicism and exists only "in and through its own differentiation."[14] Bad faith is *métastable*—a word Sartre uses to designate the evanescent, abruptly transitional nature of its psychic structures.[15] At this point he claims neither to reject nor to understand it. Although he acknowledges its "very precarious" existence, he is still prepared to say that (note!) "it can even be the normal aspect [way?] of life for a *very great number* of people."[16] Keeping in mind our question, we must attempt to understand the ambivalence of Sartre's position and, by looking at key aspects of his more developed view, come to some determination as to its salvageability and consequences.

The "ideal lie"

To be noted first is that, even in his preliminary discussion, Sartre makes a point of telling us that the lie he has described is the "ideal lie."[17] In the present context, this is important, I believe, for two reasons. First, although for the sake of relieving the problem we might wish the opposite, Sartre does not, at this point, suggest that bad faith involves anything less than an *ideal* lie.[18] On the contrary, he tells us that the "common, popular forms of the lie," in which the liar only "half-persuades" himself of it, are "degenerate aspects" of the lie and represent "intermediaries between falsehood and bad faith."[19] Hence, we cannot, at this stage, circumvent the problem by affirming that this project (of lying to oneself) lacks either clarity[20] or persuasion. Second, this discussion is important for its introduction of the concept of "half-persuasion." Although Sartre cannot cash it in here, this concept may be the main wedge into his culminatory treatment of bad faith and his confrontation with "the true problem of bad faith."[21] We shall see later that the issue of non-persuasion and persuasion bears significantly, though problematically, on Sartre's subsequent notion of a peculiarly *non-persuasive* evidence.[22]

"Facticity" and "transcendence"

Sartre realizes that the problem he faces has led many to take recourse in a theory of the unconscious. For reasons that are generally consistent with his view of the translucency of consciousness, but which others have analyzed and found wanting,[23] Sartre rejects the Freudian psychoanalytic theory. Concluding that his problem is left "untouched" by the psychoanalytic alternative,[24] he turns to his well-known descriptions of "patterns of bad faith." *Assuming* that these are instances of bad faith, even though he has offered no further claim to comprehend it, he asks, "What must be the being of man if he is to be capable of bad faith?"[25]

Sartre's reply is prompt and definite. His phenomenological description of the erratic, transitory behavior of a coquettish woman pending imminent sexual advances appears to give him a basic insight into the mechanism of bad faith. The human being for Sartre, as we saw in Chapter 1, is at once a *facticity* and a *transcendence*—roughly speaking, both a "given" and the possibilities associated with its freedom, both a "what is" and a "what is not." The coquette uses to her advantage this "double property" of human reality.[26] She is aware of the possibility of "the first approach" but chooses to recognize only the "respectful" and "discreet" in her companion's attitude. She is aware of the desire she evokes but purifies it of anything humiliating by acknowledging it only as "pure transcendence"[27]; "she refuses to apprehend the desire for what it is."[28] She leaves her hand to be held but at that moment becomes all intellect. She reduces her companion's actions to *what they are*, while enjoying his desire as transcendence *(as not being what it is)*, as being only among his possibles. Despite her translucent self-awareness, she attempts to transform facticity into transcendence and vice versa. She plays "seesaw" with the two aspects of her being. By doing so, she feels that she is escaping all reproaches. But she does so at the price of arresting, of "gluing down," of thingifying, her possibilities—of objectifying her transcending freedom. She is in bad faith.[29]

As two aspects of human reality, facticity and transcendence (as we saw in Chapter 1) should be susceptible to what Sartre calls a "valid coordination." But bad faith wants neither to coordinate them nor to overcome them in a synthesis. Rather, "bad faith seeks to affirm their identity while preserving their differences."[30] The coquette affirms her intellect or respect in the mode of being of a thing even while distinguishing between herself as object of desire (body) and herself as the intellectual or wholly respectful being she could become. Bad faith "must affirm facticity as *being* transcendence and transcendence as *being* facticity, in such a way that at the instant when a person apprehends the one, he can find himself abruptly faced with the other."[31] Hence, the *métastable* double property of transcendence-facticity becomes a condition for the possibility of the *métastable* phenomenon of bad faith.

Although this point serves to illuminate what Sartre "intends" by bad faith, it does not eliminate his dilemmas concerning it. For, even given the facticity-transcendence character of human reality, consciousness, it must be recalled, "affects itself with bad faith."[32] And, as a consequence of its prereflective nature, consciousness, for Sartre, must be aware of its intention of hiding the truth from itself—in this case, of its deceptive project of "sliding back and forth"[33] from facticity to transcendence.

Being for-itself

There is a closely related way of viewing human reality, which is at the root of Sartre's facticity-transcendence analysis and is more directly responsive to his question concerning the necessary ontological prerequisite of bad faith. Anyone familiar with even a skeletal outline of Sartre's phenomenological ontology is acquainted with it. (Indeed, we saw this in Chapter 1.) As early as the Introduction of *Being and Nothingness*, Sartre offers a preliminary distinction between "being for-itself" *(l'être-pour-soi)* and "being in-itself" *(l'être-en-soi)*, between the being of consciousness and the being of the phenomenon, between self-referential being and being "what it is." Sartre sees the former as distinctive human reality and defines it as a being "which *is* what it *is not* and which *is not* what it is."[34] Unlike being in-itself, being for-itself or consciousness (as we have seen) is not a "what" or an object or a thing. That is, it is not "what it *is*"; it lacks identity or "a certain coincidence [or oneness] with itself"[35]; it has no nature or fixed essence. On the other hand, it "is what it is *not*"; it is its possibilities, its future undetermined projects, its potential for "transcendence." In different words, the *being* of human reality is not what it is and is what it is not because it is *free*. For Sartre, being for-itself or human reality *is* freedom. "The essence of the human being is suspended in his freedom," says Sartre. "What we call freedom is impossible to distinguish from the being of 'human reality'; . . . there is no difference between the being of man [sic] and his *being-free*."[36]

The connection between this paradoxical manner of viewing human reality and Sartre's alleged relation of facticity-transcendence to bad faith should now become more apparent. Bad faith (*assuming* for the moment that it is possible) could not affirm facticity as *being* transcendence and transcendence as *being* facticity, in the abruptly evanescent manner Sartre suggests, unless human reality were a being "which is what it is not and which is not what it is"; that is, unless it were "ambiguous," "fluid," and without self-coincidence. This game could not be played between facticity and transcendence unless, within human reality itself, there were the possibility of free interplay between "what it is" and "what it is not"; unless, to put it more radically, there were a "built-in" tension or dialectical "to-and-fro" between the "what is" and "what is not" aspects of human reality. It is because the human being's "essence" is *suspended* in freedom, because human *being* as consciousness (or, more exactly, as "conscious body") exists "at a distance from itself" (if I may be permitted later terminology),[37] that it can move freely and elusively between facticity and transcendence and *attempt* to treat each in the mode of being of the other. It is because I both am and am not what I have been, both am and am not *only* my past or present, for example, that I can try to escape from my past or present by appealing to the "perpetual re-creation" my freedom entails.[38]

A brief return to Sartre's coquettish woman might add clarification here. It is because she "*is* what she is not" and "*is not* what she is," *qua* human reality, that she can try to convince herself of the *possibility* that she is in intellectual discussion with her companion when in fact she is being "advanced to" sexually and is eliciting the desire of her companion. After all, she is not just body, and she is more than her present emotions or behavior. Involvement in intellectual conversation, being "intellectual," is among her possibilities. Her freedom cannot foreclose this. So, given the situation—which (in Sartre's view of "situation") she in part created through her choosing—she shifts disingenuously to what she is not. In so doing, she not only denies that she is mere body but also arrests her transcendent intellectual capability and turns it into the mode of being of a thing or in-itself (facticity). She "glues down" her transcending possibility. She is said to be in bad faith, for she cannot be "all intellect" in the manner that an inkwell is an inkwell. She is a being who *is not* what she is and *is* what she is not; as human reality, she is free and without identity. To borrow a passage from the last part of *Being and Nothingness:* "To the extent that the for-itself wishes to hide its own nothingness from itself and to incorporate the in-itself as its true mode of being, it is trying also to hide its freedom from itself."[39]

We now have the more basic answer to Sartre's question as to what must be the *being* of humans if they are to be capable of bad faith. As we saw in the preceding chapter, "The condition of the possibility for bad faith, in its most immediate being, in the intra-structure of the pre-reflective *cogito* must be what it is not and not be what it is."[40] "If man is *what he is,* bad faith is forever impossible"[41]; bad faith "requires that . . . there be an imponderable difference separating being from non-being in the mode of being of human reality."[42] Were human reality not so constituted, the fluctuating interchange between our transcendence and facticity could not be attempted, and we could not, in bad faith, be involved in the self-destructive enterprise of treating ourselves as identities, of fleeing our freedom, of tying ourselves down.

But, despite this elucidation and the interconnections we have observed, we must ask whether we are brought any further toward accepting the feasibility of lying to oneself, on Sartre's terms. I submit not. However directly Sartre speaks to the ontological requirements needed for human *being* to be capable of bad faith, he has not shown how that *being* of human reality allows lying to oneself. However well he shows that "a beginning which *is* what it is not and which *is not* what it is" makes possible the game of reciprocal metamorphosis between facticity and transcendence, he has not shown how this game involves lying to oneself, in his initially defined sense of lying. No matter how sensitively he unveils the double property of human reality and describes its inner workings, he cannot get away from his own view, as we have noted, of the "total translucency" of consciousness. It would appear that no interworkings between the "two aspects" of human reality (or free, conscious being or subject-being), however deceptive in intent, can escape this translucency.[43] To suggest that they do would not only violate a critical dimension of his theory of consciousness but would also appear to break the "psychic unity" on which he insists against Freud and the psychoanalysts.

We are left to wonder if Sartre's view of bad faith as lying to oneself is salvageable. Perhaps, as his position develops, lying to oneself takes on a modified meaning. We must probe further.

Faith, belief, and "non-persuasive evidence"
In an important and demanding section entitled "The 'Faith' of Bad Faith,"[44] Sartre affirms that the "true problem" of bad faith originates in the fact that bad faith is "faith." We are not dealing here, he maintains, with certainty, if "certainty" is to be understood as "the intuitive possession of the object."[45] However, if

"belief" is taken to mean "the adherence [adhésion] of being to its object" when the object is either "not given" or "given indistinctly," then bad faith is belief, and the fundamental problem of bad faith is a problem of belief.[46] Our question concerning the possibility of bad faith as lying to oneself then becomes a question, roughly speaking, of whether and how it is possible, given one's consciousness of one's attempts to lie, to believe (have faith in) one's own would-be lies to oneself.

At this point, so much depends on the nature of "faith," the relation of belief to evidence, and, perhaps most importantly, the manner in which one "puts oneself in" (or "affects oneself with") bad faith. All of these issues come together here. Sartre now tells us that, in its original project and in its coming "into the world," bad faith makes a conscious decision regarding the precise nature of its requirements. For it realizes that "faith is decision and that after each intuition, it must decide and will what it is."[47] It thus stands forth "in the firm resolution not to demand too much, to count itself satisfied when it is barely persuaded, to force itself in decisions to adhere to uncertain truths."[48] This means that, although bad faith perceives evidence, it resigns itself in advance to not being "fulfilled" by the evidence. In other words, it commits itself ahead of time to a "non-persuasive evidence" which it designs as nonpersuasive. Prima facie, this bears resemblance to the common lies of "half-persuasion" which Sartre has earlier dismissed as "degenerate aspects of the lie" and has distinguished from bad faith.[49]

In any case, what we can now infer, according to Sartre, is that the primitive project of bad faith is itself in bad faith. Or, to put the matter in a slightly different way, the initial enterprise of bad faith is to be seen as a decision made in bad faith about the nature of faith. Because faith is not certainty, the consciousness of bad faith (or "bad-faith consciousness") decides to be content with an insufficiency of evidence; to determine arbitrarily the amount of evidence by which it will be persuaded, while "knowing" that the amount it requires is not sufficient to persuade *fully*. In a passage that is germane to this point, Sartre says the following:

> I am not only in bad faith at the end of my effort when I have constructed my two-faced concepts *[concepts amphiboliques]* and when I have persuaded myself. In truth, I have not persuaded myself: to the extent that I could be so persuaded, I have always been so. And at the very moment when I was disposed to put myself in bad faith, I of necessity was in bad faith with respect to this same disposition *[ces dispositions mêmes]*.[50]

And he adds poignantly:

> The decision to be in bad faith does not dare to speak its name; *it believes itself and does not believe itself* in bad faith; *it believes itself and does not believe itself* in good faith.[51]

What we see, then, is that from its very inception bad faith is aware of its structure and attempts to exploit the mercurial "nature" of consciousness and faith by setting up weak requirements for the acceptance of *non-persuasive* evidence. Bad faith begins with an awareness that human reality is *métastable*, that it *is* what it is not and *is not* what it is. On this intuition, it sets out to forge the instruments of its own (non)self-persuasion. It "decides" that "non-persuasion is the structure of all convictions." As consciousness is a being that is always "in question," that always has nothingness at its heart, so belief must be a being that constantly "questions its own being." This means that belief can realize itself only at the price of self-destruction, that it can make itself known to itself only by simultaneously denying itself as the known. This is what Sartre is getting at when he says, "To believe is to know that one believes, and to know that one believes is no longer to believe."[52] To believe is not to believe, so "pure belief" is impossible.[53] This allows him to say also that it is the impossibility of perfect good faith (of totally believing what one believes) that makes bad faith possible. The reason for him is evident: consciousness is evanescent; it is constantly fleeing from identity with itself; it is "perpetually escaping itself." Hence, in its being, the immediate "becomes" mediate, the absolute becomes relative, and belief becomes nonbelief.[54] In other words, because of the nature of consciousness, *everything* in it must be "in question" or *métastable;* otherwise, the translucency of consciousness would be spoiled by the opaqueness of the *en-soi.* As a consequence, every belief "falls short" *(n'est pas assez croyance[55])* and can never believe enough *(ne peut jamais assez croire),* and one never fully believes what one believes. Belief then becomes "impossible belief." So my failure to *believe* that I am courageous, for example, does not dispirit me, since believing always comes short of believing. This applies to "good faith"[56] as well as to "bad faith."

Hence we see that for Sartre the primitive project of bad faith makes use of and exploits the constant "autodestruction" of "the fact of consciousness" *(fait de conscience).* As we have observed, because of the alleged nature of consciousness and of faith, we are able, in bad faith, to set conditions for our being "persuaded" even when we are not persuaded. Similarly, the stage is set for "believing" even when our belief comes short of believing. For Sartre, it follows, of course, that if "bad faith" is "faith" and includes "its own negation" in its "primitive project,"[57] then at the outset a faith that wants itself to be "not quite convinced" *(mal convaincue)* has to be possible. The faith of the coquette, for instance, in "deciding" in advance not to be fully convinced in order to convince itself that she is not what she is (a flirt) is in *bad* faith from the start.

We are advanced in understanding the project and intentions of bad faith. Yet, again, we must not forget our critical question as to the possibility of lying to oneself, on Sartre's terms. In reconsidering this question in the light of what has immediately preceded, we bring to a head Sartre's position regarding bad faith.

Sartre appears to offer a direct reply to the question. He says, "I shall not be able to conceal from myself that I believe so as not to believe and that I do not believe so *as* to believe."[58] How then can one be in bad faith if bad faith involves "lying to oneself" and "lying to oneself" involves concealing the truth from oneself?[59] In fact, does not this admission totally annihilate "bad faith"? Sartre concedes that "knowing" I am a coward, for instance, at the moment that I wish to believe myself courageous serves eventually to destroy my belief. But he is quick to make three qualifications, the third of which is most pertinent here. First, considered in terms of the mode of being of the in-itself, I *am* not any more courageous than cowardly. Second, "I do not *know* that I am courageous," for any such view of myself must be accompanied by belief (for it goes beyond reflexive certainty). Third, it *is* the case that bad faith "does *not* bring itself to believe" (*ne s'arrive pas à croire*[60]) what it wants to believe. However, *"it is precisely as the acceptance of not believing what it believes that it is bad faith."*[61] In contrast to good faith, which attempts to perform the converse, bad faith flees being by finding refuge in "not-believing-what-one believes." By exploiting the identityless nature of consciousness, by including its negation in its primitive project, bad faith disarms in advance all beliefs—both those it would like to grasp and those that it wishes to flee. That is to say, in "willing" the self-destruction of belief, bad faith at the same time spoils beliefs "which are opposed to it"; namely, those "which reveal themselves as *being only* belief." For, given that consciousness is "perpetually escaping itself,"[62] that the being of consciousness as consciousness is to exist "at a distance from itself,"[63] beliefs which are apprehended as beliefs can no longer be "only belief": they are already no longer belief; they are what Sartre later calls "troubled belief."[64]

A modified sense of "lying to oneself" and the possibility of bad faith

Two inferences may now, I believe, be drawn from these observations. First, given the totally translucent nature of consciousness and the troubled nature of belief, we must still say that, in the strict sense of successfully and completely hiding a truth from oneself, within the unity of a single consciousness, "lying to oneself" is not possible for Sartre. The consciousness (of) belief cannot miss questioning its own belief; the bad-faith consciousness cannot escape an awareness of its own self-destroying and disarming project; the consciousness (of) belief or disbelief, cannot be ignorant of its believing so as not to believe, or its not believing so as to believe (for that, as we saw, would suggest an "unconscious," a "consciousness ignorant of itself," which, for Sartre, is "absurd"[65]); consciousness cannot flee an awareness of what it is trying to hide, flee, or negate. If consciousness is self-conscious, if it involves a pre-reflective awareness of itself, it cannot alter or hide anything from itself.

But to say that "lying to oneself" is not possible in Sartre's strictest sense of this expression is not *necessarily* to say that bad faith is impossible in Sartre. It is only to say that it is precluded by his initial, strict sense of "lying to oneself." But weaker, modified senses are possible. I submit that the substance of Sartre's developed position on the phenomenon of bad faith—particularly as expressed in his section on "The 'Faith' of Bad Faith"—allows us to infer that he finally adopts a qualified sense of the expression. We have seen much evidence for this. In its original project, "bad faith" (as Sartre perhaps prematurely calls it) structures itself to accept *non-persuasive* evidence, to count itself satisfied when it has met only minimal requirements for persuasion, to regard itself as persuaded when it is only partially or half-persuaded. It constructs "two-faced," ambiguous concepts (of persuasion, belief) by which this can be done. Bad faith *decides* that nonpersuasion is constitutive of all convictions. It exploits the nature of belief (belief always "falls short" of belief; "to believe is not to believe," given the instability and elusiveness of consciousness) by accepting to believe what it cannot *fully* persuade itself to believe, given the translucency of consciousness. And to repeat: "it is precisely as the acceptance of not believing what it believes that it is bad faith."[66]

This statement is surely an important key to understanding both Sartre's modified sense of "lying to oneself" and his developed view regarding the possibility of bad faith. I submit that "the *acceptance* of not believing what one believes" (italics mine) represents one articulation of the qualified sense in which Sartre finally understands "lying to oneself." To revert to the language of "persuasion," we can perhaps also say that "lying to oneself" turns out to have the modified sense of "the acceptance of not being *fulfillingly* persuaded even when one is "persuaded." In any case, one can accept "not-believing-what-one-believes" not only because of the dialectical, *métastable* nature of belief but because, as I have stressed, the primitive project of bad faith sets weak evidential requirements for persuasion. One can meet these requirements, be "persuaded" on that count, and yet be aware that the "required" evidence is inadequate for complete, fulfilled persuasion. One can, in this manner, not believe while "believing" and presumably believe while "not believing."

If this qualified sense of lying to oneself is endorsed and if bad faith is, as we saw from the start, lying to oneself, then it follows that bad faith, *in this qualified sense of lying to oneself,*

is possible. By presupposing and acknowledging the translucency of consciousness—its total "openness"—this qualified
usage answers our repeated question about the possibility and
manner of lying to oneself in the full translucency of consciousness. This modified meaning of the expression also allows a
viable reply to Sartre's own question: "How can we believe by
bad faith in the concepts which we forge expressly to persuade
ourselves?"[67] In addition, it has other advantages: I mention
only a few. It sees bad faith precisely in terms of what Sartre
ultimately views the problem of bad faith; namely, in terms of
belief.[68] It is grounded on the assumption, thoroughly compatible with the translucency of consciousness, that bad faith does
not fully succeed in believing what it wishes to believe or not
believe. In attaching itself to the phenomenon of "not-believing-
what-one-believes," it testifies anew to the "distance" that exists
at the core of the *being* of consciousness, and it elucidates further the *métastable* "double property" ("transcendence-facticity") of human reality.[69] To refer to one concrete illustration, it
allows us to see how, finally, the bad faith of the coquette involved precisely her *acceptance* of her believing (that she was
involved in intellectual discussion, not bodily flirtation) even
though, given the translucency of consciousness, she did *not*
believe and was *not fully persuaded.*

What shall we say then? Has Sartre met what he calls his
"true problem of bad faith"?[70] I believe the answer to this is a
heavily qualified, problematic "yes." Insofar as he has given us,
within the context of *faith* and *belief,* a sense in which a "lie
to oneself" is possible on his own ontological premises (that
consciousness is totally translucent and that there is an idiosyncratic unitary structure to "single consciousness"), I believe
that he has moved towards resolving both his "essential" problem and our central difficulty with his initial definition of bad
faith. Certainly, he has provided us with a sense in which the

"lie to oneself," because of bad faith's primitive resolution in respect to evidence, need not necessarily collapse or "fall back,"[71] in the face of the translucency of consciousness.

Nonetheless, there are at least two qualifications or difficulties that must be expressed. *First,* as I already anticipated, because Sartre's qualified sense of "lying to oneself" presupposes a conscious decision to be content with evidence that does not fully persuade, it appears to be a "lie" in a weak sense of that word. As such, it seems to be a lie of "half-persuasion," which Sartre earlier characterizes as a common, degenerate form of the lie and rejects as an instance of bad faith.[72] Either there is an inconsistency here, or Sartre, without having specifically expressed it, has altered his approach to "half-persuasion" while developing his account of bad faith.

Second, given again his view of the primitive project of bad faith, there is no question that the modified sense of "lying to oneself" involves a *deliberate* intention to accept as persuasive what is not fully persuasive, and to "believe" (according to criteria that one "knows" are inadequate for *full* persuasion) what one consciously does not fully believe. This suggests a cynical element in Sartre's modified sense of bad faith. But Sartre clearly states in a number of places that bad faith does *not* involve a *cynical* lie.[73] To be sure, Sartre early describes the "cynical consciousness" as one that, though affirming truth within itself, is involved in the "doubly negative attitude" of both denying it in words and "denying that negation as such."[74] Although the qualified sense of bad faith which I have been attributing to Sartre is not so overtly cynical (it seems more like a game of "pretend" which consciousness plays with itself in respect to persuasion and belief), it does seem to make "knowing preparations"[75] for offering to oneself as "truth" a "pleasing untruth."[76] Moreover, insofar as bad faith for Sartre finally *denies* the "inner disintegration" (*désagrégation*)[77] or freedom of human reality, which it both attempts to *flee* in the human search for identity and to *utilize* in its wish to escape the in-itself, it appears to share—at least partly—in the cynical consciousness. In any case, if this qualified sense of bad faith is to hold, and Sartre continues to insist that bad faith is not cynical, he will have to differentiate it clearly from both the "cynical lie" and "cynicism."[78] We shall probe this issue in detail in the next chapter.

In conclusion, one point merits explicit affirmation. However adequately this *acceptance* of not-believing-what-one-believes might qualify as a weakened version of lying to oneself, it is a far cry from the view of bad faith (suggested in the early part of Sartre's analysis) that requires a *successful concealment* of truth from consciousness in the full translucency of consciousness.

Doesn't seem to have truly overcome the problem.

3

The Cynicism
of Sartre's
"Bad Faith"

At the end of his treatment of "Bad Faith" in *Being and Nothingness,* Jean-Paul Sartre concludes that "In bad faith, there is no cynical lie nor knowing preparation for deceitful concepts."[1] A few pages earlier, at the beginning of the highly important section "The 'Faith' of Bad Faith," he announces: "The true problem of bad faith stems evidently from the fact that bad faith is *faith*. It *cannot* be either a *cynical* lie or certainty—if certainty is the intuitive possession of the object."[2] And having suggested early in his analysis that "the ideal description" of the liar would be "a cynical consciousness,"[3] he now wants, again, to separate bad faith from the cynical lie or the cynical consciousness:

> The decision to be in bad faith does not dare to speak its name; it believes itself and does not believe itself in bad faith; it believes itself and does not believe itself in good faith. . . . For me to have represented it to myself as bad faith would have been cynicism.[4]

These and other statements Sartre offers in his oft-quoted analysis of bad faith make it clear that Sartre does not regard bad faith as cynical; that he does not, finally, see the bad-faith consciousness as a cynical consciousness; and that he repudiates the view that bad faith involves a cynical lie. In only one spot—immediately after pointing out, in the light of "total translucency of consciousness,"[5] the autodestructiveness of any deliberate and cynical attempt to lie to oneself—does he explicitly suggest that the bad-faith consciousness might have a cynical dimension. Here he allows that, as a mercurial, evanescent consciousness, bad faith "vacillates continually between good faith and cynicism."[6] And a few lines later he adds that a bad-faith "style of life" does not preclude "abrupt awakenings to cynicism."

IN THE present chapter, I wish to show that, in spite of his insistence to the contrary, the deceptive consciousness that Sartre characterizes as bad faith is a cynical consciousness; that the project of bad faith is a cynical project; and that bad faith, though not an "ideal" lie, is a form of cynical "lying."

In arguing my main thesis, I am pursuing a suggestion I made at the conclusion of my preceding chapter on "Bad Faith and 'Lying to Oneself.' " In the closing pages, I barely suggested a basis on which my reconstruction and modification of Sartre's view of bad faith—as "lying to oneself"—reflects a cynical aspect of bad faith. In what follows, I wish to elucidate my suggestion and make evident the grounds on which I maintain that bad faith, as Sartre analyzes it, turns out to be a cynical project. Thus, though I have tried to salvage Sartre's view of the possibility of lying to oneself, I have offered no intention—or pretension—of delivering his view (of self-deception) from cynicism. Rather, as the present chapter will confirm, I have raised the question of whether, on Sartrean terms, lying to oneself—even in a qualified sense—can ever be without a cynical element. In what follows, my suggestion will become an argued contention.

To set the stage for my thesis, I must first seek out Sartre's use of the word "cynical." This clarification will enable us to comprehend better what Sartre is denying when he denies that bad faith is cynical.

Sartre's use of *cynical*

In the context of *Being and Nothingness* and his discussion of bad faith, Sartre does not say much directly to explicate his meaning of "cynicism" or "cynical." The most he says is hardly self-explanatory: "The ideal (description) of a liar, as we have seen, is a cynical consciousness, affirming the truth in himself, denying it in words, and denying for himself that negation."[7] This "doubly negative attitude," he tells us, "rests on the transcendent: the fact expressed is transcendent since it does not exist, and the original negation rests on a *truth*, that is, on a particular type of transcendence."[8] Sartre goes on to state:

> As for the inner negation *(négation intime)* which I effect correlatively with the affirmation for myself of the truth, [it] rests on *words*, that is, on an event in the world. [Moreover], the inner disposition of the liar is positive; it could [become] the object of an affirmative judgment. The liar *intends* to deceive and he does not seek to hide this intention nor to disguise the translucency of consciousness; on the contrary, he has recourse to it when there is a [matter] of deciding secondary behavior.[9]

Despite its parsimony and lack of elucidation, Sartre's account of the twofold negation involved in the "cynical consciousness" of an "ideal lie" is directive here. Sartre seems to be saying that, in telling an ideal lie, one negates the inner truth of which one is aware (which one "possesses," if you like) in the very project of trying to conceal it from the Other. That is to say, in lying, the liar denies in his words *(dans ses paroles)* to the Other a truth that he "knows" and affirms within himself. He exercises that negation "correlatively" with affirming the truth to himself. But the "ideal lie" does not end with this "original negation." The cynical consciousness of the liar involves a "*doubly* negative attitude" *(double attitude négative)*[10]: the liar, still translucently conscious of the truth he is trying to conceal, and not trying to hide the deceptive intent from himself, also denies to himself the deceptive falsity that he is trying to convey to the Other. Yet that does not stop him from telling the lie to the Other. His consciousness is *cynical:* it continues to reflect a blatant disregard for the truth.

As for the liar's "flaunted intention" (*l'intention affichée*[11]) to tell the truth—as expressed, for example, in his words "I'd never want to deceive you!" "This is true! I swear it!"—Sartre insists that it is the "object of [this] inner negation." But, Sartre tells us, it is not recognized by the liar as *his* intention; rather it is "played" and "imitated"; "it is the intention of a character *[personnage]* which he plays in the eyes of his questioner," but his feigned character, "precisely because *he does not exist* [*parce qu'il n'est pas*[12]], is a transcendent."[13]

Before drawing this clarification to a head, two tangential but relevant points now deserve mention. First, we see from the above how the lie is for Sartre a "phenomenon of transcendence." It is transcendent, first, because it is directed beyond the liar to the Other whom the liar is trying to persuade; second, because, as a denial of a truth, the "fact" expressed—as Sartre puts it—"does not exist" yet rests on a certain kind of transcendent truth; and third, because it requires the taking on and playing of a role (the feigning of a "character") which does not "exist," which is outside the nature of consciousness. As Joseph Catalano has pointed out, the whole structure of the lie can be called a "phenomenon of transcendence" in Sartre because it is shaped toward persuading the Other to accept an untruth as a truth.[14]

But we must note that Sartre is dealing here with what he calls "lying in general" and, more particularly, the "ideal lie." Although the machinations of strict lying—as an Other-directed phenomenon—are cynical, Sartre disclaims cynicism for the kind of phenomenon that he labels "lying to oneself" (that is, bad faith or self-deception). This kind of lying does not, according to Sartre, share the same transcendent aims or features noted above.

Second, we must observe again that Sartre considers bad faith under the rubric of "the attitude of 'self-negation.' "[15] He chooses to examine it as "one determined attitude . . . essential to human reality . . . which is such that consciousness, instead of directing its negation outward, turns it towards itself."[16] This means, as we have seen in earlier chapters, that Sartre sees bad faith right from the start as a negative attitude, an attitude of negation toward the self, which prompts him to ask the question: "What, are we to say, is the being of man who has the possibility of denying himself?"[17] Bad faith, as lying to oneself, is a negative attitude, but does it represent the "doubly negative" attitude by which Sartre marks the "cynical consciousness" of the strict lie? And does it rest on and aim at the transcendent in the manner that the cynical consciousness does? By affirming that bad faith cannot be a cynical lie, Sartre seems necessarily to be saying "no" to each of these questions.

Perhaps Sartre has misjudged the nature of the cynical consciousness. Perhaps he has failed to see part of the negative attitude that a bad-faith consciousness "self-consciously" adopts toward truth (and falsity). Whatever the case, I intend to show that the attitude of self-negation in which bad faith is said to consist is, without question, cynical. That it may not be cynical in exactly the same manner that a strict lie or falsehood is cynical does not save it from cynicism.

At this point, we are able to understand that Sartre sees in the "ideal lie" a model of the cynical consciousness. The ideal lie, one might say, is for him an instance of "ideal" cynicism. The liar's consciousness is, as we have seen, doubly negative: it doubly denies the truth of which the liar is conscious and attempts to hide from the Other. In *expressing* to the Other the opposite, or a deceptive variation, of what he believes, he manifests a callous disregard for what he takes to be the truth. His pretended assurances to the Other—which he recognizes as untruth and denies to himself—that he is telling the truth show again a dismissal of and a lack of concern for truth (and goodness). All this he does "in entire lucidity" *(en toute lucidité)* and with full understanding of the truth he is masking or altering. The liar deliberately exploits, for his own deceitful ends, the ontological duality of myself and the Other, of myself and myself for the Other ("du moi et du moi d'autrui"[18]). His project of intentionally misrepresenting the truth of which he is aware is unambiguously cynical. Although the negations that constitute this consciousness are transcendent in the sense of aiming outside consciousness, they nonetheless betray the taking of a negative attitude toward one's consciousness, toward "oneself," so to say.

With this focus, and in these terms, we must now attempt to understand why Sartre does not regard bad faith as cynical. We shall then be in a better position to challenge Sartre directly.

Why, for Sartre, bad faith is not cynical

In my preceding chapter on Sartre's analysis of bad faith, I tried to make clear Sartre's distinction between "lying in general" and "lying to oneself," between the "strict lie," for example, and the lying that takes place in bad faith. I pointed out that "what changes everything" for Sartre is that, in bad faith (as "lying to oneself"), it is from myself that I (try to) conceal the truth, that the ontological duality between the one who deceives and the one who is deceived disappears. Because of this, Sartre initially views the possibility of lying to oneself as severely problematic. Given the translucency of consciousness, "if I deliberately and cynically attempt to lie to myself," the intended lie self-de-structs; it is destroyed "from behind" by my very awareness of my trying to deceive myself.

I am persuaded that this point, now seen in terms of con-sciousness's acts of denial and negation, remains the essential reason for Sartre's refusal to attribute cynicism to bad faith as a form of lying to oneself. If bad faith is lying to oneself, how can the negative attitude that constitutes lying subsist if, to use Sartre's words, "the duality which conditions it is suppressed"? If, as a form of lying, bad faith involves taking a negative attitude toward oneself; if it necessarily involves denying to oneself a truth about oneself of which one is aware; if it must be such a crassly mendacious and deceptive attitude, how can it possibly occur or succeed in the unitary structure of consciousness? And, even if some form of lying to oneself is feasible, as count-less examples in everyday life seem to attest, how, given a uni-fied consciousness, can it be cynical in the sense that an ideal lie is cynical? That is to say, how would it be possible—given the fact that the one who lies and the one to whom the lie is told are the same person—to adopt the doubly negative attitude of (1) denying to oneself the truth that one "knows" and has affirmed, and (2) then denying to oneself that negation? How would this be possible without—to use Sartre's language—"annihilating" "the whole psychic system"?

For Sartre, the answer is straightforward: this consciousness is simply *not* possible. The answer is in the question, as he is apt to say. Although bad faith is a form of lying—specifically, lying to oneself—it cannot be *cynical* lying. The unitary struc-ture of consciousness precludes that. To resort to Sartre's dom-inant terminology, that which "affects itself" with bad faith "must be conscious (of) its bad faith"; it must be non-thetically aware of its bad faith, "since the being of consciousness is con-sciousness of being."[19] A bad-faith consciousness is incapable of the deliberate distortion of truth, of the *cynical* self-negation, that takes place in the "ideal lie," in lying to the Other. The unity of a single consciousness precludes and prohibits such a possibility.

But I want to argue that Sartre is wrong in this inference. What Sartre has done is this: he has reasoned that, because bad faith, as lying to oneself, must be distinguished from lying in general (and from the strict lie in particular), and because, unlike the "ideal" lie, lying to oneself precludes the possibility of completely concealing the truth from the one whom one is trying to deceive (specifically, oneself), therefore the bad-faith consciousness cannot be cynical. Sartre seems to have made the possibility for complete success of the project of lying (for completely concealing the truth) a decisive condition for its being cynical. I urge that Sartre is justified in concluding only that bad faith cannot be cynical in exactly the same way that lying in general is cynical, or that a "strict" lying (to the Other) consciousness is a cynical consciousness. It is one thing, and understandable, for Sartre to contend, prior to his analysis of bad faith and on the basis of a preliminary awareness of bad faith as "lying to oneself," that bad faith cannot be cynical. It is quite another—and certainly less understandable—for him to maintain the same after he has differentiated more carefully the deceptive structure of bad faith's lying from that of the "ideal"[20] lie. In focusing on the single and unified consciousness of lying to oneself, while inadvertently allowing the duality of consciousness to become a necessary condition for both lying in general and cynicism, Sartre has failed to acknowledge the blatantly cynical aspects of the kind of lying that, by his own admission, goes on in bad faith or self-deception.[21]

IN WHAT follows, I shall try to make clear some of the cynical aspects in bad faith as "lying to oneself." In doing so, I shall, of course, assume the essential correctness of the heavily qualified sense of "lying to oneself" which I have earlier attributed to Sartre's meaning of bad faith. To make my thesis unambiguous, I intend to show that, even in the distinctly qualified sense of "lying to oneself," bad faith, for Sartre, turns out to be cynical. While heeding Sartre's peculiar sense of "cynical," I shall also include in the meaning of "cynical" the notion of having a blatant disregard for, or indifference toward, truth. This, of course, is one of the common usage and dictionary senses of "cynical"—one that I have already invoked in a number of places in this book. I intend to show that bad faith, as analyzed by Sartre, is cynical in both of these senses.

The cynicism of bad faith

Initially, I want to make evident the more obvious. I propose to show that Sartre's analysis of the project and structure of bad faith betrays cynicism in the common usage sense to which I have been alluding.

"Cynical" in a common usage sense

First, we must note again that, for Sartre, "consciousness affects itself with bad faith." We do not "undergo" bad faith; we are not afflicted with it; we do not have it inflicted on us. We "put ourselves" in bad faith as we put ourselves to sleep,[22] so to say. As Sartre states it, there must be "an original intention and project" of bad faith; this very project entails "a comprehension of bad faith as such and a pre-reflective apprehension (of) consciousness as affecting itself with bad faith."[23] That is to say, bad faith involves a conscious decision to be in bad faith; it decides and wills what it is; it is "conscious of its own structure."

As I showed in the last chapter,[24] the very project of bad faith, for Sartre, is itself in bad faith. The bad-faith consciousness forges for itself "two-faced concepts" (des "concepts amphibo-

liques"[25]) by which to persuade itself when it is not persuaded. In its initial enterprise, it exploits the nature of faith (faith is belief, not certainty) and the evanescent nature of consciousness by deciding on weak evidential requirements for its persuasion and for "truth." By choosing to regard non-persuasion as the structure of all beliefs, bad faith "stands forth in the firm resolution not to demand too much," to count itself satisfied when it is not fully persuaded, "to force itself in decisions to adhere to uncertain truths."[26] At its inception, bad faith consciousness includes its own *negation:* I determine myself to be "convinced" or "not quite convinced" (*malconvaincu*[27]) in order to convince myself that I am not what I am or am what I am not. Because consciousness is always "in question," I, in bad faith, take advantage of the continuous autodestruction of the "fact of consciousness" *(fait de conscience)* by deliberately setting up mechanisms for my own (pseudo) "persuasion": I set up instruments by which I can persuade myself to "believe," on the basis of limited and selective data, even when I do not believe. And I am not dispirited by my unbelief, for I have told myself, in preparation for my "belief," for my "persuasion," that one can never believe enough ("ne peut jamais assez croire"), that all belief "comes short" of belief ("n'est pas assez croyance"[28]), that good faith is an "impossible belief" *(croyance impossible).*

These two points make clear, beyond reasonable doubt, that the bad-faith consciousness must be called "cynical" in the common usage sense I have invoked above. If consciousness "affects itself" with bad faith in the translucency of consciousness, it is surely responsible for the consciousness with which it has affected itself. And if the very project of bad-faith consciousness is itself in bad faith; that is, if it structures itself in advance to accept as "persuasive" that which it "knows" is *not* fully persuasive and if it (consciously) sets for itself the mechanism by which to "lie to itself," then it cannot escape the charge of having an indifference to or disregard for truth. Despite Sartre's assurance to the contrary, the bad-faith consciousness does make "knowing preparations" (*préparation savante*[29]) for "deceitful concepts" (*concepts trompeurs*[30]) and for its own deception. (I have shown this in the foregoing chapter.) It connives to hide the truth, to disregard it, to provide itself with a phony rationale for not asking itself to be fully persuaded, for believing what is transparently not fully believable. By exploiting the perpetual self-destruction of consciousness, it disarms in advance *all* beliefs, including all those that are opposed to it. By regarding all believing as not believing enough, all belief as "impossible"[31] or "troubled belief,"[32] bad-faith consciousness sneers at the possibility of "good faith"—of "believing what one believes"—and becomes disparagingly indifferent to the possibility of truth. Although, as I have tried to show, bad-faith consciousness does not succeed in believing completely what it wishes to believe, it goes on believing nonetheless. It is, I believe, blatantly "cynical" in the common usage sense of "cynical" to which I have been referring. This cynical attitude—of preparing to believe what one does not believe and to not believe what one does believe—is part of the "upsurge" of bad faith and is determinative of what Sartre calls the ulterior attitude (*l'attitude ultérieure*) and *Weltanschauung* of bad faith.[33]

LET US consider for a moment one of the most controversial of Sartre's examples: the illustration taken from the psychiatrist Steckel's account of the woman whom marital infidelity (*une déception conjugale*) has rendered frigid, who reaches a point of hiding from herself the sensual enjoyment that the sexual act brings her.[34] For Sartre, she is an example of "pathological bad faith."[35] Although such women frequently give to their husbands "objective signs of pleasure," under questioning they invariably deny having given such signs. They are involved in a pattern (Steckel called it "distraction") in which they apply themselves in advance to becoming distracted from the pleasure they dread. At the time of the sexual act, they deliberately turn their thoughts away from it and try rather to focus on daily housekeeping chores or the maintaining of household accounts. They prepare themselves ahead of time not to experience, not to acknowledge, the pleasure. But, Sartre contends, the conscious, deliberate efforts "not to confirm this experienced pleasure" (*ne pas adhérer au plaisir éprouvé*[36]) imply the recognition that the pleasure is experienced. Although, for Sartre, this is a clear instance of bad faith, it is not an instance of cynicism. Sartre says, "If the frigid woman distracts her consciousness from the pleasure she experiences, it is by no means cynically and in full agreement with herself: it is in order to prove to herself that she is frigid."[37]

But surely, if Sartre's non-Freudian analysis of the "frigid woman" is correct, the frigid woman illustrates not only bad faith but also the cynical element in bad faith: the cynicism of bad faith, if you will. She makes "knowing preparations" for her self-deception: she "deliberately" chooses to think about domestic chores to prevent herself from believing that she might enjoy the sexual act with her husband. By choosing the "distracted" consciousness, she "disarms" in advance any counterbeliefs (for example, that she experiences pleasure in this sexual act): she prepares "not to believe" what she believes and to "believe" what she does not believe. Who would want to say that this inner conniving to prove to herself that she is frigid is not cynical, that is, blatantly deceitful in a way that clearly exhibits an indifference to truth? The fact that this woman "is not in full agreement with herself" (*n'est point . . . en plein accord avec elle-même*) does not exclude—as Sartre suggests—her being cynical. In fact, this failure to agree with herself is testimony not only to her believing-what-she-does-not-be-lieve—the mark of the bad faith consciousness—but to her re-solve to continue to "believe" (that she does not experience any pleasure in the sexual act) in spite of her awareness of the "truth" (that she does). What is this but the *Weltanschauung* of bad faith and cynicism?

I could, of course, multiply examples from Sartre. The case of the coquette[38]—who exploits the *métastabilité* and double-property of human consciousness, who forges a strategy by which to "fixate" on her intellectual possibilities, who "glues down" her intellectual capacity while recognizing her male companion's desire as being only "transcendent"—is sufficient to show again the cynical aspects of bad faith in Sartre. But we shall not dwell on it here. That Sartre misses these cynical aspects; that, toward the end of his analysis, he can say that the project of bad faith is not a matter of a "reflective and voluntary decision"[39] (*il ne s'agit pas d'une décision réfléchie et volon-taire*[40]), is both a puzzle and a violation of his own analysis of the devious project and mechanism of bad faith[41] I have sug-gested above that Sartre appears inadvertently to have made the ontological "duality" of consciousness (mine and the Other's) a necessary condition for both an ideal lie and cynicism (I cannot, he urges, conceal the truth from my own translucent con-sciousness as I conceal it from the Other). Sartre's doing so appears to have predisposed him to pass over some ordinary but distinct marks of cynicism in bad faith's project.

But I must now proceed to my remaining task of showing that, even if we go by Sartre's technical analysis and meaning of the cynical consciousness, we have grounds for contending that the bad-faith consciousness is cynical. In short, I want to show that, although bad faith is not an ideal lie in Sartre's strict sense, its deceptiveness still involves the "doubly negative attitude" that characterizes what Sartre calls the "cynical consciousness."

"Cynical" in Sartre's idiomatic sense

We may begin by acknowledging that the person of bad faith—the self-deceiver—cannot, by definition, exploit—as does the "ideal" liar—the ontological duality of my consciousness and the Other's, or of myself and myself for the Other ("du moi et du moi d'autrui"[42]). This point is a truism and not arguable. But it does not follow from it that bad faith is not a cynical consciousness. For, first, as we have seen earlier, bad faith, as a modified form of lying (to oneself), involves the adoption of a negative attitude toward oneself: "consciousness, instead of directing its negation outward, turns it towards itself."[43] In the very project of bad faith, I take a negative attitude toward myself by setting up a pattern by which I can deny the truth of which I am aware and which I "correlatively" affirm. I set up the mechanism by which to count myself "persuaded" even when I know that I am not. Like the "strict" liar, I have an awareness or "comprehension"[44] of the truth which I should like to conceal from myself, and I proceed with the enterprise of the would-be lie in spite of that "comprehension." The man or woman of bad faith shares with the strict liar this part of the self-negating attitude by which Sartre characterizes cynicism.

But, given the translucency of consciousness, how can the man or woman of bad faith be said to be involved in the "doubly negative attitude" of the "cynical consciousness"? And in what sense?

My reconstruction,[45] in the preceding chapter, of Sartrean bad faith in terms of a highly modified sense of lying to oneself allows us to see the cynical intent and strategy that occur in bad-faith consciousness. In "lying to oneself"—in the qualified sense I have proposed—I do "deny" to myself a "truth" of

which I am translucently aware. Although the denial is not necessarily "in words," it is yet a negation—one based on the contrived and disingenuous criterion of "half-persuasion," according to which my bad-faith consciousness has determined itself
to be "satisfied" or "persuaded." It is important to note that,
though I cannot succeed in hiding the truth entirely from my
consciousness (I correlatively affirm it), I do succeed (at least in
"successful" cases of bad faith) in meeting the deliberately weak
evidential criteria for "persuasion." In other words, a modified
form of the cynical lie does take place. I submit, moreover, that
in bad faith, as in the case of strict lying (or "lying in general"),
I do, in turn, inwardly deny ("negate"), on the basis of my pre-
reflective awareness of the truth I am trying to hide, the *falsity*
of which I am trying to persuade myself. To be sure, the "lie"
in this case cannot be the same as the lie to the Other. But, as
I've shown, because of bad faith's primitive resolution[46] in respect to evidence, it does not follow that this attempted lying-
to-oneself "falls back" or collapses in the translucency of consciousness. By contrived criteria and the choice of selective evidence, the bad-faith consciousness decides that it is "persuaded" even when it is not. The cynical motive is there; and so
is the "doubly negative" attitude of the cynical consciousness,
despite the fact that it cannot succeed in the same complete
manner that the "ideal" lie does.

But how about what Sartre calls the liar's "flaunted intention" (*l'intention affichée*[47]) of telling the truth—his deceptive
assurances to the Other that, of course, he is telling her the
truth; that he would never want to deceive her, and so on? Does
and can the practitioner of bad faith make such reassurances
to himself? Is this process, too, "the object of an inner negation"[48]? And may we say of the practitioner of bad faith—who,
after all, is trying to persuade himself of something that is in

question—what Sartre said of the liar; namely, that he does not recognize this intention as his own?

I suggest that the person in bad faith, like the "liar to the Other," *does* attempt to reassure himself; to tell himself as he draws self-deceptive conclusions—based on ambiguous and selected data—that he is an honest man, that, of course, he is not that other "kind" of man—a liar, a deceiver, a flirt, a seducer, or what have you. These reassurances are important reinforcement for his holding fast to the criteria of *half-persuasion* which he sets up in advance to "persuade" himself, to bring himself to *accept* "believing what he does not believe." He can reassure himself in this way—despite his translucent awareness of the truth that he is trying to hide—because of the double-property, the "facticity-transcendence," of human reality. Just as I, in the basic movement of bad faith, can play see-saw[49] with these two aspects of human reality or consciousness and can exploit the metastable "nature" of all belief, so can I, in spite of the unity and translucency of consciousness, accept these reassurances as "believable" even though I do not fully believe them. I can accept "believing" the reassurance that I do not (fully) believe because the evanescent, identityless makeup of consciousness allows me to tell myself that all believing is "not believing enough." So—as we've seen—I count myself satisfied even when I'm not "fulfilled" by the evidence.

Hence, the "flaunted intention"—to oneself it would be more "deliberate" and persistent than "flaunted"—can be utilized also in bad faith in a manner comparable to the way it is in an "ideal lie." To get a better sense of this, one can imagine the coquette's[50] reassurance to herself that her interest and motives are intellectual, not bodily: "I'm involved in an intense, exciting discussion of *Being and Nothingness:* might anyone doubt that?" The project of bad faith and the instruments of "half-persuasion" allow her to accept her self-reassurance. So this aspect, too, of the cynical consciousness can be exercised by the bad-faith consciousness.

In the light of the above, we may now understand that the modified "reassurances" that we give to ourselves in bad faith can certainly become an "object of an inner negation" (l'objet d'une négation intime).[51] Although I cannot conceal the truth from myself in the manner that I conceal it from the Other during an "ideal" lie, I am still—because of the unity and translucency of consciousness—aware of the truth I am trying to hide from myself. Thus, while remaining "barely convinced" (malconvaincu), I can "negate" the phony but adamant reassurances that I am giving myself. But, as long as I abide by my criterion of half-persuasion, I can continue with my self-deception. This criterion—carefully prepared to deceive—together with the métastable makeup of consciousness, allows me to go on "believing" even when I do not believe. And the unity of a single consciousness, for which Sartre argues strongly, does not prohibit, as Sartre maintains, my negating the "reassurances" (of my truth telling) that I give to myself. Given the translucency and ambiguous structure of the bad-faith consciousness, I am in fact congenitally disposed to negating these persistent reassurances (or insistences) I give to myself. Thus, this inner negation, as part of the liar's cynical consciousness, is also part of "lying-to-oneself," part of the bad-faith consciousness.

One issue of comparison remains. Regarding the "flaunted intention" of the cynical "ideal" lie, Sartre—one may recall—says: "It is not recognized by the liar as his intention. It is played, imitated, it is the intention of the character which he plays in the eyes of the questioner, but the character, precisely because he *does not exist,* is a transcendent." "The lie" he continues, "does not put into play the inner structure (intra-structure) of present consciousness; all the negations which constitute it bear on objects which by this fact are removed from consciousness."[52] The question now arises: "Is this general aspect of the ideal, cynical lie applicable to bad faith, too?"

One might be quick to say that the negations of bad faith cannot "bear on objects . . . removed from consciousness"; that, unlike the strict lie, bad faith is not a "phenomenon of transcendence" or of ontological duality and thus cannot share in this aspect of the cynical lie. At one level, this seems obviously true. But at another, one might say that just as in the strict lie the "flaunted" intention is the intention of a character one plays, so in lying to oneself (bad faith) my intention of self-(re)assurance is the intention of a character *(un personnage)* that I play and pretend (albeit, to myself) to be, but that does *not* exist. If, in the case of the "strict" lie, the feigned character is "transcendent" because "he does not exist" (he does not have concrete being here and now), so in the case of bad faith (as a modified form of "lying to oneself") the character I pretend to be may be said to be "transcendent" because he does *not* exist. Although in lying to oneself, I do not play a character in the "eyes of an [outside] questioner," yet, in trying to articulate reassurances to myself of my truth telling, I can take on the "character" of the one I want to take myself to be but "am" not. Sartre's coquette, for example, can take on the character of an intellectual who is "beyond reproach" in matters of sexual morality. From that vantage point she can tell herself that she is doing no more than discussing with her male companion the philosophical issues of *Being and Nothingness*. This can be done by the same deceptive mechanism of half-persuasion, which I discussed above and in the preceding chapter.

To be sure, I cannot persuade myself completely, as I can persuade the Other completely (when in "entire clarity" I alter and conceal the truth from her); I cannot take the "lie to myself" for "truth," as the Other can take my lie. Nor can I take my adopted feigned character as my "true" character in the manner in which the Other can. Yet, as I have tried to show above, this does not preclude my being able—even in the modified lying to oneself that constitutes bad faith—to offer intended reassurances of my truth telling from the perspective of a "character" I have assumed and adopted. So, though not entirely the same, this possible aspect of the pattern of bad faith meets another of Sartre's conditions for the cynical consciousness; to say the least, it is compatible with the structure of cynicism in the cynical lie, though in a modified form of lying and persuasion.

But what about Sartre's point that the liar does not recognize the "flaunted intention" of the lie as *his* intention? Given the unit and translucency of consciousness, may this be said also of the practitioner of bad faith?

I submit that, if it applies to the strict or ideal lie, it can apply also to bad faith; that is, to "lying to oneself" in the modified sense I have been advocating. For, in spite of the fact that, for Sartre, the deception of the "ideal lie" is based on ontological duality, and this flaunted intention is the intention that the liar attributes to the character he is playing before the Other, my non-recognition of the "flaunted intention" "as *mine*" does not require the presence of the Other (or the consciousness of the Other): It requires only that there *be* a character that I play and from which I can offer the deceitful intention of reassurance. On this ground, the person in bad faith—the "self-deceiver"—may also fail to recognize his self-reassuring, though deceptive, intention of truth telling as his own intention. For *if* my preceding suggestion and analysis are correct, *then,* even in the translucency of a unitary consciousness, one can take on a "false character," insist from that adopted perspective that one is telling the truth, and because one is "half-persuaded" of the falsehood on which one is insisting, not recognize this intention of (false) reassurance as one's own. Again, the *métastable*, fluid structure of consciousness allows this, for consciousness is always at a "distance from itself" and is "evanescent," so to speak. Thus, as we have seen, the person in bad faith can "pretend" to believe, ground assurances of truth telling on this pretense, and yet, because of his translucent awareness of the truth he is hiding, negate the deception he is affirming. The strategy of bad faith and the elusive, seesaw nature of human reality permit the self-deceiver's failure to "recognize" his deceitful reassurance of truth telling. Hence, even this secondary, rather technical detail of Sartre's cynical consciousness (as incorporated in the "ideal lie") turns out to be structurally compatible with bad faith.

Conclusion

If my foregoing analysis and argument are sound, I have shown that, both from a common usage perspective and from the perspective of his frustratingly brief technical account of the cynical consciousness, Sartre's bad faith may be said to be cynical. Bad-faith consciousness exploits the nature of faith, makes "knowing preparations" for its deceitful maneuvers and concepts, and in so doing exhibits a blatant disregard for truth. It is cynical in this sense. Moreover, although bad faith is a heavily qualified form of "lying to oneself," it shares, in a qualified way, the pattern of double denial (or the "doubly negative attitude") which Sartre places at the heart of the "ideal description" of the "cynical consciousness." Bad faith is also cynical in this idiomatic technical sense; that is, on Sartre's own terms. Although I do not necessarily uphold the skeletal details of Sartre's characterizations of the cynical consciousness, I believe that I have shown that the project and structure of bad faith bear most of the marks of Sartre's cynical consciousness. I have argued that the unity of bad faith's "single consciousness" does not, as Sartre seems to think, preclude a basic cynicism in its project and pattern. I have suggested a way—compatible with Sartre's terms—in which bad-faith consciousness can be cynical without "annihilating" its "whole psychic system," without "falling back" and "collapsing" "beneath my look." Although, as I have attempted to show in the preceding chapter, "lying to oneself" turns out to be a lie of "half-persuasion," a "degenerate" form of lying, it is still a lie and it is still—in spite of Sartre's insistence to the contrary—cynical. If I am right in the above account, it is bad faith's strategy of "half-persuasion" that can accommodate this cynicism in the unitary structure of consciousness.

4

Good Faith:
Can It
Be Salvaged?

Careful readers and scholars of Sartre are often baffled by the relatively brief analytic attention Sartre pays to the notions of "good faith" and "authenticity" in *Being and Nothingness* and in other of his early and pivotal philosophical works. In *Being and Nothingness*, for instance, Sartre assures us—in an important footnote that continues to tantalize many scholars—that the possibility of radically escaping bad faith "supposes a self-recovery of being which was previously corrupted." "This self-recovery," he adds, "we shall call authenticity, *the description of which has no place here.*"[1] Even his discussion of good faith—which, in his detailed chapter on bad faith sometimes appears to be presented in conceptual opposition to bad faith—is so skeletal that it leaves the reader bewildered by implications which, on first reading, appear to conflict. Moreover, his diverging suggestions, in "The 'Faith' of Bad Faith",[2] both that good faith, like authenticity, can be contrasted to bad faith; and that good faith, like sincerity, shares the bad-faith, and impossible, "ideal of being in-itself,"[3] make a comprehension of Sartre's view of the relationship between good faith and authenticity even more perplexing.

In the next chapters, I wish to complete my study of Sartre's fundamental "attitudes."[4] I plan to do so by exploring the relation, in Sartre's early works, between Sartre's concepts of good faith and authenticity, particularly as they relate to bad faith. My intention is to help reconstruct good faith and to elucidate authenticity in a way that will make them recoverable fundamental "attitudes" toward human reality; that is to say, possible, alternate modes of human existing—or of "existing" our freedom—to bad faith. In doing so, I shall attempt to differentiate authenticity from good faith and to make evident why, though they are often treated as synonymous (sometimes even by Sartre), the two concepts should not be identified in Sartre. In short, I shall aim to show the marks of their differentiation. And, in passing, I shall also hope to show, as a subsidiary consideration, the grounds on which we can be said to be responsible for our attitudes of bad and good faith, and for the authenticity or inauthenticity of our fundamental existential "orientation" or "attitude." If I can complete the present study with at least a working grasp of the meaning of and distinction between good faith and authenticity in Sartre's early writings—a grasp that often appears to be absent in much of Sartrean scholarship—I shall have succeeded.

In proceeding, I wish to acknowledge that I have gained from some earlier exploratory work done on this general topic by a limited number of Sartrean scholars. Although Robert V. Stone, for example, in "Sartre on Bad Faith and Authenticity",[5] informs us that "Sartre tells us little of the positive character of authenticity," he both helps us to note the Other-involvement of the bad faith consciousness and indicates the kind of externalization from which an "authentic" person is liberated. But more than anyone else, I believe, the American commentator on Sartre, Joseph Catalano, has—especially in recent years[6]—struggled to understand some of the curt but perplexing statements Sartre makes about good faith in *Being and Nothingness*, and the evolution of the meaning of authenticity in Sartre's early works. Although I have learned considerably from Catalano's studies—and have delighted in professional exchanges with him—I am not persuaded that he has offered the last word on these topics. Though his efforts to clarify these concepts are admirable, his articles continue to exhibit, in places, a common tendency to conflate good faith and authenticity.[7] In the exploration that follows, I hope to go beyond Catalano's interpretation and to set in clearer focus the relationship between good faith and authenticity. In the process of doing so, I shall try to make clear some of the places where I question or part from Catalano's basic interpretation.

"Good faith" in *Being and Nothingness*

It is within the context of Sartre's intense analysis of "bad faith"[8] that Sartre offers a secondary account or, rather, outline of what he takes good faith to be. Having referred early in his analysis to the "idea of sincerity" as the "antithesis of bad faith,"[9] he goes on not only to contend that the project of *sincerity* "must be in bad faith"[10] but also to draw a contrast between *bad* faith and *good* faith, as though the latter were the antithetical concept."[11] If good faith turns out to be the antithesis, for Sartre, of bad faith, then it would be tempting, at least from a common usage perspective, to understand "good faith" as interchangeable with "authenticity." But this conclusion—hardly acceptable to Catalano—could not be squared with selected passages in Sartre. "The ideal of good faith (to believe what one is) is," says Sartre, "like that of *sincerity* (to be what one is), an ideal of being-in-itself."[12] But this can hardly be the way of "self-recovery" from bad faith, for it seems to share in it. We need to attend more closely to the rest of Sartre's sketchy story.

Early in his crucial—and most directive—section, "The

'Faith' of Bad Faith,'' Sartre begins to give us clues about his use of ''good faith.'' He tells us that the disposition to put oneself in bad faith is itself in bad faith; that to have represented it (the disposition) to oneself as bad faith ''would have been cynicism,'' and ''to believe it sincerely innocent would have been in *good faith*.'' Moreover, he tells us—in a passage that baffles the more casual reader and testifies to the metastable condition of consciousness—that ''the decision to be in bad faith does not dare to speak its name: it believes itself and does not believe itself in bad faith; it believes itself and does not believe itself in *good faith*.''[13]

Then, just a few lines later, Sartre starts, more decisively, to offer points of contrast between *bad* and *good* faith. Bad faith ''does not hold the norms and criteria of truth as they are accepted by the *critical* thought of good faith.'' And, though bad faith ''apprehends evidence'' (*saisit des évidences*[14]), ''it is resigned in advance to not being fulfilled by this evidence, to not being persuaded and transformed into *good faith*'' (''à ne pas être persuadée et transformée en bonne foi''[15]).

So Sartre's suggestion, from the start, is that whereas bad faith is unwilling to be persuaded by critical evidence, good faith is willing; that, whereas the ''spontaneous determination of our being''[16] in bad faith—in other words, the ''original project'' of our bad faith—is a closed, uncritical attitude toward available evidence, the fundamental attitude or original determination of being in good faith is an open, critical attitude toward evidence. And while bad faith has ''taken precautions by deciding . . . that non-persuasion is the structure of all conviction,''[17] good faith has, presumably, not.

Next, Sartre readily gives us an illustrative but problematic instance of good faith. ''I believe,'' he says,

> that my friend Pierre feels friendship for me. I believe it in *good faith*. I believe it but I do not have for it any self-evident intuition.

> . . . I believe it; that is, I allow myself to give in to all impulses to
> trust it; I decide to believe in it, and to maintain myself in this
> decision. I conduct myself, finally, as if I were certain of it—and
> all this in the synthetic unity of one and the same attitude. This
> which I define as good faith is what Hegel would call the *immedi-
> ate*. It is simple faith.[18]

It is what, in still everyday language, we might refer to as "unwavering firmness of belief."

But Sartre is quick to point out that "Hegel would demonstrate at once that the immediate calls for mediation and that
belief, by becoming *belief for itself*, passes to the state of non-
belief."[19] "This gets to the heart of Sartre's theory of consciousness and of belief. Consciousness is an "elsewhereness" of
being; it is always at a distance from itself[20]; is metastable, mercurial, abruptly transitional, evanescent, always elsewhere,
never one with itself. Unlike certainty, which is characterized
by "the intuitive possession of the object," belief is the "adherence of being to its object when the object is not given or is
given indistinctly."[21] "To believe is to know that one believes,
and to know that one believes is no longer to believe." This
means, for Sartre, that the "non-thetic consciousness (of) believing is destructive of belief." "To believe is not to believe."[22]
Belief, as a being which continually "questions its own being",
can "realize itself only in its destruction . . . only by denying
itself." "We see the reason for it," Sartre says: "The being of
consciousness is to exist by itself, thus to make itself be and
by that to surpass itself."[23] So, "in this sense, consciousness is
perpetually escaping itself; belief becomes non-belief, the immediate mediation, the absolute relative and the relative absolute."[24]

But note what has happened. No sooner has Sartre given us
a basis for distinguishing between good and bad faith in terms
of contrasting "determinations" of our being, or attitudes

toward critical evidence, than he makes it more difficult to maintain the distinction. In suggesting that good faith is "simple faith," that "it appears to one as pure subjective determination without external correlative," and also that the belief of good faith, like bad faith, passes to the state of non-belief, Sartre draws *good* and *bad* faith closer together again. Suddenly he tells us that "the ideal of good faith (to believe what one believes) is, like that of sincerity (to be what one is), an ideal of being-in-itself."[25] And if it is, then good faith, as I suggested earlier, shares the bad faith goal of *self-coincidence;* or to put it as Catalano does, "the *ideal* of good faith is in bad faith."[26]

In my earlier chapters, I have tried to show how the bad-faith consciousness attempts to exploit the autodestructiveness of "the fact of consciousness," the "elsewhereness" of consciousness, and the corollary fact that "every belief falls short of belief." I shall not repeat my analysis here. But we must now take note of Sartre's contention—which follows immediately—that if "one never wholly believes what one believes," if "every belief in good faith is an impossible belief," "then there is a place for every impossible belief."[27] Given Sartre's rapprochement between good and bad faith, how can he possibly make this statement (which allows for impossible belief), and how can he continue to distinguish between *good* and *bad* faith? Let me explore further.

Two types of "faith"

Part of the answer is, I believe—and here I follow the lead offered by Catalano without going where he goes—that Sartre is using the expression "good faith" in two different senses. On the one hand, as I have already suggested, good faith, at the beginning of this section, "The 'Faith' of Bad Faith," connotes an openness to critical evidence, an openness to being persuaded, whatever the evidence. (Later, I shall try to elucidate how "good faith" connotes not just an epistemological attitude toward evidence but what I might call an *ontological* attitude toward our freedom—a spontaneous attitude of accepting it rather than trying to run away or flee from it.) On the other hand, in the latter part of this section, Sartre seems to be using good faith in a radically different way—in a way that is not only similar to the way he employs sincerity but virtually identical to it. "Good faith wishes to flee the 'not-believing-what-one-believes' by finding refuge in being."[28] And if every belief falls short, and the "ideal of good faith" is "to believe what one believes,"[29] then every belief in good faith is an "impossible belief" because "self-destruction" exists at the basis of all faith."[30]

Is this not the same situation, for Sartre, as "sincerity"? The goal of sincerity, we saw, is "to bring me to confess to myself what I am in order that I may finally coincide with my being; in a word, to cause myself to be in the mode of the in-itself, what I am in the mode of 'not being what I am.' " Isn't the *ideal* of good faith the same as the "ideal of sincerity"—what Sartre refers to as the "second mode of being," which "I'm prevented by nature from attaining"[31]? Certainly, as I said above, Sartre has acknowledged them as the same.[32]

But if the goal and "essential structure" of good faith are the same as that of sincerity, and if the "essential structure of sincerity does not differ from that of bad faith," then is the structure of good and bad faith the same? And are we left in a situation where we are not able to distinguish between good and bad faith? And, to return to our earlier question, how can there be "a place for every impossible belief"?

It seems to me clear that Sartre intends to maintain a firm distinction between the two types of faith. Sartre tells us that the "original project of bad faith is a decision in bad faith about the nature of faith."[33] As I have tried to show in preceding chapters, bad faith—viewed epistemologically—takes advantage of, exploits, the "unstable," *métastable*, fluid nature of belief or faith. It is because "to believe is not to believe enough" ("n'est pas assez croyance"[34])—in short, because consciousness is not what it is and is what it is not—that bad faith can be possible at all. In bad faith, I tell myself that because all belief "falls short," "non-persuasion is the structure of all convictions,"[35] and thus I can continue to "believe" I am courageous even when I am aware of counterevidence and am not persuaded that I am courageous. If every belief is autodestructive, if the ideal of even *good* faith is "impossible belief," then I can accept believing what I don't quite believe and make room for the "impossible" beliefs against which there is evidence that I cannot conceal. Realizing that "annihilation" is at the root of all faith, I can, in bad faith, assure myself than I am no more cowardly than courageous: "I shall" says Sartre, "define the impossible belief as my belief"; I shall not allow myself to be discouraged by not quite believing.[36] While bypassing critical evidence, I can allow myself to be persuaded by *uncritical* evidence. I cannot know that I am courageous but—never mind—the intuition of certainty does not accompany *any* belief, so let me be content with faith's insufficient or only "selective" evidence, so to say. Because "belief is *nothing other* that the consciousness (of) belief,"[37] and consciousness is metastable, I "persuade" myself, in bad faith, that my not-believing-what-I-believe is just the *normal* metastable "state" of all faith. My bad-faith consciousness disarms in advance all beliefs—both "those it would like to take hold of and, by the same stroke, the others, those which it wishes to flee."[38] In this way, *bad* faith abuses faith and allows for "impossible" belief: it adopts a deceptive attitude toward the ambiguity and self-destructiveness of belief. In Catalano's language, bad faith undermines "all critical attitudes by justifying all uncritical attitudes."[39]

It is important, at this stage, to stress a point that Catalano emphasizes in his analysis of good faith; namely, that Sartre's contentions regarding good faith are made within his discussion and analysis of the *possibility of bad faith*. I, too, have pointed this out earlier. Indeed, Sartre seems centrally concerned with the question, "What are the conditions for the possibility of . . . [bad] faith"[40]? But, as we attempt to probe further the meaning of good faith, we must note that it is in the context of his explication of the possibility of "bad faith" that Sartre discusses "sincerity" also. In fact, one of his concluding claims is that "in order for bad faith to be possible, sincerity itself must be in bad faith," for "the condition of the possibility for bad faith is that human reality . . . must be what it is not and not be what it is."[41] And in another place—as I have already pointed out—Sartre tells us that "Bad faith is possible only because sincerity is conscious of *missing its goal* inevitably, due to its very nature."[42]

So what are we to say? *Is* good faith the same as sincerity, as the latter part of this section on faith suggests? If so, what happens to the earlier notion—already touched on—of good faith as an "attitude" of openness to one's freedom and critical evidence? Do the earlier distinctions collapse because of Sartre's puzzling comments about the *ideal* of good faith?

Two points must be made immediately. First, it should be noted that Sartre—insofar as he is likening good faith to sincerity—is referring here to the *ideal* of good faith and sincerity, *not* to a "good-faith" or a "sincerity" consciousness. Second, we should observe—as I have already noted—that, for Sartre, bad faith is a "bad," "deceptive" decision ("a decision in bad faith") about the nature of faith,[43] and good faith, as a form of "simple faith," may be presumed to involve a "good," though possibly mistaken, "decision" about the "nature of faith." In bad faith, we have seen, we adopt a deceptive project by telling ourselves that the "total annihilation" of bad faith "exists at the basis of *all* faith."[44]

These two points clear a path for our seeing that Sartre's perplexing comments comparing the *ideal* of good faith with the *ideal* of sincerity can be reconciled with his preliminary distinction between good and bad faith, and that good faith need not be identified with sincerity as a "phenomenon of bad faith." To begin, let us note that both bad faith and good faith are *faith,* and each type of faith, though aware of its metastable structure, aspires to an "unwavering firmness of belief." Ontologically considered, this is because free human reality is congenitally and permanently inclined to fill the "hole in Being"—a disposition which, in his *Cahiers,* Sartre refers to as the "hell" of the "pursuit of Being,"[45] for "every attempt of the For-itself to be In-itself is by definition doomed to fail".[46] And although both types of faith, as "projects" of consciousness, are aware of the impossibility of self-coincidence of consciousness, they do not employ that awareness, or—now, to borrow Catalano's words—do not "face and use the impossible ideal of faith"[47] in the same way. To put the matter another way, good-faith consciousness and bad-faith consciousness do not confront or respond to faith—or to our freedom—in the same manner. Both good faith and bad faith initially want "to believe what one believes" in the absence of a "self-evident intuition" of certainty; bad faith, one might say, takes this over from good faith.[48] But, because consciousness is not what it is and is what it is not, bad faith exploits this impossibility of belief, assumes that good faith is impossible, decides on requirements that will allow it to count itself "persuaded" when it is not persuaded, and thus "forces itself in decisions to adhere to uncertain truths."[49] As Catalano would likely put it, bad faith assumes that the ideal of good faith is impossible and uses that as an excuse for accepting "unjustified belief" (for example, "I am not a coward").[50]

Bad faith flees being (for example, that "I am cowardly") by in-voking "not-believing-what-one-believes": it tries "to flee what it cannot flee"[51]—the factity of what it has done, or, indeed, its freedom. And, as we have seen, "it believes and does not believe itself in good faith."[52] It exploits the "good faith" *ideal* of "believ-ing what one believes" by declaring all such belief to be *impos-sible* and then allowing non-persuasive belief to be accepted as "faith." Once more, good faith is discussed mainly within the context of the possibility of *bad faith*.

Reading between the lines: Agreeing and disagreeing with Catalano

Much of what may now be developed concerning good faith emerges from between the lines. The *ideal* of good faith, of "be-lieving what one believes," is, as we saw, an ideal of *in-itself,* an ideal of *being*[53] and, as such, is vulnerable to the criticisms Sar-tre has made of the *ideal* of sincerity. Good faith, like sincerity, initially aspires to believe what it believes. But as Sartre points out earlier in *Being and Nothingness*—to which I have made mention above—the original structure of our "not being what we are" makes this movement impossible ("renders impossible in advance all movement toward being in itself"), and, far from being "hidden from consciousness," this impossibility is the "very stuff of consciousness."[54]

Given what Sartre says, I believe—and I am perhaps in dis-agreement with Catalano here—that we must acknowledge that the *ideal* of good faith, like that of all faith, is a simple, perfect, though impossible, faith. But the difference is that good faith, now viewed *epistemologically* as faith, does not, as does bad faith, attempt to exploit this impossibility, or set up mechanisms ("forge" instruments) by which to excuse, bypass, or ignore critical evidence. Good-faith consciousness does not try to put itself "beyond reproach" or "ruin all belief."[55] In spite of sharing with bad faith an ideal of *being* ("of unwavering firmness of belief"[56]), it remains open to its freedom, to criticism, to its distance from itself, without trying to ignore or destroy it or put itself out of reach. In short, unlike bad faith,[57] the project of good faith is *not* in bad faith. It does not, as does bad faith, *will* the "self-destruction of belief." Good faith does not try to take refuge in not-believing-what-one-believes, and thus permit itself to believe what it does not fully believe on the grounds that it is only "belief." Good faith is a distinctly different "immediate attitude" that we take "in the face of our being"[58] or free consciousness. Good faith, in spite of faith's ideal of "unwavering firmness of belief," accepts its metastable consciousness (its freedom) without making "impossible belief" an excuse for accepting insufficient evidence for its belief, without constructing "two-faced concepts" to persuade itself that it is what it is not (for example, courageous) or is not what it is (for example, cowardly).

I agree entirely with Catalano when he says that "good faith does not accept the *ideal* of faith as the goal of faith." This is an important distinction: for though good faith initially believes what it wants to believe," it prereflectively accepts itself as "in question" and is unwilling to violate its metastable being. Catalano is, I think, right in saying that "the project of good faith carries within it the critical awareness that the *ideal* of faith is in *bad faith*."[59] But, for me, this means that, though good faith consciousness, like all faith, shares the ideal of "perfect belief" or "believing what one believes," it recognizes that accepting "unwavering" or "impossible" belief is in bad faith and constitutes a failure to accept human reality as freedom, or to carry an open attitude toward its "believing"—that is, its consciousness (of) believing.

In this regard, it is important to note that, for Sartre, bad

faith is "not restricted . . . to not seeing the being which I am."
For "it attempts also to constitute myself as being what I am
not." This helps us to understand another of Sartre's points of
contrast: "But if I were not cowardly in the simple mode of not-
being what-one-is-not, I would be in *good faith* by declaring that
I am not cowardly."[60] In good faith I acknowledge not only that
I am not what I am, but, because I am free, metastable human
reality, also that I am not what I am not, for consciousness cannot be tied down or "filled" either way. In short, good faith
prereflectively accepts the ambiguity of consciousness. While
bad faith views good faith as impossible by identifying the goal
of good faith (the "unwavering firmness" of belief) with the unwavering ideal of faith, good faith, in spite of its ideal, recognizes and accepts the factity of its freedom. To put it in somewhat different Sartrean terms, good-faith consciousness
accepts itself as "troubled," as inescapably "unhappy."[61] While
bad faith uses its comprehension of the (impossible) ideal of
good faith as a basis for lying to itself and fleeing what it is ("If
every belief in good faith is an impossible belief, then there is
no place for every impossible belief"[62]), good faith accepts the
anguish associated with its freedom—with the impossibility of
its self-coincidence—and *assumes responsibility* for the authorship of its beliefs and actions. For good faith, the fact that consciousness is always in flight or is never at one with itself does
not become an excuse for accepting "unjustified beliefs" as acceptable, or for accepting "believing what it does not believe,"
or for regarding all beliefs as equivalent, or for trying to escape
one's freedom or responsibility. While the attitude of bad faith
(and sincerity) is to "miss itself"[63] and its chosen intent, the attitude of good faith is to confront itself, not miss itself and its
choices.[64] While the attitude of bad faith is to flee its freedom
and its anguish, the attitude of good faith is to face its freedom
of consciousness; that is, the autonomy and responsibility to

which consciousness is condemned. While bad faith both exploits and pursues the impossible goal of attaining oneness with one's beliefs—of attaining coincidence with consciousness—good faith, aware of the impossibility of faith's ideal, confronts its freedom, accepts the "interrogation" or "distance" within all consciousness, refuses to *pursue* faith's impossible ideal, and accepts responsibility for the choices it makes towards its own non-coincidence. Far from trying to reach the ideal of in-itself, or to bypass critical evidence, or to put itself "out of reach," or to tie itself down, or to justify its belief by distorting the impossibility of a "perfect" faith, or to flee freedom, good faith faces its evidence, its mercurial, unstable, consciousness, its freedom, and takes responsibility for the attitude it adopts toward that freedom.

Before proceeding further, I must pause to point out that the analysis I am providing has not only profited from Catalano's pioneering work on this topic but in many respects appears to concur in the general line of his interpretation. But there is at least one basic point on which we appear to disagree. Catalano seems to read everything that Sartre says about the *ideal* of good faith not only from the perspective of Sartre's discussion of the possibility of bad faith but *in terms of* bad faith. And at times he appears to perceive the *ideal* of good faith solely as the *ideal* that bad faith deceptively projects onto good faith as its impossible-to-realize ideal. Catalano says, for instance (in Sartre's name): "bad faith makes [the] impossible ideal of faith to be *its* ideal of good faith." He says also—in the same paragraph—"the *ideal* of good faith is thus the conception of good faith that bad faith forges for itself."[65] For Catalano, the *ideal* of good faith is interpreted entirely as a distorted creation of bad faith; it appears to be completely independent of a good-faith consciousness. The ideal of good faith is, for Catalano, but an ideal which bad faith imposes on good faith in order to justify its own "bad-faith" beliefs. To put it another way, the ideal of good faith seems, for Catalano, to be but bad faith's way of understanding good faith. To use the language Catalano employs in his most recent rearticulation, this ideal is of a "perfectly justified belief,"[66] but, as we have seen, this ideal of a perfectly justified belief is the ideal by which *bad faith* has succeeded in deceiving itself.

I do not separate these notions so strongly. As much as I acknowledge the distortion and exploitation of faith's ideal by bad faith, I do not divorce the *ideal* of good faith so emphatically from good faith. In my judgment, Sartre's text does not allow it. As I have already mentioned, Sartre says quite plainly that "The ideal of good faith (to believe what one believes) . . . is an ideal of being in-itself."[67] One might say that this "unwavering firmness of belief" is an ideal of all faith—even of *good* faith. And, on my interpretation, good faith is *good,* among other reasons, because in recognizing the congenital, "built-in," non-coincidence of all belief, it refuses to require or pursue this ideal as an ideal of "in-itself"; that is, in recognizing its freedom, it refuses to tie itself down in order to flee the anguish of its consciousness. As much as it initially aspires to "believing what it believes," to unwavering belief, in recognizing its freedom, it refuses to adopt a project of giving itself up as freedom.

To be sure, Catalano says clearly that good faith "sees that its own belief is in question but it accepts this condition as the situation of freedom."[68] And he also acknowledges that good faith "does not require the impossible of itself."[69] But that is not where we disagree. I am questioning, rather, Catalano's view of the ideal of good faith and the relation of that ideal to good faith. On my interpretation, the ideal of good faith is *neither* only, to use Catalano's terms, a mistaken "common sense notion" of good faith, completely apart from Sartre's notion of good faith, *nor* simply bad faith's projection of what good faith *ought* to be.[70] As difficult as it may be to fathom, good faith, I repeat, like all belief, aspires initially to "glue itself down": like all consciousness, it is "unhappy"[71] and prereflectively desires completion in (and of) Being. As Sartre will tell us in the *Notebooks*, this constitutes the "a priori ideal of all consciousness."[72] As Sartre says, consciousness wants "to flee the not-believing-what-one-believes"—which bad faith has so deceptively "accepted" and exploited—"by finding refuge in being."[73] The *initial ideal of good faith* may well be an ideal of Being—an ideal of self-coincidence or substantiality—and thus an impossible ideal. But this does not turn it into solely a bad-faith conception of good faith. Good faith, like all faith, initially has an ideal which, if *pursued* as a project, would lead to bad faith. But, as I have insisted above, good faith does not, as does the project of sincerity, pursue this ideal or try to "bring it into being" (if I may exploit a pun). As Catalano puts it in respect to what he calls Sartre's "rethought" good faith, "good faith does not aim at an ideal" but at accepting its "situation of freedom" and "resolving itself responsibly and critically in action."[74] Catalano's interpretation disowns any *ideal* of good faith for good faith. The *ideal* of good faith is for him the impossible ideal which bad faith attributes to good faith and exploits for its own purposes. But I urge that, because any ideal of faith—insofar as it aspires to self-coincidence and desires to flee from the freedom of consciousness—might be said to be a bad-faith ideal, it does not follow that the ideal of good faith can only be a bad-faith version of good faith, a version which Sartre contrasts with good faith as an attitude of accepting one's freedom (and responsibility). Catalano is *right* in pointing out that there is ambiguity related to Sartre's use of good faith, but *wrong*, I think, in viewing the ideal of good faith only in terms of bad faith.

It seems to me that Sartre's concluding paragraph in "The 'Faith' of Bad Faith" section—to which Catalano is attentive and even quotes partially—once more confirms the interpretation I give to the ideal of good faith. Sartre says that "good faith seeks to flee the inner disintegration of my being in the direction of the in-itself which it should be and is not."[75] Good-faith consciousness, like all consciousness, cannot escape either the metastable condition of all consciousness or its "innate," congenital desire to attain self-coincidence and substantiality. Human reality cannot evade its natural "impetus toward substantiality."[76] As Sartre tells us later in *Being and Nothingness,* "Human reality may be defined as a being such that in its being its freedom is at stake because human reality perpetually tries to refuse to recognize its freedom."[77] Or, to use the language of Sartre's "Conclusion" (of *Being and Nothingness*), "the for-itself is effecting a perpetual project of founding itself *qua* being and a perpetual failure of this project."[78] The for-itself "lacks," and what it lacks is in-itself. Human reality or consciousness is free "because it is *not enough*"[79]; it wants an essence; it is "haunted" by this value, this *ideal.* This "in-itself-for-itself" becomes the "fundamental value" which the for-itself posits.[80] The consciousness that projects good faith cannot escape this value, this unreflective passion for completion or oneness. The for-itself as lack spontaneously and unreflectively seeks self-coincidence; it wants to be for-itself-in-itself. To invoke and anticipate Sartre's language in the *Cahiers pour une morale,* not even an *authentic* individual can "suppress the pursuit of being through conversion, for there would be nothing else."[81] But, as I have stated and wish to develop further, consciousness can, in good faith, recognize its freedom and incompleteness and take responsibility for its free acts and creations. To put the matter in a somewhat different Sartrean way, even though phenomenological ontology reveals to us that "in-itself-for-itself" is the "ideal meaning of all human attitudes,"[82] it does *not* follow that (1) good faith is impossible or (2) Sartre's proper, "rethought"

sense of good faith is entirely independent of the *ideal* of all
faith.

Good faith: Epistemological and ontological

The above analysis suffices to show that good faith in Sartre
may be viewed from at least two dominant perspectives: the
epistemological and the ontological. In spite of differences between Catalano and me, I believe we are in essential agreement
on this point. From the point of view of belief—or, more specifically, faith as belief—we have seen that good faith is an epistemological attitude which, though disposed to believe what it
believes and to be "unwavering," does not "accept" "non-persuasive evidence"[83] as persuasive and refuses to allow the "freedom" of belief—the non-coincidence and evanescence of belief—to become an excuse for pursuing and accepting
"unwavering belief" in the mode of being in-itself. And, in
marked contrast to bad faith, good faith, as an *epistemological*
attitude, accepts itself as faith and not certainty, retains a critical perspective on evidence, and refuses to construct two-faced
concepts (*des "concepts amphiboliques"*[84]) by which to exploit
the "self-distancing" of consciousness and to "persuade" itself
of its deceptive beliefs. That is to say, it is an open and critical—
not a deceptive—attitude. Good faith does not allow the impossibility of the self-coincidence of belief to become a reason for
suspending critical criteria related to persuasion. It is not, as is
bad faith, a faith "that wished itself to be not quite convinced."[85]
In spite of the *ideal* of faith—all faith—good faith confronts
openly its evidence, its "freedom," the troubled "nature" of its
"unhappy" consciousness. It "accepts" that it is not what it is
in spite of faith's "congenital" disposition toward self-identity,
toward filling itself up or making itself "substantial" and "sta-
ble." Unlike both bad faith and sincerity, good faith does not

pursue a project of tying itself down, does not pursue stability of belief, even though it "naturally" "wishes to flee" the "inner disintegration of [its] being."[86]

But we have seen that good faith is also—and perhaps more dominantly—what I have called an *ontological* attitude. That is, good faith is an "original" attitude toward human reality, toward our freedom, toward our "existing" as freedom, which differs radically from the bad-faith attitude. Sartre refers to it as one of "the two *immediate* attitudes we can take in the face of our *being*."[87] And at the very end of *Being and Nothingness*, when discussing the possibility of putting "an end to the reign" of the "God" value ("in-itself-for-itself"), he mentions the "fundamental attitude" which freedom can take so as "not to coincide with itself but to be always at a distance from itself."[88] *Being and Nothingness* is replete with such references, but they normally do not mention good faith. Yet, as I tried to show above, Sartre's analysis of bad faith, together with his passing references to good faith, make clear that good faith cannot be understood only in epistemological terms, only in terms of belief, but must be interpreted more basically in terms of how freedom "responds" to itself, how the free being of consciousness deals with its "troubled" freedom. Good faith is precisely the human being's (freedom's) project of accepting its abandonment to freedom and the anxiety of its ontological distance. In the good-faith attitude, we accept the facticity of our freedom—our "autonomy"[89]—and our accompanying abandonment to responsibility, to our being "the incontestable author"[90] of our actions and our "world." In *bad faith*, in contrast, we refuse our freedom and make fleeing our freedom our basic existential disposition. "Most of the time," Sartre tells us, "we flee anguish in bad faith."[91]

But that does not mean that good faith is a futile project. It is only when the project of good faith has been distorted by the bad-faith goal and project of pursuing and attaining the impossible *goal* of self-coincidence that good faith can be ruled out as a possibility. But despite the fact that, ontologically, freedom (or consciousness) is lack and intends completion, it is free either to affirm or to try to hide from its freedom. Free consciousness can try to obscure "all its goals in order to free itself from anguish."[92] The human being who tries to flee the "consciousness of his freedom"—whom Sartre calls the "serious man"—is "of the world": he "dismisses human reality in favor of the world," gives to himself "the type of existence of the rock," and *is in bad faith.*[93] "If there's self-deception [i.e., bad faith]," Sartre informs us in *The War Diaries,* "it's a lie carried out with the totality of human reality."[94] But "anguish, abandonment, responsibility," Sartre tells us, "whether muted or in full strength, *constitute the quality of our consciousness* in so far as this is pure and simple freedom."[95] Later he adds: "The one who realizes in anguish his condition as *being* thrown into a responsibility which extends to his very abandonment has no longer either remorse or regret or excuse: he is no longer anything but a freedom which perfectly reveals itself and whose being resides in this very revelation."[96] These lines in Sartre come perhaps as close as any to encapsulating Sartre's notion of good faith. If good faith is nothing else, it is the basic attitude of accepting ourselves—without regret, remorse, despair, or excuse—as anguished "freedom" and of taking responsibility for our choices, projects, attitudes. Good faith, as an ontological attitude, is, we might say, the *"acceptance" of our abandonment to both freedom and responsibility.*

To many readers of Sartre, this account of good faith as an ontological attitude may sound strikingly similar to what many regard—sometimes before analysis—as Sartre's conception of *authenticity.*[97] Certainly some of my own earliest writing or Sartre has conveyed this impression to some readers.[98] In the next chapters, I shall want to focus on Sartre's concept of authenticity and, as I promised at the outset, attempt a better understanding of the relationship between these concepts and "attitudes." It is of interest to note in passing that I have not, here, discussed good faith in *moral* terms. This is not to suggest that, on my interpretation, good and bad faith are necessarily unrelated to morality or that they have no moral dimensions. Indeed, I have, at times, contended the opposite.[99] But, in attempting to develop Sartre's concept of authenticity, I want to keep in mind Catalano's contention, at the end of "On the Possibility of Good Faith," that authenticity and inauthenticity, but not good faith and bad faith, are to be viewed as *reflective* and *moral* categories. Certainly, as I shall show subsequently, there is in Sartre's writings persuasive evidence to corroborate the view that for Sartre it is authenticity, not good faith, that places the human being in the *moral* dimension.[100] I shall attend to this matter in considerable detail in the following chapters.

5   Sartre's Concept of "Authenticity"

As I mentioned at the beginning of the preceding chapter, Sartre's references to "authenticity" in *Being and Nothingness* are sparse, and they generally refer to the possibility of "self-recovery" or of "deliverance and salvation."[1] And his few references, both explicit and implied, suggest alternatively that authenticity is the same as and different from good faith.[2] While Sartre sometimes describes attitudes as authentic when they reflect an acceptance and affirmation of one's freedom in the manner we have characterized good faith above,[3] he also appears to suggest in places that authenticity, like sincerity, can become—perhaps on Heidegger's terms—a form of bad faith, or a project of fleeing from one's freedom. Hence, it is to works other than *Being and Nothingness* to which we must turn for elucidation of Sartre's formative notion of authenticity.[4] Because of Sartre's self-proclaimed struggle for authenticity in the situation of "la drôle de guerre,"[5] and because his wartime "Carnets" include a first record of his punctuated formulation of the ontology he systematizes in *Being and Nothingness,* I turn first to Sartre's *War Diaries,*[6] where his discussion of authenticity is both more directive and more generous in scope.

"Authenticity" in *The War Diaries:* Sartre's formative view

Sartre's initial view of authenticity comes relatively early in *The War Diaries* (1939–1940). "Authenticity," he says, "can be under-

89

stood only in terms of the human condition, that condition of a being thrown into a situation. . . . Through the authentic realization of the being-in-situation, one brings to plenary existence the situation on the one hand and human reality on the other." To be authentic, he adds, "is to realize fully one's being-in-situation, whatever this situation may happen to be." "This presupposes," he says, "a patient study of what the situation requires, and then a way of throwing oneself into it and determining oneself to 'be-for' this situation."[7]

Although the present chapter is not the place to summarize all of the terms and ontological structure assumed by this characterization, we can see, by following some of Sartre's remarks and contentions in *The War Diaries*, that his view of authenticity here relates centrally to his view of the "human condition," to his phenomenological ontology, to his account of the human project and the way in which human reality faces its "condition." Human reality is free; this means that "it is never anything without motivating itself to be it." It exists without foundation; it "falls into the world"; it is a "gratuitous" nothingness. "Numbed" by this gratuitousness, human reality wants to be "its own foundation." "Throughout all [of human reality's] undertakings, he seeks, not to preserve himself . . . nor to increase himself, but to found himself." In fact, Sartre contends—with a brevity that is tantalizing—that "human reality is *moral* because it wishes to be its own foundation."[8] Yet each undertaking reveals anew to the human being that he or she is "gratuitous to the marrow." This "original fall" and "striving for redemption" make up human reality.[9] But "human reality loses its way trying to found itself."[10] Searching its own foundation, trying to "found substantiality for the future," it struggles to tie itself down, to flee its own gratuity. But it grows weary trying to "deliver itself from the torment of freedom."[11] Out of weariness, it "self-motivates itself" to *conceal* from itself "the fact that it is condemned to self-motivate itself."[12] In its search for substantiality, for the "absolute," it resigns itself to being a "buffeted consciousness," to becoming a "thing." This, Sartre says, is self-motivated *inauthenticity*. To anticipate Sartre's later language (still in *The War Diaries*), "Inauthenticity . . . consists in seeking out a foundation in order to 'lift' the absurd irrationality of facticity"[13]—that is, the irrationality of the gratuitous or superfluous character of human reality. Even in love, we posit the Other as the foundation of our existence; we desire the Other as lover to "lift our facticity." Thus our being-for-Other in love is also *inauthentic*.

But this state of "uneasiness," this "unhappiness," can become a reason for consciousness to motivate itself to stop fleeing from itself, to take a more lucid view of itself. The complicit soldier, for example, tired of trying "to *flee* what he's *making of himself*," may motivate himself "to return to an accurate view of [himself] and stop fleeing [himself]." Self-motivating consciousness may seek to "recover" itself by proposing authenticity as its value. Yet Sartre makes it clear that authenticity is *not* a "primary value." It, too, emerges out of the "first impetus towards substantiality," for all human consciousness seeks substantiality. It is out of this impetus that human reality "must draw the value-reason that allows it to *recover itself*'; it offers itself as a "*means* to arrive at substantiality."[14] Given the congenital disposition of all consciousness, it even "suppresses that which, in the search, is *flight*."[15] So how can this "conversion," this new attitude of "authenticity" happen, and, given consciousness's perennial lack, what does it turn out to be?

At this point in *The War Diaries*, Sartre offers important insights into his early and formative conception of authenticity. "The search for a foundation," he says, "requires that one *assume* that which one founds," and one assumes in order to make "use of what [one is] assuming."[16] In this case, one assumes "in order to found." To assume, here, is "to adopt as one's own, to claim responsibility." To put it another way, the "assumptive conversion" that "presents itself as a value for consciousness" is the willed "adoption of reality as one's own," that is, the willed acceptance to live the freedom, the "break in being," to which one is "condemned." All that consciousness is, "it makes itself be." Consciousness is free; it "self-motivates itself." So the first assumption that human reality is required to make when "looking back on itself" is the "assumption of its freedom." This implies one's recognition that one is the "incontestable author" of one's choices,[17] that "one never has any excuses"—a key contention which he revises in *Being and Nothingness* to say "I am without excuse."[18] All that happens to me, to consciousness, is by my own doing. This is the "law of freedom," the law of human reality. The value of authenticity which consciousness proposes to itself "bids human freedom to do what it is doing." Free consciousness cannot plead—as does "buffeted consciousness"—the excuse of its facticity or its givenness. To *assume* in the context of authenticity's project is "to adopt reality as one's own, to claim responsibility." In assuming my freedom, I appropriate it and I refuse excuses for "every excuse invokes Necessity."[19] I take responsibility. I do not blame it on the situation. In my "assumptive conversion," in the *new* attitude which I adopt, I not only recognize that I am condemned to be free and am without excuse; I also *will* it. "My freedom becomes *mine*."[20] I take responsibility for all my actions, for all my situations—for "all my cowardice, all my stupidities, all my lies."[21] I recognize that I have no *right* to be exempt from any "situation," for it is through my free choice that my situation comes to be: "no situation is ever undergone."[22] This is the awesome responsibility to which I am condemned and which I *will* when I convert to "authenticity" and adopt human reality (freedom) as my own. "To be authentic," Sartre has told us, "is to realize fully one's being-in-situation, whatever

this situation may be."[23] We may now add that it is also to realize, and to take responsibility for, one's being-in-situation,
whatever that situation may be. At one point in *The War Diaries*,
Sartre even refers to this authenticity as "the only absolute"[24]:
"I can't . . . see anything," he says, "but a moral code based on
authenticity."[25]

This view of authenticity, as involving a kind of "assumptive
conversion" or "self-recovery" by human reality from its "fall"
into the world, gains other points of clarification in *The War
Diaries*. "Authenticity," Sartre tells us, "is achieved en bloc; one
either is or is not authentic"[26]; "there's no middle course"[27];
"authenticity can't be divided"[28]; "there's no room for a third
estate."[29] But that does not imply that when one attains authenticity, one has it once and for all. Because human reality is free,
the present has no "purchase" on the future: "every instant,"
every situation[30] is new and requires a "new authenticity to be
invented."[31] "It isn't enough," Sartre says, "to have acquired it
once, in respect of a particular, concrete circumstance, in
order for it to extend itself spontaneously to all the situations
into which we are plunged." Authenticity has to "conquer new
territory." It has to "consolidate," renew, revise, "extend" what
is already there.[32] Nothing from the authenticity of the present
"moment" protects me from falling into inauthenticity in the
next. Anguish—which in *Being and Nothingness* is said to be the
reflective awareness of one's freedom—remains "at the heart
of all authenticity."[33] The desire "to acquire authenticity", Sartre remarks tellingly in *The War Diaries*, "is a desire *to see
things more clearly*" (italics mine) and not lose that clarity: it is
a desire to call into question. But the calling into question on
the part of human reality is also always in question. Desiring to
call into question is always "against a background of authenticity," but it is always "not enough," "for it is always necessary to
change." Human reality continually envisages situations which
are "on the horizon," "out of reach." As Sartre puts it: "it is by

no means enough to be authentic: it is necessary to adapt one's life to one's authenticity."[34] Authenticity is "true fidelity to ourselves"[35]; it involves living one's freedom, living—not refusing—one's human reality, which is always "not enough," which is never complete.

From my piecing together of Sartre's account of authenticity in *The War Diaries*, we can note that the view he articulates here is seminal for his references to and discussion of authenticity in subsequent works. The position outlined, though problematic in its implications, certainly gives content to his bare mention in *Being and Nothingness* of authenticity as "self-recovery of being which was previously corrupted."[36] And it enables us to see better the grounds on which Sartre holds open—in the latter part of *Being and Nothingness*—the possibility of an "ethics of deliverance and salvation."[37] By embracing freedom as its value, by adopting it as its own, human reality can—in spite of its lack of being and desire for substantiality—stop trying to flee its freedom, stop trying to "make itself akin to things."[38] To use the language of *Being and Nothingness*, radically escaping "bad faith" *is* possible (as I suggested in the preceding chapter). But this possibility of "deliverance" can be "realized" "only after a radical conversion,"[39] only after the "assumptive conversion" Sartre elucidates in *The War Diaries* has taken place—that is, only after one has *willed* to take responsibility for the freedom and responsibility to which one is condemned. As we saw earlier in respect to good faith, authenticity implies an awareness of our being responsible for the direction of our fundamental project, of our life's orientation.[40]

Moreover, *The War Diaries* give us an early indication of the tenuousness of authenticity, of the uneasy status of the acceptance of one's freedom. Though human reality can self-motivate itself to make freedom and responsibility its own, it remains perennially threatened—because of the emptiness of its being—by inauthenticity, by consciousness's temptation to tie down its freedom, to fill itself with something, to adopt the mode of being of in-itself. As Sartre says in *Being and Nothingness*, "human-reality is free because it is *not enough*"; "human reality is a being such that in its being its freedom is always at stake because human reality perpetually tries to refuse to recognize its freedom."[41] Hence we are congenitally inclined to "getting enough" even when we resolutely lay claim to our freedom. Because of its nothingness, consciousness intends completion and, as we said earlier, constantly runs the risk of tying itself down, of returning to buffeted consciousness, to what he here calls self-motivated inauthenticity. To put aside, for the time being, the question of whether Sartre's conception of "authenticity" and "inauthenticity" in *The War Diaries* can be identified with "good faith" and "bad faith" in *Being and Nothingness*, we may note that in *The War Diaries* Sartre exhibits plainly his concern that even authenticity might become a project for escaping one's freedom. He asks: "Is authenticity . . . going to reinstill in me the spirit of seriousness?"[42] Although his answer is a clear "no" ("For to grasp oneself as a person," he explains, "is quite the opposite of grasping oneself in terms of the world"), his question seems to anticipate his concerns regarding the "serious man" in *Being and Nothingness*.[43] It also prefigures his worry at the end of *Being and Nothingness* about the *possible* "bad faith" of the "freedom" that chooses "to be always at a distance *from* itself," that "wills to hold itself in awe."[44] The project of tying down one's authenticity can also become—as does sincerity—a project of *inauthenticity* and/or bad faith. Perhaps this reveals part of the reason for Sartre's malaise at times with the terms *authenticity* and *inauthenticity*[45] and for his declaring, in *Being and Nothingness*, that Heidegger's use of them is "dubious and insincere."[46] In the recently translated *Notebooks for an Ethics*, Sartre seems to confirm this point when he says that "if you seek authenticity for authenticity's sake, you are no longer authentic."[47] For if one were to act "in this way in order to confer on oneself the being or quality of an in-itself-for-itself," one would be in "a project of bad faith."[48] But I shall defer until a subsequent chapter my consideration of Sartre's focal discussion of authenticity in the *Notebooks*.

"Authenticity" in *Anti-Semite and Jew*

For the purpose of further elucidation and development of this concept in Sartre's early works, I turn now to Sartre's *Anti-Semite and Jew*,[49] a work which, I believe, draws significantly from the view he struggles to develop in *The War Diaries*.

"Authenticity," he tells us here, "consists in having a true and lucid consciousness of the situation, in assuming the responsibilities it involves."[50] And "to be in a situation . . . is to choose oneself in a situation." The human being, he reaffirms, is "first of all a being 'in a situation.'" What human beings "have in common is not a 'nature' but a *condition*."[51] Put another way, the human being can be defined "as a being having freedom within the limits of a situation." And this freedom may be considered *authentic* or *inauthentic* according to the choices he or she makes in the situation. "Authentic liberty assumes responsibilities."[52] Jewish authenticity consists in "choosing oneself as a Jew," that is to say, in realizing, choosing, and accepting "one's Jewish condition,"[53] one's Jewish "situation," one's Jewish "reality." Authenticity is, for the Jew, "to live to the full his condition as Jew."[54]

The anti-Semite, on the other side, "flees responsibility as he flees his own consciousness"; he chooses "for his personality the permanence of rock"; he chooses "the irremediable out of fear of being free."[55] He lives in "fear of the human condition."[56]

Moreover, the inauthentic Jew, like the anti-Semite or other in-authentic person, denies his "situation," his "Jewishness," de-cides to run away from it,[57] to "flee . . . Jewish reality."[58] The inauthentic Jew "represents two extremes of his possible be-havior: in anti-Semitism, he denies his race in order to be more than a pure individual . . . ; in masochism, he repudiates his liberty . . . in order to seek the repose and passivity of a thing."[59] He chooses the mode of being of in-itself rather than the mode of a free, metastable for-itself that he is.

Although I cannot focus here on the differences between the inauthenticity of the anti-Semite and the inauthenticity of the Jew, I must make at least two passing observations. First, let us note that the anti-Semitism of the Jew is, for Sartre, a "bor-rowed" one—a "secondary" one, we might say: the inauthen-ticity and "disquietude" of the Jew in the face of the anti-Se-mitic Jewish "situation" is primarily a *social*, not a "metaphysical" inauthenticity,[60] as it is for the anti-Semite. The Jew is "the social man, par excellence," says Sartre. "His con-cern is not yet the place of man in the universe, but his place in society." For anti-Semitic society to reproach the inauthentic Jew for his "metaphysical inauthenticity" is to fail to recognize that the Jew "is condemned to make his choice of himself on the basis of false problems in a false situation." It is we—the anti-Semites—who "force" the Jew into "the dilemma of Jewish authenticity or inauthenticity"; that is, "to choose to be a Jew whether through flight from himself or through self-asser-tion."[61] It is the anti-Semite who "makes" the Jew and "forces" him or her to accept or reject the "Jewish reality" he has cre-ated.

Second, we must observe that, when discussing inauthentic-ity in this context, Sartre seems to place an uncharacteristic emphasis on the "limits" and power of the "situation." Given his insistence, in *The War Diaries* and elsewhere, that "no situation is ever undergone," that "no mechanical force can [ever] decide on history,"[62] that in war, for instance, "there are no innocent victims,"[63] it is disconcerting to find Sartre contending, for example, that "the Jew is social because the anti-Semite *has made him* so."[64] To be sure, Sartre defines *situation* in *Being and Nothingness* as "the common product of the contingency of the in-itself and freedom," and acknowledges that it is impossible to distinguish what "the *plenum* of being of the world"— the in-itself—contributes to it from what "freedom contributes."[65] Yet because the "in-itself" or "brute given" constitutes part of the situation, it does not, either in *The War Diaries* or in *Being and Nothingness*, become a basis for qualifying the responsibility one must assume for one's situation and one's choices. The for-itself "discovers itself as engaged in being," "hemmed in," and "threatened" by being. But it is the for-itself that "freely posits the end in respect to which the state of things is threatening."[66] Authenticity demands (and we have seen this as a dominant theme) the recognition that we are without excuse.[67] Sartre cannot "plead excuses." In appropriating my freedom, he has insisted, I must "refuse excuses," for any excuse "invokes Necessity."[68] Whether we are talking about the "human condition" or "the basic human situation,"[69] or any particular less global, "situation," it is human reality that "hatches the situation"[70]: "there is no non-human situation."[71] Or, as Sartre puts it earlier in *Anti-Semite and Jew*, "to be in a situation . . . is to choose oneself in a situation."[72] And although "situation" and "motivation" are really one for Sartre,[73] Sartre, both in *The War Diaries* and in *Being and Nothingness*, regards the attribution of blame to a situation to be an instance of bad faith or even *inauthenticity*. For, though we may have encountered a "real limit to our freedom," "it is still necessary to understand," he says in *Being and Nothingness*, that "the limit imposed does not come from the *action* of others."[74]

Parenthetically, I must be quick to point out—lest I be misunderstood—that Sartre's early view of freedom as "absolute"
and "unconditioned" does not remain unaltered in the course
of his philosophical development. In the trajectory of his writings, he appears increasingly to recognize the "power of circumstances" *(la force des choses)* and even to acknowledge social conditioning.[75] As early as in his "Présentation" (1945)—his
inaugural editorial for *Les Temps Modernes*—Sartre acknowledges "situations which condition." And then, a few years later
in *St. Genet: Actor and Martyr*, he allows for passivity, inertia,
and social alienation. In the opening part of an interview entitled "The Itinerary of a Thought" (1959), Sartre admits—to explain "why [his] outlook changed so fundamentally after the
Second World War"—that life taught me *la force des choses*—
the power of circumstances.[76] And, in the *Critique of Dialectical
Reason* (1960) and later in *The Family Idiot* (1981), the notion of
"pure freedom" or the "pure individual" is replaced by a medi-
ated social "concrete" individual: material conditioning is given
even more weight. And though, in *Sartre by Himself* (*Sartre par
lui-même* [1977]), Sartre states that he "still remains faithful to
the notion of freedom," he says unequivocally that "There's no
question that there is some basic change in [my] concept of
freedom."[77] This is borne out—the decade before his death—in
his "plural thoughts" with Benny Lévy, in which Sartre sees
human reality further as both "constituted" and "constituting,"
passive as well as active, and acknowledges alterity as enabling
as well as alienating. Hence, in spite of my focus here on the
early Sartre, I do not want to leave the impression either that
consciousness remains completely unconditioned for Sartre or
that there is no shift in Sartre's thinking concerning freedom
and external conditions. And, though I remain with my present
focus on the formative Sartre, I remind the reader in passing
that unequivocal or unqualified statements can hardly be made

about thinkers like Sartre who continuously reexamine themselves and even "think against" themselves.

Diverging but complementary: A brief comparison

In spite of what appears to be an aberrant use of the "situation" in which one "chooses" inauthenticity (or authenticity), one may see clearly that the view of authenticity he presents in *Anti-Semite and Jew* overlaps with the view he developed in *The War Diaries* and has doubtless emerged from it. Whereas, for example, in *The War Diaries*, he has said that "To be authentic is to realize fully one's being-in-situation, *whatever this situation may happen to be,*"[78] in *Anti-Semite and Jew* he affirms that authenticity consists of choosing oneself in a situation, in having a "lucid consciousness of the situation, in assuming the responsibilities it involves."[79] In each work, it is clear that "situation" is used widely enough to include the human situation or the "human condition."[80] And in each description, authenticity *requires* facing the facticity of one's unjustifiable freedom, of one's condemnation to freedom and responsibility in a "resisting world"—in a world from which human reality realizes a "nihilating rupture."[81] This, of course, is the "human condition."

But there is a clear difference in emphasis in these accounts. Whereas Sartre's analysis in *The War Diaries* is dominated by the latter ontological analysis (authenticity "can be understood only in terms of the human condition"[82]), by the manner in which human reality "confronts" its own freedom and condition and effects a "radical conversion," his account of authenticity and inauthenticity in *Anti-Semite and Jew*—perhaps because of its intense social significance—is slanted more toward the *situation,* or more particularly toward the specific historical, social, or what I might call "local" situation. It seems clear, as Catalano attempts to show in his exploratory work on authenticity, that in *Anti-Semite and Jew* Sartre understands the project or task of authenticity to vary according to the "givens" of one's situation and one's position in the social strata. To be authentic, the Jew has to confront the Manicheanism, the anti-Semitism, the bad-faith oppression "built into" his historical and social situation. Almost as a prelude to what he does in the *Critique of Dialectical Reason*[83] years later, Sartre seems here to be anticipating his concern for collective responsibility and to be framing the issue of authenticity in the context of "bad-faith" historical and social institutions in which we inevitably find ourselves participating (for example, historical structures of racism).[84] Given that there is no freedom except in a situation and no situation except through freedom,[85] does it follow, we might ask, that the Jew is in part responsible for the historical, "bad-faith" Jewish social "reality"?: or that he cannot be authentic unless he not only lucidly recognizes but also changes that anti-Semitic "situation" or "reality"?

My intention, here, is not to answer these questions but to affirm two related points. First, whether the situation is ontological, historical, global, or regional, freedom is, for Sartre, always "situated," and never independent of a situation. Second, whether one is talking about freedom with respect to one's human ontological condition, or freedom in relation to any particular historical or social/existential context, *any* attempt on the part of human reality (or human freedom) to hide, flee from, or refuse its freedom in relation to the "situation," is for Sartre—at least in these writings—*inauthentic*. The anti-Semite's project is "objectively an attempt to hide from one's freedom and responsibility"; it is a "project aimed at limiting the freedom of a Jew," at making the Jew completely "responsible" for the "bad-faith" anti-Semitic situation in which he finds himself.[86] Human freedom is never unsituated. But the acceptance or refusal of one's freedom with respect to given historical and social structures—however petrified these structures may be—is never *merely* situational, contextual, or regional. It is inseparably bound up with the ontological, with the attitude one adopts to one's awesome freedom and responsibility-in-situation. Although the Jew or African American or any of us may be "forced" to participate in a society in which structures continue to objectify her, she is completely free to affirm or deny her freedom in relation to the structures and facticities of the situation. One's ontological freedom is an abstraction apart from one's existential freedom, apart from the way one "exists" or "lives" that freedom; and the way one exists or "practices" one's freedom is an abstraction apart from a concrete situation of which one is, in part, the creator.[87]

To be authentic is, indeed, to "realize fully one's being-in-situation"[88]—that is, one's freedom-in-situation—and to take responsibility for it. Catalano is right in concluding from this that an authentic life for Sartre "reveals human action [and, I might add, choice] to be at the root of all accepted values" and that this ontological given implies "the possibility of altering the very historical structures that we have collectively produced."[89] This insight is surely compatible with Sartre's contention, at the end of *Being and Nothingness*, that "when freedom becomes conscious of itself, it will reveal itself in anguish as the unique source of value."[90]

Authenticity and "self-recovery"

I cannot take leave of those two diverging but mutually supporting accounts of authenticity without attending briefly to a key theme which is emphasized in Sartre's more "ontological" *War Diaries* account but is virtually unmentioned in his later, more situational, *Anti-Semite and Jew* account. I refer specifically to his notion of "self-recovery" and the related notion of "deliverance." We have seen, in his formative *War Diaries* account, that, in spite of consciousness's "congenital" disposition to fill its emptiness, to relieve its "troubled," non-substantial being by trying to secure a foundation, consciousness can choose to "recover" itself by an "assumptive conversion," by a willed "adoption of reality as one's own." This, in effect, turns out to be consciousness's project or "proposal" of "authenticity"—the willed adoption of an attitude in which consciousness accepts its gratuitous freedom and claims authorship and responsibility for all of its actions, whatever its "situation" might be. In assuming freedom and adopting it as one's own, in accepting the "angst" of its non-coincidence, human reality *converts* to a lucid recognition of its "self-motivation" and refuses excuses. This new attitude, which constitutes a *conversion* from consciousness's futile (and bad-faith) "natural" search for a foundation and for self-coincidence, represents human reality's "recovery" from its "fall" into the world. Rather than try to make itself "akin to things"[91]—or akin to God for that matter—human reality, by affirming itself as freedom and proposing to live consistently with that lucidity, makes *authenticity* its value and in so doing finds the possibility of "deliverance."

It may seem peculiar that Sartre does not mention "self-recovery" in a later work which focuses and depends so strongly on the concepts of inauthenticity and authenticity. Yet one should not conclude that the omission is problematic or that *Anti-Semite and Jew* is inconsistent with his early views on authenticity in *The War Diaries*. In my judgment, Sartre takes for granted in *Anti-Semite and Jew* the relevant ontological analyses he has provided in *The War Diaries* and has developed in *Being and Nothingness*. There is no suggestion that he has here denied the "self-recovery" and "deliverance" contentions. If anything, as I already suggested, Sartre seems concerned, in *Anti-*

Semite and Jew, with applying his ontological analysis of authenticity to a particular social context and problem—more specifically, with drawing out the implications of his ontological account of "authenticity" and "self-recovery" for the phenomenon of racism. He makes it clear, as we have seen, that the anti-Semite is not able to accept the human condition, his being-in-situation; that he tries to flee his own consciousness and responsibility; that, fearing the human condition, he continues to choose "petrified values" over his own freedom.[92] The anti-Semite cannot resist the "impetus towards substantiality,"[93] cannot tolerate the non-coincidence of consciousness; so he chooses instead the "impenetrability" of a rock rather than the uneasiness of freedom. He chooses to continue his "natural" bad faith—to seek a foundation and justification for himself—rather than the way of authentic self-recovery, which is always open to him. The *authentic* Jew, on the other hand, accepts the "value" of "living" the unsettledness and "dis-ease" of an elusive, non-substantial consciousness, and of taking full existential responsibility for her freedom and her choice of being. In so doing, she delivers herself from her natural bad faith. Hence, Sartre's development of "authenticity" in *Anti-Semite and Jew* presupposes rather than departs from his original view of authentic self-recovery in *The War Diaries*. It extends and elucidates but does not defeat the former.

My interpretation of authenticity in Sartre's early philosophy as presupposing a willed "conversion," and my insistence that, even when unsaid, authenticity, for Sartre, is intimately connected with the for-itself's "self-recovering" or reclaiming the "identityless" freedom which one is, are strongly supported by Francis Jeanson's interpretation of Sartre's concept of authenticity in *Being and Nothingness*. And, because of Sartre's unequivocal praise for Jeanson's grasp of his thinking ("You have so perfectly followed the development of my thought"),[94] I must at least take note of Jeanson's explication. For Sartre's glowing assessment makes Jeanson's analysis of his early works a standard against which any other interpretation must be tested.

Testing against Jeanson's "approved" account

At the heart of Jeanson's interpretation is his pervasive contention that, for Sartre, the human being is, through and through, ambiguous.[95] Consciousness is a being that exists ambiguously in the mode of not being what it is and being what it is not; non-coincidence with itself lies at the heart of this "freedom."[96] This non-coincidence, this ambiguity, makes subjectivity "susceptible to bad faith."[97] Human reality "naturally" "desires" to attain being-in-itself, to escape from its ambiguity and radical contingency. Human reality is in perpetual flight toward what it can never be. This is the human condition.

It is precisely this ontology of ambiguity that, on Jeanson's account, allows for a passage from the "natural attitude" of our ontological condition to a "new, more fundamental attitude"[98]—specifically, to a *moral* attitude in which I "valorize" (give value to) my ontological non-coincidence.[99] Freedom itself is ambiguous. "Factual freedom"—the ontological freedom to which I am abandoned—allows a "radical conversion" to a "freedom-as-valued," to my free choice of "valorizing" my metastable, unsteady, troubled freedom.[100] In freely choosing it, I "imbue it with value." I choose to stop pursuing the impossible self-coincidence: as "freedom" I accept and affirm my freedom; I pass beyond my "natural" attitude to a "moral" attitude, yet without disowning my "natural" ontological tendency, without pretending—to use the language of *The War Diaries*—that human reality can ever eliminate its "natural" or "first" "impetus towards substantiality."[101] In recognizing and affirming my "nothingness," my "self-distance," my non-coincidence, I recognize that the ambiguity at the heart of human subjectivity is "the sole source of values"; and I "see" the possibility of "deliverance," of genuine "self-recovery." Accordingly, I refuse the reassurances and self-justifications made in my "natural" disposition to bad faith; I reflectively *convert* toward "moral agency"[102]; I begin to "value" the non-substantial freedom which I am. On Jeanson's interpretation, the coming to be of this *moral* attitude is not an "episode in the evolution of the human species"; it is rather a "conquest by the individual" that always "refers back to the singular act of individual *conversion.*"[103] It is a move from "bad faith"—where unreflective freedom pursues a "preset goal"—to the "moralization" of human consciousness, where even the goal "may be placed in question" and where the individual reflectively affirms her non-coincidence and takes full responsibility for her freedom and responsibility.[104]

For Jeanson, it is clear that this conversion or metamorphosis is the beginning of genuine "self-recovery" (in Sartre), the beginning of authentic "self-knowledge" and "self-making." This passage from "factual" or "natural" freedom to "freedom as valued" always requires a "radical conversion" and constitutes a passage to "authenticity." Although one can never abandon the natural or ontological freedom to which one is condemned, one can stop "realizing" oneself in bad faith and freely choose, by a "purified" and reflective effort, to take hold of one's freedom to pursue the project of authenticity (of *living* one's ambiguous freedom), to develop one's own humanization. To put it in Jeanson's words, "The human condition may be either ignored in *bad faith* or understood and lived in such an effort at *authenticity*"[105]; but there is no absolute sign that justifies one attitude over another.[106] In my adoption of a "moral" attitude—that is, in my conversion—my freedom wills itself as ambiguous, resolves to maintain its ambiguity, and does so in the knowledge that this "liberation" can never be total or final. I cannot deliver myself completely from "my incessant problem of the situation" (my relationship to others and to the world). My authentic choosing of myself is not an attainment of lucidity once and for all; it is, rather, a "point of departure"[107] for making myself "authentic." In adopting this new attitude, human reality *recovers* itself as freedom and responsibility; that is, it accepts the gratuity of its being, surpasses "illusory justification," and accepts the "burden of [its] initiatives,"[108] the *facticity* of its responsibility. This conversion marks the start of one's "self-recovery," the passage from one's "spontaneous initial choice"[109] to one's authentic making and remaking of oneself. But this does not mean that authenticity is a "state attainable by man"; for, because human reality is always at a distance from itself and is always metastable and ambiguous, nothing concerning it can ever be finished.[110] Human authenticity is the continued task of being authentic: one must, as Sartre suggests in the *The War Diaries*, "adapt one's life to one's authenticity."[111]

My summary of Jeanson's account of Sartre on authenticity allows me now to reaffirm certain points with additional confidence and, I hope, clarity. First, we may observe that Jeanson's account, though written without access to *The War Diaries* and intended as an exegesis of *Being and Nothingness*, parallels closely the details of authenticity that Sartre himself has given in *The War Diaries*. Jeanson's interpretation of Sartre's "factual" or "natural" freedom and of the passage from "factual freedom" to "freedom-as-valued" closely approximates what Sartre says in *The War Diaries*. And, more specifically, Jeanson's account of the conversion from "natural" attitude to "moral" attitude, though placing much greater emphasis on the moral existence that the "willed" conversion generates, is virtually identical, in terms of analytic structure, to Sartre's *War*

Diaries account of the "assumptive conversion." On each account, this passage marks the movement by which human reality reflectively reclaims its freedom and responsibility and takes on the humanizing project of authenticity.

Second, we see clearly that Jeanson's account completely corroborates my tentative interpretation of the vital role of "self-recovery" in Sartre's analysis of authenticity. Jeanson's discussion of Sartre's reflective conversion, of freedom's recognizing and affirming its non-coincidence as value, is faithful to Sartre's account, in *The War Diaries,* of the attempt by self-motivating consciousness to recover itself by proposing authenticity as its value. And certainly this form of "self-recovery" in respect to authenticity is consistent with what Sartre maintains—all too briefly—in selected passages in *Being and Nothingness.*[112] *Conversion* and *self-recovery* thus appear as essential conditions for authenticity in Sartre. I shall address this specific issue in much greater detail in the following chapter.

Third, Jeanson's interpretation strongly suggests that the willed conversion on which Sartre insists in *The War Diaries* and mentions in *Being and Nothingness* is a conversion *from* our "natural" ontological condition of "bad faith." More exactly, this is in line with Sartre's contention, in *Being and Nothingness,* that consciousness's choice of authenticity is a "self-recovery of being which was previously corrupted," that is, was in bad faith[113]; or with his contention in *The War Diaries* that human reality's choice of authenticity is a choice to cease its "natural" "bad-faith" attitude of fleeing from its freedom and trying to make itself "akin to things." On Jeanson's reading, it is clear that human consciousness, because of its non-coincidence with itself—its ontological "dis-ease"—exists "naturally" in bad faith and, "starting from that," may either decide *reflectively* to consolidate its bad faith or convert to authenticity.[114] Whether or not, as I'm inclined to believe, Jeanson has overinterpreted the bad faith of "factual" or "ontological" freedom, Jeanson clearly sees Sartre's authenticity as freedom's self-affirming alternative—even antithesis—to the human being's "natural" condition, to his ontological disposition to "bad faith."[115] And this both enlightens some of Sartre's skeletal references to authenticity in *Being and Nothingness* and serves, generally, to confirm my interpretation of Sartre's notion of authenticity.

Finally, Jeanson's "approved" interpretation of Sartre's phenomenological ontology seems to make clear that my movement from a "natural attitude" of flight, from a "natural bad faith" (his words![116]) to a "willed" acceptance and self-affirmation of my freedom and responsibility—to authentic self-recovery—constitutes a *moral* conversion. To put the matter somewhat differently, the "effort at authenticity" is a *moral* effort; the reflective adoption of one's freedom as one's own is a moral choice; "self-recovery" is the moralization of human reality; authenticity (or inauthenticity) is, for Sartre, a moral category. With the human being's new valorization of "non-coincidence," she becomes a moral agency. She stops pursuing the unreachable justification of herself; instead, she acknowledges herself as "unjustifiable" and recognizes that the non-coincidence, the "nothingness" at the heart of human reality is the only source of values.[117]

6

Authenticity and Good Faith: An Analytic Differentiation

My attempt in the two preceding chapters to reconstruct and analyze Sartre's sometimes elusive notions of good faith and authenticity return us to one of the central questions that generated my inquiry of the last two chapters. If one is to redeem any constructive sense of good faith in the early formative writings of Sartre—as I have tried to do—how is one to distinguish it from Sartre's concept of authenticity, to which Sartre gives more repeated attention and detail, and in respect to which he offers greater clarity? I have argued that Sartre's analysis allows a positive sense of "good faith" at both an epistemological and an ontological level. At the epistemological level, I have contended that good faith is an attitude that is open to the metastability of consciousness, to the ambiguity and incompleteness of all belief, to critical evidence. In respect to the ontological level, I have suggested that good faith may be viewed as an attitude that confronts and affirms, rather than flees from, the freedom and responsibility to which (for Sartre) we have been abandoned. And I have also contended that, in spite of human reality's desire for Being, it can affirm its freedom, its nothingness, its *lack* of being, without making that affirmation a bad-faith project.

But, in my interpretation of "authenticity" in Sartre, I have

110

shown, likewise, that, for Sartre, authenticity, as a willed "conversion" *from* one's "natural" attitude of trying to flee one's freedom *to* a lucid recognition of one's situation, also invokes the acceptance, affirmation, valorizing, and living of one's freedom, one's "non-coincidence" of being, one's ontological abandonment to responsibility. At a number of places in the foregoing chapters, I have alluded to the marked resemblances among commonly held interpretations of Sartre's "good faith" and "authenticity," whether these views were adopted before or—as in our case above—after close analysis of the Sartrean texts. And I have even suggested that Joseph Catalano, one of the pioneers among North American inquirers on these topics, has sometimes conflated the two concepts.[1]

The question remains: How, after analysis, are we to differentiate—if at all—these two important Sartrean concepts? Are we to assume, following our immediately preceding conclusions, that (1) "conversion" is a necessary condition of "self-recovery" and of authenticity, but *not* of ontological good faith; and (2) it is the case, as Joseph Catalano sometimes insists, that while good and bad faith are categories of the non-reflective consciousness, authenticity is a category of the reflective, voluntary consciousness? And, finally, (3) may we conclude, following the highlights of our characterizations of good faith and authenticity, that, whereas good faith may be salvaged as a creative ontological and epistemological "attitude," it does not share authenticity's ethical or moral dimension; namely, a moral "conversion" from corrupted being,[2] from ontological bad faith, to a new moral attitude in which, as Jeanson interprets the matter, I reclaim my freedom and valorize and live my "non-coincidence"? Let us look at these overlapping issues, one at a time.

"Conversion" as a necessary condition

First, I must restate, at the price of sounding repetitious, that both Sartre's discussions of authenticity, as we have viewed them above, and Jeanson's approved interpretation elucidate and corroborate Sartre's contentions, made principally in foot-notes in *Being and Nothingness,* that "deliverance," "self-recovery," authenticity, is possible only after a "radical conversion" (a change in one's fundamental project) with respect to "corrupted" being.[3] But, though we saw grounds for saving the concept of *good faith* in Sartre, for purging it of the bad-faith connotations to which interpreters normally condemn it, we did not posit for it the "conversion" requirement or prerequisite that we attributed to authenticity. Although we granted that human reality, as non-self-coincidence, is perennially susceptible to bad faith, good faith, as a contrasting ontological attitude, appears not to be a willed attitude or an attitude adopted through a "willed," reflective *conversion* from ontological bad faith. If anything, the redeemed sense of good faith which I was suggesting appeared to be a *spontaneous* self-choosing in which freedom, though tempted by the inevitable passion for being, non-reflectively—that is, without attending to itself—accepts its abandonment to freedom without *projecting* flight from its "non-being" or "elsewhereness" of being, without trying to hide or flee from its non-coincidence. It is, as we saw, one of "the two immediate attitudes we can [spontaneously] take in the face of our being,"[4] one of the two fundamental attitudes or self-choices we can make in respect to our distinctive freedom. But though "most of the time we flee anguish in bad faith," it does not follow that we cannot be in good faith,[5] that we cannot, or necessarily do not, originally accept the non-coincidence of our free being. But it is important to note that, in spite of an inclination by some interpreters to suggest a movement or conversion from bad faith to good faith, Sartre, in his limited and frustrating discussion of good faith (in *Being and Nothingness*), does not speak this way. It is true that, in discussing bad faith's "coming into the world," Sartre speaks of bad faith's resignation to "not being transformed into good faith."[6] But overall in the pages of *Being and Nothingness*, Sartre appears to view "good faith" as a "spontaneous determination of being," and to label *authenticity*, not good faith, the "condition" in which, through "radical conversion"—by a reflective alternation in my choice of myself—I can radically escape (my "natural attitude" of) "bad faith."[7] By "pure reflection," I can, in short, "recover" myself[8] as "for itself." In fact, in *Cahiers pour une morale*, Sartre makes it clear that the conversion involves "refusing the quest for being" *(réfuser la quête de l'être)*[9] that marks the bad faith "natural" attitude, and adds that "authenticity" (not good faith) will consist in "maintaining the tension" [*maintenir la tension*][10] of the "break in being," of the non-coincidence of for-itself. Only by this "*pure* reflective consciousness"[11] can the for-itself "recover" itself as the "for-itself reflected-on in its reality."[12] If this is so, it follows—as I shall reaffirm later—that authenticity, not good faith, constitutes for Sartre "deliverance" from bad faith.

But, in this regard, Catalano has, I believe, offered an important qualifying point. He has pointed out that in Sartre there is a "close relation between the way the will appears on the reflective level and the way freedom functions at the pre-reflective level."[13] "At the pre-reflective level," he continues, "freedom does not exist as a 'will'." And, as Sartre himself contends, "The will in fact is posited as a reflective decision in regard to certain ends" which it did not create.[14] So if bad faith, at a pre-reflective ontological level, has an "original, non-thetic awareness of itself" as freedom, then there is at least the possibility for bad faith to escape its condition. The will can emerge, in *good faith*, as a joyous acceptance of freedom without regret or remorse, rather than a mode of freedom that is trying, in bad faith, to escape freedom. In other words, the relation between ontological bad faith and the reflective awareness of the possibility of good faith "lays the foundation" for the possibility of "conversion."[15] That is to say, given "original freedom" as its foundation, the will can be posited as a reflective decision to decide the attitude of being which the for-itself wishes to assume in relation to the "ends" it has already posited and which "characterize" its being.[16] The will is produced within the limits of what Sartre calls our "initial project."[17] In order words, the will is not opposed to our fundamental choice of being but is to be understood only within "the perspective of our fundamental choice."[18] And, as Sartre also tells us in *Being and Nothingness*, "the for-itself can make voluntary decisions which are opposed to the fundamental ends which it has [pre-reflectively] chosen." But these can only be reflective and derive from errors.[19] This does not mean that "conversion" or "self-recovery" is a necessary feature of "good faith," but only, I repeat, that the reflective awareness of the possibility of good faith lays the groundwork for the possibility of a reflective conversion; that is, a change in fundamental project from bad faith, to an authentic mode of "existing" or "living" one's freedom. Hence, this qualification does not alter, in any substantive way, our hypothesis—gained from our study of some of Sartre's earlier works—that radical *conversion* is one of the marks that differentiates authenticity from our redeemed ontological sense of *good faith.*

"Reflection" as a mark of differentiation

Whether we relish it or not, we have already begun to respond to our second culminating query—namely, whether, as suggested in our preceding accounts, authenticity and good faith are, finally, to be distinguished from one another in respect to the difference between the non-reflective and the reflective consciousness. Certainly, Catalano has suggested, in a number of places,[20] that while good and bad faith are pre-reflective ontological "attitudes," authenticity and inauthenticity are better understood as functions of the reflective, voluntary, and (hence) ethical consciousness. (We shall defer a discussion of "ethical" until we confront the next question.) And Catalano cannot be charged with failing to attempt to clarify the levels or "states" of consciousness in relation to these two pairs of concepts. For in "Authenticity: A Sartrean Perspective," he has tried carefully to distinguish these levels of consciousness from "perfect reflection,"[21] and to relate them, in turn, to both authenticity and *good* and *bad* faith.

But we must return to Sartre himself. To be sure, Sartre distinguishes between pre-reflective and reflective consciousness, and to be sure, he relates these forms of consciousness to good and bad faith. As early as *The Transcendence of the Ego*, Sartre distinguished between an *unreflective* consciousness, which is directed outside of ourselves and our (conscious) acts, and a *reflective* consciousness (or "reflection"), which "takes consciousness as an object" and directs its attention onto itself.[22] As such, reflection is a "second-order" and distinctly human activity, while unreflective consciousness, though also conscious (of) itself, is first order.[23] And, in the early pages of *Being and Nothingness*, Sartre distinguishes between the "reflective" and "pre-reflective" (or "non-reflective") consciousness: he assures us that, though all consciousness is "positional" (in that it "transcends itself in order to reach an object"[24]), there is "a pre-reflective cogito which is the condition of the Cartesian cogito," and that it is this "non-reflective consciousness," this "non-thetic" consciousness (of) consciousness, which renders all reflective, thetic, consciousness possible.[25] Further, there is no question that, in his provocative analysis of "bad faith,"[26] Sartre admits that the "original intention and . . . project of bad faith implies . . . a *pre-reflective* apprehension (of) consciousness as affecting itself with bad faith."[27] And, because "that which affects itself with bad faith must be conscious (of) its bad faith," it follows, for Sartre, "that I must be in good faith, at least to the extent that I am conscious of my bad faith."[28] Combined with his statement, at the end of his chapter on "Bad Faith," that bad faith cannot be a "cynical lie," this early evidence seems strongly to support the judgment of Catalano and others that good faith and bad faith are, for Sartre, categories of the pre-reflective consciousness. But we must probe further.

Following some of our observations in respect to question (1) above, we can now, however briefly, add some clarification from a later section of *Being and Nothingness*. In "Being and Doing: Freedom"—and particularly in his brilliant analysis of "causes," "motives," and "ends"—Sartre brings his distinction between pre-reflective and reflective consciousness to a head. While the *unreflective* consciousness is a "spontaneous self-projection towards its possibilities"[29]—that is, is an "involuntary spontaneity" or a "non-positional self-consciousness"[30]— the reflective consciousness appears to be a *voluntary* consciousness. Although I should hesitate to use the words *unreflective* (or *pre-reflective*) and *reflective* interchangeably with *involuntary* and *voluntary* in Sartre, it seems clear—if I may move in a converse direction—that, for Sartre, the voluntary "requires the appearance of the reflective consciousness,"[31] that the "voluntary" is often identified as the "reflective,"[32] and that the involuntary is understood in terms of a "purely unre-flective consciousness."[33] Catalano puts it well, I think, when he suggests that the latter consciousness is the one that is "absorbed in activities," whereas the former (reflective voluntary) is the consciousness that seeks, for instance, "to discover what these activities [or actions] mean."[34] Sartre tells us directly that reflection "is the for-itself conscious of itself"[35] and is an effort of a for-itself to recover a for-itself "which it is in the mode of non-being."[36] "The meaning of reflection," he adds, "is thus its

being-for." In particular, "the reflective is the reflected-on nihilating itself in order to recover itself"[37] as distinctive nothingness or "non-coincidence." That is to say, reflection is for-itself's attempt "to recover the for-itself by a turning back on
itself"; in other words, it is for-itself's effort to "be for-itself
what it is for-itself"—flight.[38] Even in *Cahiers pour une morale*—his most concentrated work on morality—he states
(again) that "l'origine de la réflexion est un effort de récupéra-
tion du Pour-soi par soi-meme, pour arriver à un pour-soi qui
soit Soi" ("The origin of reflection is an effort at recovery of the
for-itself by itself, to arrive at a For-itself which is Itself").[39] Sartre's reference to self-recovery here reminds us of the differentiating role we have attributed to "conversion" in authenticity
and returns us to the issue of whether the reflective consciousness has any role in good or bad faith or must, rather, be
viewed as a differentiating characteristic of authenticity alone.

Sartre offers us more to go by. He tells us that "The for-itself
which exists in the *voluntary* [reflective] mode wishes to recover
itself in so far as it decides and acts. It does not wish merely to
be carried towards an end; . . . it wishes [rather] to *recover itself*
as a spontaneous project towards this or that particular end."[40]
But Sartre also makes it clear that, because "a *voluntary* decision finds its motive in the fundamental free choice of my
ends," it is only within the compass of my fundamental project
that the will can be efficacious.[41]

Take Sartre's example of an "inferiority complex," the initial
project of choosing oneself "as inferior in the midst of others."[42]
The inferiority that we feel and live "is the chosen instrument
to make us comparable to a thing; . . . to make us exist as a
pure outside in the midst of the world."[43] The will here is not
"opposed to the fundamental choice"; on the contrary, "it is
understood in its ends and in its fundamental bad faith only
within the perspective of a fundamental choice of inferiority."[44]

In other words, the "divorce between the spontaneous and willed consciousness" is "projected by . . . our fundamental freedom" and "can be conceived only in and through the profound unity of our *fundamental project,* which is to choose ourselves as inferior."[45] Moreover, to "choose" to live a pre-reflective project of an inferiority complex is to choose to live in *bad faith* in relation to one's fundamental freedom or one's original consciousness. As Sartre puts it, the choice of inferiority "implies the constant realization of a *gap* between the end pursued by the will and the end obtained." The will to maintain this "divorce" is in *bad faith,* for "it flees the recognition of the true ends chosen by the spontaneous consciousness and it constitutes false psychic objects as motives" (for example, "love of the beautiful"). "Whereas in the form of *reflective* consciousness," Sartre says, "the will constitutes in *bad faith* false psychic objects as motives, on the other hand in the capacity of a *nonreflective and non-thetic* self-consciousness, it is consciousness (of) being in bad faith and consequently (of) the fundamental project pursued by the for-itself."[46] That is to say, the will's fundamental bad faith here—the voluntary deliberation that wants to conceal our inferiority from ourselves "precisely in order to *create* it" and "measure it"[47]—is recognized and is "chosen" within the limits of our pre-reflective, spontaneous, initial project of inferiority, our being of consciousness.[48] In Sartre's words, "This inferiority which I struggle against and which nevertheless I recognize, this I have chosen from the start."[49]

Catalano puts the matter well in his account of Sartre's analysis of the bad faith involved in an "inferiority complex." At a *pre-reflective* level, the person with an inferiority complex may well have a project to be superior. But he is "afraid of committing himself to his own freedom." He fears failure, but he is not prepared to abandon his project of being superior. So he "creates the [self-deceptive] belief in himself as having an inferior nature"; he would be superior "if nature had not cursed him with an inferiority complex." (In Sartre's language, "The inferiority which is felt and lived is the chosen instrument to make us comparable to a *thing,* "that is, to make us exist as a pure outside in the midst of the world."[50]) So, on the *reflective* level, "his will now appears as a struggle against his inferior nature," as a struggling "will to power" that attempts to "rise above" an "inferior condition," which he himself has created. The person with an inferiority complex flees from his freedom and thus is in bad faith by regarding himself as a "will to power" in a given ("inferior") "essence," which he, in fact, has created. His will emerges in bad faith not because it wills "bad objects" but because it "constitutes the self-deception that brings about the inferiority complex itself."[51]

The above makes clear what we have already anticipated; namely, that the voluntary exists at a reflective level, that the involuntary exists at a pre-reflective, and that, at a pre-reflective level, our fundamental freedom cannot exist as "will." We have also seen that, in spite of appearances to the contrary, the reflective choices of the will—and its fundamental bad faith in the case of an "inferiority complex", for instance—can be understood and can be "efficacious" only within the framework of one's pre-reflective, spontaneous choice of one's being, one's fundamental project. "When I deliberate," Sartre says, "the chips are down"[52]; that is to say, all my deliberations are in the context of my pre-reflective project, my *original choice* of myself. Sartre brings to a head the implications of this point when he says: "By means of the will, we can *construct* ourselves entirely but . . . the will which presides over this construction finds its meaning in the original project [with its ends] which it can appear to deny."[53] And, finally, we have even seen how this relation between reflective will and non-reflective or pre-reflective choice of being can lay the foundation for a "conversion." Given our pre-reflective choice of being, there can be a *reflective* awareness of the possibility of good faith. In reflecting on the meaning of my acts, I face the freedom of confirming my project or of altering it. This is a key consideration, given what I have contended about the role of reflection in self-recovery and the entry into authenticity.

But the question remains: "Can this reflective conversion be from bad faith to good faith?" None of the above speaks directly to the question. But Sartre's concluding statements about "inferiority complex" suggest an answer: "So long as I'm 'in' the inferiority complex," he says, "I cannot even conceive the possibility of getting out of it . . ."; "I can be freed from my inferiority complex only by a *radical modification* of my project."[54] And it would be hard to conceive of such a modification—as we have seen in *The War Diaries* and *Jeanson's* approved interpretation—without a *reflective* decision; or, as Sartre puts it earlier, a "systematic and reflective effort" to alter my fundamental project.[55] But a reflective adoption of one's freedom as one's own, a voluntary embracing of one's ambiguous freedom and one's responsibility, a reflective *conversion* from one fundamental project to another, would seem to mark consciousness's move—as we've seen in our earlier analysis—from bad-faith consciousness ("inferiority complex") to authenticity, but not from "bad faith" to "good faith." Let us, however briefly, look further at this matter.

The issue, again, is not whether bad faith can escape what Jeanson—and, indeed, Sartre in the *War Diaries*—regards as its natural attitude of flight. Sartre makes it clear that this is possible[56]—in fact, the very relation of one's reflection and will to one's pre-reflective choice of one's being and ends opens that possibility—but that it requires an "abrupt metamorphosis" of one's "initial project," "a new choice of oneself and "one's ends,"[57] for everything within the *Weltanschauung* of bad faith is in bad faith. Sartre tells us, in fact, that such a radical "modification is *always* possible," and that the anguish which "manifests our freedom to our consciousness is witness of the perpetual modifiability of our initial project."[58]

The issue, rather, is whether there can be a radical conversion from a "natural" and pre-reflective or non-reflective bad faith to an acceptance and affirmation of one's freedom, which Sartre—I argue—allows as "good faith." To be sure, as we have seen, Sartre has told us that the consciousness that exists at a reflective or voluntary level wants to "recover itself as a spontaneous project" toward certain specific ends.[59] But, for Sartre—at least as I have argued—good faith viewed ontologically is a fundamental human attitude and original project in which human reality accepts the non-coincidence of its freedom and the facticity of its responsibility. Putting aside the related issue of whether bad faith, as flight from freedom, is our "natural" or "factual" ontological condition or attitude for Sartre (and there is persuasive evidence that it is!), we must yet insist that, insofar as a radical conversion or radical modification of our fundamental project involves a reflective consciousness ("a consciousness *directed upon consciousness*"[60]) and insofar as our original choice of our freedom, of our fundamental attitude, is, for Sartre, pre-reflective, then *good faith* cannot be the form of "deliverance" to which we can arrive by reflective or "willed" conversion. For although, as we have seen, pure reflection is an effort on the part of for-itself to "recover" itself as "nothingness," to recognize and affirm its elsewhereness or non-coincidence of being, it does not—at least in key passages in *Being and Nothingness*—appear to have any role in the "immediate attitude" of good faith—of accepting the anguish of for-itself's non-being—as one of the possible fundamental choices of "being-in-the-world."[61] Reflection is necessary for the *conversion* from the bad-faith pursuit of necessary being (the desire to be God or In-itself-For-itself) to the authentic choosing and recognizing of oneself as a "break in being," as elusive, gratuitous, ambiguous being. Although *reflection on* my pre-reflective awareness of my bad faith can exhibit an awareness of the possibility of good faith, and even prompt me to modify my fundamental project radically, my "willed" radical conversion to the project of affirming and living my free, ambiguous, evanescent being, constitutes a "deliverance" and "self-recovery" which Sartre generally labels "authenticity."[62]

As we have seen in respect to (1) above, good and bad faith, viewed ontologically, represent the fundamental and original ways in which freedom approaches itself pre-reflectively: either by confronting the angst of freedom or by fleeing from it. And this project of being is the context for all our reflections and deliberations. But, despite the fact that "freedom is always at stake,"[63] that consciousness always pursues Being,[64] that human reality is continuously threatened by bad faith, my "corrupted" freedom, through a reflective conversion, may deliberately choose to recover itself as freedom and live consistently with the freedom (and "responsibility") to which it is condemned.[65] This reflective (and radical) conversion, this *deliverance from* bad faith, is precisely what Sartre means by authenticity, not good faith. To put the matter another way, the "willed conversion" of which Sartre speaks as early as in *The War Diaries* is the necessary condition and distinguishing characteristic of our move from bad faith (our "natural attitude" of fleeing from freedom and responsibility) to what Sartre calls our "self-recovery," our "authenticity," our "salvation."[66] That is to say, the reflective consciousness that is necessary to any radical transformation of one's fundamental project, to any choice of radically altering one's *bad faith* way of being-in-the-world, represents the *second* basic feature that differentiates authenticity from the closely related fundamental but—Sartre seems to want to say—pre-reflective and non-thetic ontological attitude of good faith.

Before ending my investigation of question (2) at the beginning of this section, I must drive home a concluding implication and then raise another closely related point. First, it is to be noted again that if the foregoing reconstruction of Sartre is correct, then one has strong grounds for inferring that authenticity rather than good faith (viewed ontologically) may more accurately be viewed as the antithesis of bad faith. Although I have struggled to save Sartre's concept of good faith from the tentacles of bad faith, and have gone out of my way to show the common characteristics between a redeemed sense of good faith and authenticity, I have tried to make clear that whereas good faith, at the ontological level, is to be viewed as one's unreflective "choice" of, or attitude toward, one's freedom, *authenticity*, as a lucid recognition, acceptance, and living of one's ontological freedom (and responsibility), requires, as prerequisite, a *reflective* radical choice to convert *from* the bad faith to which one is "naturally" inclined and in which one is living. Although, as I have tried to show, my pre-reflective awareness of my "affecting" myself with bad faith[67] returns me to my original project of freedom, that is, to my "being," to my "free project" of being,[68] and confronts me with the possibility of good faith, it is only by a "willed conversion," by a reflective act of radically changing my fundamental project, by consciousness "operating" on and redirecting consciousness, that I can "recover" myself as freedom and (rather than try to flee from it) take full responsibility for it and begin to "live" its ambiguity and non-coincidence. For Sartre—and for Jeanson, who gives a pronounced emphasis to Sartre's move—it is this *new* attitude,[69] this reflective passage from bad faith to taking hold of one's freedom, that begins the project of *authenticity* and constitutes a "radical escape," a "salvation," from bad faith[70] or "corrupted" being. This means that, although good faith can be viewed as an original attitude (of facing one's freedom) that *contrasts* with bad faith, and although the awareness of bad faith implies a kind of ontological precomprehension of good faith, it is the *post-conversion* authentic life that marks for Sartre the mode of being that is opposite (or antithetical) to living in bad faith. Freedom—and I shall say more about this later—now becomes "valued."[71] I am even tempted to say that the reflective conversion, by which the bad faith consciousness adopts, or perhaps returns to, good faith's non-thetic, "joyful" affirmation of freedom, not only marks the start of the project of authenticity but also turns good faith "into authenticity." But I should better leave that issue to another occasion.

One might argue, of course, that it is inauthenticity, the reflective decision to continue in the bad-faith patterns of fleeing freedom, that may better be viewed as the opposite of authenticity. But because for Sartre we are ontologically predisposed to bad faith and are continually threatened by it, we have a strong case for viewing the way of "self-recovery" of freedom, the way of authenticity, as the antithetical mode of being—the mode of assuming one's gratuity, of making and remaking oneself without excuse and without permanence. This point is certainly confirmed by the main line of Sartre's reasoning in *Being and Nothingness*[72] and in *Cahiers pour une morale*. In the latter he says—if I may offer representative quotes—that "reflection is born as an effort on the part of consciousness to recover itself"[73] ("la réflexion naît comme un effort de la conscience pour se récupérer"[74]), and he refers to the "new 'authentic' manner of being-to-oneself and for-oneself" as "transcending the dialectic of sincerity–bad faith" (*nouvelle manière*, 'authentique,' *d'être à soi-même et pour soi-même, qui transcende la dialectique de la sincerité–mauvaise foi*[75]). He calls this authenticity the new manner that man has to "exist his existence" *(d'e-xister son existence)*.[76] The corroboration, I think, cannot be stronger.

And now—secondly—in concluding this section, I wish to raise an issue and make a brief point or two about it. In distinguishing between the unreflective and reflective consciousness, Sartre contends, as we have seen, that the unreflective consciousness "is a spontaneous self-projection towards its possibilities." And, having characterized it in this way, he goes on to affirm that, since it is so, "it can never be deceived about itself," and thus we "must take care not to hold it responsible for making a mistake about itself."[77]

I wish, for a moment, to focus on the first part of this statement. If we are to take seriously Sartre's contention that, because it is spontaneous, the unreflective consciousness "can never be deceived about itself," and if, in fact, bad faith is a pre-reflective consciousness,[78] then it would appear to follow that, insofar as bad faith is self-deception,[79] bad faith is not possible. But clearly this would be an outlandish conclusion, for Sartre has not only given us an analysis of the "patterns of bad faith,"[80] but has provided us with concrete examples of bad faith that are clear instances of self-deception.[81] And certainly in some of my own earlier writing, I have sought to make clear the sense in which and the mechanism by which, in spite of the translucency of consciousness, one can, for Sartre, successfully lie to oneself in a modified sense of lying.[82] As regards "attitude" toward evidence, I have tried to show that bad faith—whether viewed epistemologically or ontologically—involves the selection or bypassing of evidence, thus self-deceptive belief.[83] Moreover, I have argued that, because the bad-faith consciousness exploits the autodestructiveness and evanescence of consciousness and forges for itself "two-faced" concepts *(des concepts amphiboliques*[84]) by which to count itself satisfied or "per-

suaded" even when it is not persuaded, bad faith may be said
to be "cynical,"[85] despite Sartre's allegation to the contrary. And,
if bad faith is a cynical consciousness, particularly because it
makes "knowing preparations" (*préparation savante,*[86]) for its
own deception, then it would seem to follow that bad-faith consciousness is not just pre-reflective but, as I have maintained
elsewhere, at least in part, a reflective consciousness that is directed upon itself. But Sartre has maintained that bad faith, in
spite of its "pre-reflective apprehension (of) consciousness as
affecting itself with bad faith,"[87] is not a matter of a "reflective
and voluntary decision"[88] (*il ne s'agit pas d'une décision réfléchie et voluntaire*[89]). For Sartre to concede that it is reflective
would, of course, radically lessen the possibility of our differentiating, as I have done, authenticity and inauthenticity from
good faith and bad faith by virtue of the reflective consciousness. As unsettled as I am with this differentiation, I must concede that, overall, the texts *do* suggest that the reflective consciousness is one of the differentiating marks of authenticity
that Sartre intends.[90]

So, in passing, I wish to take exception again to Sartre's statement that, because the unreflective consciousness is a "spontaneous self-projection towards its possibilities" (of which it is the
sole source), it cannot be deceived about itself[91] (*ne peut jamais
se tromper sur elle-même*[92]), that is, cannot deceive itself. It
seems to me that, although this statement allows Sartre to
maintain that bad faith, as unreflective, is not cynical, it fails to
cohere with Sartre's overall reference to and analysis of widespread self-deception. Moreover, it has provided nurture not
only to those interpreters of Sartre who—I think, wrongly—
exclude cynicism from the translucent project of bad faith, but
also to those who wish to deny, on the grounds of bad faith's
unreflective consciousness, that the practitioner of bad faith is
"responsible" for his or her bad faith. (We shall consider this

further in respect to question 3.) Although, to be sure, Sartre is right in reminding us that "we must take care not to hold [the unreflective consciousness] responsible for making a mistake regarding itself when the error is actually a false evaluation of the objective situation," his statement does not eliminate either the possibility of self-deceit or the attribution of "responsibility" to one for one's bad faith. And Catalano's reminders—with which I agree—that the pre-reflective awareness "does not have to be a thetic comprehension," and that the pre-reflective consciousness "does not have to be distinct," do not do away with either cynicism or deceit in bad faith.[93] So, although Sartre seems to want to make the pre-reflective/reflective distinction a mark of the distinction between, let us say, bad faith and inauthentic, good faith and authentic, consciousness, he is left with the problem of showing how, while he excludes a Freudian "unconscious," the self-deceptive "attitude" of bad faith can take place without reflection, without consciousness attending to consciousness, and within a non-thetic consciousness. But having rearticulated this problem, I must now move on to the final issue raised at the beginning of this chapter; namely, whether authenticity may be differentiated from good faith by virtue of its *moral* or *ethical* dimension.

The advent of the moral dimension

In the discussion above of the first two questions, we have seen how radical conversion through a reflective consciousness marks the passage from bad faith to authenticity and the difference between the "original attitude" of good faith and authenticity. And I have at least suggested the likelihood that the for-itself's conversion to a project of authenticity constitutes human reality's move into the moral realm, into what in the *Cahiers* he calls a "new *authentic* way of being to oneself and for oneself."[94] Moreover, in my preceding chapter on authenticity, I have not only tried to show the closeness between Sartre's discussion of authenticity in *The War Diaries* and Jeanson's "approved" interpretation of Sartre's relevant views, but have also pointed out that both the Sartre of *The War Diaries* and Jeanson's Sartre see the transition—the "willed" conversion from a "factual freedom" to a "freedom as valued" (Jeanson), from a disposition to flee one's freedom to an attitude of affirming and *valuing* one's freedom—as a *moral* conversion. The new attitude of "valorizing" one's non-coincidence becomes the beginning of moral agency in human reality. The conversion, I suggested, seems to mark the "moralization" of the human being, and authenticity becomes for Sartre a moral category. I now want to pursue this suggestion within the context of my attempt to provide features by which to differentiate Sartre's conception of authenticity from what I have called Sartre's "redeemed" sense of good faith.

First, it does us well to remember anew that, in a number of places in *Being and Nothingness*—footnotes in particular—Sartre, as we have seen, states that the radical conversion of which we have spoken is a prerequisite for the "self-recovery," for the "authenticity," that is required for an "ethics of deliverance and salvation."[95] Moreover, in these same pages we have seen Sartre raise questions about Heidegger's use of "authentic" and "inauthentic" because such projects and expressions have an "implicit moral content"[96] and are "tainted with an ethical concern."[97] Generally speaking, the *Being and Nothingness* references, as sparse as they are, seem to confirm the suggestion, which is so strong in *The War Diaries* and in Jeanson, that embarking on the project of authenticity constitutes a transformation, a "metamorphosis"[98] from a *natural* (bad-faith) attitude of trying to hide one's freedom to a moral attitude of "adopting freedom as one's own"[99]—in other words, of making freedom one's fundamental value and project.

But one cannot say that Sartre's treatment of the distinction is entirely without ambiguity and problems. In discussing, for instance, the "ethical implications" at the end of *Being and Nothingness*, he makes contentions that seem to preclude an easy distinction of this type. The "spirit of seriousness," which considers values as "transcendent givens," "puts forward the opacity of the desired object and posits it in itself as a desirable irreducible." This attitude is, he claims, in bad faith but is also on a moral level: "Thus we are already on the *moral* plane but concurrently on that of bad faith, for it is an *ethics* which is ashamed of itself and does not dare speak its name. It has obscured all its goals in order to free itself from anguish."[100] That is to say, the "serious" consciousness, which "hides" from itself its "free project,"[101] is a *bad-faith* consciousness that, if we are to take this passage as a guide, already appears to reflect a moral awareness. And, if that is the case, the distinction between the good faith/bad faith attitudes and authenticity/inauthenticity cannot be drawn so readily in terms of a differentiating *moral* dimension. This would give weight to my earlier point that Sartre himself is not entirely clear, or even consistent, in his use of these terms.

The commentator Joseph Catalano, who also presses for the differentiation I have been pursuing, is similarly aware of contentions by Sartre that make the moral differentiation problematic. Acknowledging that "good and bad faith—in contrast to authenticity and inauthenticity—are not described as moral categories" by Sartre, he points out, as I have tried to show in a preceding chapter, that they are to be distinguished by the manner in which the for-itself relates to responsibility. In good faith, the for-itself accepts responsibility; in bad faith the for-itself flees it. But doesn't the acceptance and/or rejection of responsibility constitute a moral dimension? That is to say, might not good faith and bad faith also be moral categories?[102]

Catalano's answer (to which I have already referred in the second section above), though somewhat sketchy and inconclusive, is *generally* consistent both with what one can infer from *Being and Nothingness* and with the foregoing analysis. He proposes that we distinguish between a *pre-reflective, ontological* sense of responsibility and a *reflective, ethical* sense. Although at a pre-reflective, ontological level it might be possible to attribute "responsibility" (in fact, I am the one "by whom it happens that there is a world"[103]) to a bad-faith consciousness, it does not seem appropriate to hold bad faith "responsible" in the sense of being "*morally* accountable" for its "choices."[104] To be sure, one must make a distinction between an "ascriptive" (Flynn) or "authorship" sense of responsibility and an existential/practical/moral sense of responsibility.[105] And if good faith, in contrast to authenticity, is a pre-reflective "original" attitude to one's freedom—in contrast to a reflective "self-recovery"— then it is not possible to impute [moral] responsibility to [the person] in [good or] bad faith"[106]: that is to say, one cannot be said to be morally responsible for one's *unreflective* good or bad faith. And if this is the case, it would seem, once more, to follow that for Sartre good and bad faith are not moral categories. Though bothered by some related anomalies, Catalano remains persuaded that the "general distinction" between good and bad faith as "ontological modes," and authenticity and inauthenticity as moral projects of being, is a "fruitful" one.[107]

Surely our preceding study of authenticity in some of Sartre's formative works has made it plain that the kind of "self-recovery" that Sartre labels "authenticity" requires a radical conversion that places the human being in a moral mode of being and allows an "ethics of deliverance and salvation." In "adopting human reality as one's own," human consciousness reflectively

self-motivates itself to accept and live consistently with its gratuitous freedom and "responsibility." The consequence is that we
are totally "without excuse,"[108] both *ontologically* (for Sartre we
"make" ourselves "be"[109]; we are condemned to "self-motivate"
ourselves) and *ethically:* "One is totally responsible for one's
life"[110]; one is responsible ethically for one's authentic mode
of being, for one has "self-motivated"[111] oneself reflectively to
convert from one's flight from freedom to a mode of being that
accepts one's freedom-in-situation and one's responsibility. So
we have no difficulty in concluding that authenticity and inauthenticity are moral categories and represent ethical "dimensions" of being in Sartre.[112] Even in his oversimplified essay "Existentialism Is a Humanism," Sartre tells us that "man makes
himself by the choice of his morality."[113] Authenticity clearly involves the human being's *moral* making of herself by choosing
to accept and recover herself as freedom, as ambiguous being.

But, though I am prepared—while speaking generally—to
allow that for Sartre the moral dimension is one of the features
that differentiate authenticity (and inauthenticity) from good
and bad faith, I am not willing, for some of the reasons I have
already outlined or implied, to divorce bad faith entirely from
the moral realm. Although the dominant Sartrean texts, as well
as the consensus of Sartre interpreters, from Jeanson to Catalano, make a moral conversion *from* consciousness's "natural"
inclination to bad faith a required condition for the project of
authenticity, I believe that neither Sartre nor his interpreters
are completely successful in excluding bad and good faith from
the ethical domain.[114] Not only is it true that Sartre specifically
mentions that the attitude of "seriousness" is both one of bad
faith and on a moral plane,[115] but it is reasonably clear that
he sometimes—in both major writing and interviews—assesses
bad faith in *moral* terms. Moreover, I want to suggest before
ending that, if my interpretation of Sartre's "bad faith" as *cyni-*

cal is a correct one (that is, if I am right in contending that, given the "knowing preparations" that bad faith makes for its self-deceit, bad faith is deliberately "cynical" in its intent[116]), then bad faith—especially when it is viewed epistemologically as in Sartre's analysis in his key section of *Being and Nothingness* entitled "The 'Faith' of Bad Faith"—cannot be entirely excluded as a moral category. As a deceitful project that uses "deceitful concepts" (*des concepts trompeurs*[117]), that, in a modified way, succeeds in "lying to oneself," and that knowingly conceals the truth from [oneself],[118] the bad-faith consciousness seems to involve an ethical choice that may be judged morally in the same way that deceit and "modified" lies are normally assessed. (This reaffirms a point I have made in my earlier writing and on panels in professional meetings—panels which have included Catalano.) If I am right in contending that Sartre's "bad faith" may sometimes be evaluated and condemned morally, then it would appear blatantly inconsistent, if not absurd, for one to infer that bad faith in Sartre can never be a moral category.[119]

Thus I end my discussion of this concluding theme on the same problematic note on which I ended my consideration of the preceding question (2) of this chapter. Although our analysis of Sartre's texts and Jeanson's approved interpretation of these related texts justify, in a general way, an ethical differentiation of the categories of authenticity and inauthenticity from the categories of good and bad faith, this differentiation in Sartre cannot be said to be hard and fast or absolute. For, as much as Sartre (or Jeanson) stresses that a reflective radical conversion from bad faith to authenticity constitutes "deliverance" and a transition to moral agency,[120] there are scattered passages that provide either lapses in consistency of Sartre's use of language, or evidence that good and bad faith are also capable of having a moral dimension for Sartre. Yet this is not to suggest either that Sartre did not intend the ethical differentiation or that it is not a very helpful one.

For the opposite is, I think, true. This differentiating feature, together with the two preceding features of *conversion* and *reflection*, provide the structure for understanding what in *Being and Nothingness* Sartre failed to do; namely, to elucidate his "ethics of salvation." As close as our redeemed (Sartrean) sense of good faith may be to authenticity, it must not be given the marks of authenticity. And, in the end, to use Sartre's early words in *The War Diaries*, Sartre does not appear "to see anything but a moral code based on *authenticity*."[121]

Roots in "The Transcendence of the Ego"

Yet it would hardly be responsible, philosophically, to leave the findings of the last three chapters—or indeed the analysis in this concentrated study—without taking into account, however briefly, some of Sartre's contentions in *The Transcendence of the Ego*[122]—Sartre's early (1937) and pivotal formulation of an "existentialist theory of consciousness." Although Sartre incorporates much of this monograph into *Being and Nothingness* (1943), we must ask, because of the formative and pervasive influence of Sartre's brilliant essay on the rest of his oeuvre, whether our findings are generally consistent with what Sartre says in *The Transcendence of the Ego*, and whether some of his earliest contentions may, as I should hope, serve to confirm the interpretation and conclusions I have ventured to offer above.

To be sure, Sartre does not, in this work on consciousness, focus on the issues to which we have attended above. Nonetheless, as Thomas Busch has forcefully shown in a book just recently published,[123] *The Transcendence of the Ego* exhibits many of the roots of Sartre's thinking concerning the need to move from a "bad-faith" or "alienated" consciousness to a consciousness that affirms its own spontaneity. Transcendental consciousness is free; it is an "impersonal spontaneity."[124] "Nothing can act on consciousness because it is cause of itself."[125] "Each instant of our conscious life reveals to us a creation *ex nihilo:* . . . it determines its existence at each instant."[126] Frightened by its "vertiginous freedom," "by its own spontaneity because it senses this spontaneity as beyond freedom," it attempts to hide itself. Even the role of ego "is to mask from consciousness its very spontaneity."[127] Consciousness "projects its own spontaneity into the ego-object"; it imprisons itself in the world in order *to flee* from itself; it becomes "a degraded and bastard spontaneity,"[128] an "impure consciousness." What is this but the fundamental and "natural" attitude of "bad faith"—of "flight from freedom"—that we have seen in *The War Diaries* and *Being and Nothingness,* in Jeanson's "official" interpretation, and in my brief references to Sartre's *Cahiers pour une morale.* As Thomas Busch has said, Sartre's early discussion of "impure reflection," of the heteronomous consciousness, "mirrors Sartre's discussion of *bad faith.*"[129]

So, as early as in *The Transcendence of the Ego,* Sartre shows, while rejecting a "transcendental ego," that radically free consciousness "alienates" itself by its "natural attitude"[130] "of flight," by its attempt—we may now say—in "bad faith" to escape from its radical freedom by tying itself down to a constituted "ego" and "object." But human consciousness is not, as we have seen elsewhere, condemned irreversibly to this "alienation" or "bad faith." As Sartre says here, "it can happen that consciousness suddenly produces itself on the *pure reflective* level,"[131] where it can escape "from the ego on all sides" and yet maintain "the ego outside the consciousness by a continued creation."[132] If the commentator Thomas Busch is correct—and I regard this point as one of the outstanding contributions of his important work on Sartre—this "pure reflective level" can be viewed as "effecting a phenomenological reduction,"[133] an epoché.[134] That is to say, the "natural attitude" *(naturliche Einstellung)* of flight and, later, of impure reflection, can be "disengaged," can be "bracketed," can be overcome by what, in *Ideas I*, Husserl calls a "phenomenological attitude"—an attitude in which consciousness recognizes itself as *a failure to be,* as the source of the "constitution" of "givens" (such as the ego) and meanings, as "empty of pre-given content."[135] This attitude is one in which consciousness breaks from a "natural" obsession with objects, the world, and the "necessary." To be sure, pre-reflective consciousness's desire for self-coincidence and identity, its pre-reflective desire to have a foundation and be "necessary" is, to use Husserl's language, "put in parentheses," "bracketed," suspended, but not eliminated by pure reflection. Yet only on a *reflective* level can this epoché take place.

What we see here not only shows the influence of Husserl on Sartre but the roots of what, on my interpretation, Sartre goes on to say and develop in *The War Diaries, Being and Nothingness,* and the *Cahiers.* The pure reflection of *The Transcendence of the Ego* is not only a parallel of Husserl's epoché but, more importantly for my study, an early formulation of the reflective conversion which I have found to be one of the differentiating features of Sartre's notion of authenticity. As Busch says, "effecting the epoché is equivalent to a veritable *conversion,*" and Sartre "employs [this] reduction as the entry into assuming an authentic existence."[136] That is to say, the "pure reflection," the "epoché" in *The Transcendence of the Ego,* parallels and prefigures the reflective ("willed") conversion of *The War Diaries,* and the "radical conversion" from our desire to be *Causa Sui,* foundation, or God in *Being and Nothingness.* It constitutes the first formulation by Sartre of the necessary condition for any passage from "bad faith" (to use Sartre's somewhat later language) to authenticity. Hence, *The Transcendence of the Ego* not only makes evident some of the grounds for what Sartre later says about the nature of "deliverance"[137] but strongly supports my making the reflective consciousness—more exactly, pure reflection—and conversion two of the differentiating characteristics of Sartre's notion of authenticity.

What about the *moral* or *ethical* dimension, which I have found to be the third differentiating mark of Sartre's characterization of authenticity? Is there any hint of this feature in *The Transcendence of the Ego*? There is very limited reference there to morality or ethics. However, it is clear that Sartre's emphasis on the possibility of an epoché, on a way of converting from an "impure," objectifying consciousness, or natural attitude of flight from self, to a purified consciousness that accepts itself as a self-motivating spontaneity and as nonself-coinciding, constitutes precisely the process of genuine "self-recovery" to which Sartre later attributes morality. In fact, his suggestion in *The Transcendence of the Ego* is that consciousness purified of the "I" and disengaged from the project of hiding from itself *(bad faith)* "provides the way of a philosophical foundation for an *ethics* and a politics which are absolutely positive."[138] According to Busch, one of Sartre's distinct insights is to see the ethical implications of Husserl's phenomenological concept and reduction.[139] Sartre has remained faithful to Husserl's insistence that philosophy as a "rigorous science" will "make us aware of the responsibility we have in regard to humanity."[140] (In *Being and Nothingness* and "Existentialism Is a Humanism," Sartre virtually overwhelms us with this responsibility.) For Husserl, the "phenomenological attitude" belonging to the epoché effects a "complete personal transformation"[141]—in effect, a radical/moral/"religious" conversion—in which we assume responsibility for ourselves and our culture. That is to say, in *The Transcendence of the Ego*, Sartre, apparently following Husserl, invokes an epoché in which purified, "converted" consciousness takes responsibility for its non-coincidence, for its "break" in being, for its complete freedom, and, one might argue, for the creation of values for all of humanity. This adoption of the "phenomenological attitude" (Husserl and Jeanson), this valuing of one's non-coincidence, appears to mark, as I tried to show earlier in this manuscript, the beginning of *moral* agency in human reality. As Jeanson has contended, Sartre tends to identify the "phenomenological attitude" (versus the "natural") with the "ethical."

Hence, as early as in *The Transcendence of the Ego*, the epoché appears to instantiate a conversion from an alienated, "natural" bad-faith consciousness to an authentic consciousness which reflectively accepts itself as freedom and adopts freedom as its own.[142] For Sartre, as for Husserl, the epoché ("conversion" here) is the key to the transformation between living "naively" *(alienated)* and assuming "rational responsibility."[143] As we have seen in *The War Diaries*, this "conversion," characterized by "adopting reality as one's own" and claiming "responsibility" for it, may be said "to present itself as a value for consciousness."[144] The value it presents is said to be "authenticity" and constitutes consciousness's entry into a moral code of existing in which my consciousness, as nothing, refuses the "quest for being"[145] (*refuser la quête de l'être*[146]) and, to use the language of *Being and Nothingness,* accepts full responsibility for the for-itself and for "the entire world as a peopled world."[147]

Thus, by reading into Sartre's early writing some of the Husserlian influence his language insinuates, *The Transcendence of the Ego* may be taken to corroborate the analysis and differentiation of authenticity that I have offered above. Even the moral characteristic I have attributed to Sartre's concept of authenticity is accommodated by a Husserlian reading of *The Transcendence of the Ego*. In addition, it seems clear that *The*

Transcendence of the Ego, especially when seen in conjunction with Sartre's maturing works, offers further warrant for my qualified claim that it is *authenticity,* not even good faith in its salvaged sense, that must be seen as Sartre's intended antithesis to bad faith.

In conclusion, I offer but a passing word about how my above study and analysis might stand in relation to Sartre's *Cahiers pour une morale,* written in 1945 but published only in 1983 *after* his death. Although I shall defer to another occasion my detailed response to *Cahiers pour une morale* (I have made passing references to it earlier), I offer the preliminary judgment that these *Notebooks*—which contain Sartre's sustained notes and developing reflections for the ethics he promises on the last page of *Being and Nothingness*—generally corroborate and elucidate the differentiating features of authenticity which I have tried to delineate above. I am confident that my intermittent references above to the *Cahiers* testify to this judgment. Although a *detailed* study of the *Cahiers* will not, I suspect, eliminate some of the problems I have attached to any effort to provide a neat, unexceptionable set of categories, I believe that it will show authenticity to entail a moral passage from what Sartre regards as the "pre-conversion" natural attitude of bad faith[148] to a "new way of being . . . for oneself"[149]; that is, to a "new attitude"[150] of accepting and affirming one's contingency and finitude, one's ambiguity of being, one's freedom. This move from the "natural attitude" amounts to a "self-recovery" of for-itself as freedom in which human reality affirms itself in its "existential dimension of choice."[151] And this possibility of "recovery" in terms of self-affirmation of one's distinctive freedom is surely one of the most persistent emphases and challenges of Sartre's entire philosophy.

7

The "Unveiling" of Authentic Existence: Corroborating My Differentiation through Sartre's *Notebooks*

In the preceding chapters, I have attempted to analyze and differentiate Sartre's notions of bad faith, good faith, and authenticity without paying detailed attention to his *Cahiers pour une morale (Notebooks for an Ethics)*.[1] Although I have invoked a number of supporting passages from these *Notebooks*, I have for the most part deliberately tried to base my analysis, reconstruction, and differentiation on the early pivotal works of Sartre published during his lifetime. To be sure, I have also placed my interpretations and contentions in dialogue with those of other commentators—most prominently, Joseph Catalano—and have tested some of my core contentions against Sartre's "approved" reading of his early work by Francis Jeanson, a brilliant interpreter and collaborator.

But, for a number of reasons, it is now time to concentrate more focally on the *Cahiers*. Written in 1947–1948, a few years

after *Being and Nothingness,* but originally published only in
1983,[2] three years after Sartre's death, the *Notebooks for an Ethics* likely represents Sartre's extensive notes for the "future
work" on ethics that he promised at the end of *Being and Nothingness.* The fact that there is no unanimity of scholarly judgment as to why Sartre failed to complete his intended work or
publish these notes during his lifetime,[3] does not take away
from their distinct value for understanding Sartre's ontological
framework and the culmination of his early thought. For,
though unfinished and incomplete, these *Notebooks* not only
offer detailed elucidation of key contentions in *The War Diaries*
and *Being and Nothingness,* but also, I believe, revise and refine
them in the light of problems and criticisms that Sartre's views
generated after the 1943 publication of *Being and Nothingness.*
And in virtually no other place does Sartre focus more on or
bring greater clarity to the passage from bad faith to authentic
existence, or the meaning of my conversion from my natural
attitude of fleeing from my freedom to my adopting freedom as
my own. Although, as Pellauer suggests,[4] Sartre can be verbose
and certainly repetitive here, these *Cahiers* have the merit of
making clear what in response to his foundational views was
not sufficiently clear in *The War Diaries* or *Being and Nothingness.* The issue of the precise meaning of authenticity and how
it relates to bad faith, reflection, and conversion—an issue to
which he devotes but passing references in *Being and Nothingness*—is but one case in point. And Sartre's elaborate and
painstaking analysis in the *Cahiers* of "creation" and the "myth
of *Causa Sui*" is but another illustration.

Assuming my preceding assessment, I can hardly conclude
my study of Sartre's basic existential attitudes without giving
more detailed consideration to selected portions of the *Cahiers*
which directly concern and elucidate my analysis and argument in the preceding chapters. For, as the *Cahiers,* in my view,

represent both the beginning and the end of his ontological ethics[5]—as well as the conclusion of his more academic, less concrete philosophizing—they also represent, in retrospect, Sartre's work that deals most comprehensively with the issues and questions that have generated my inquiry, especially in my last three chapters. So, in a word, I should be remiss in my responsibility to the present study were I not to give more thought and retrospective attention to them. And, although I can read Sartre in the original, my task is made somewhat easier, and the Sartrean text more readily accessible, by the discerning translation of the *Cahiers* by David Pellauer, just published this past year (1992) by the University of Chicago Press.[6]

In this concluding chapter, then, my intention will be twofold. I want to explicate what I regard as idiosyncratic in Sartre's detailed discussion of authenticity in the *Notebooks,* specifically his notion of the *unveiling* of authenticity or authentic existence. His account, which is consistent with the notion of disclosing, rather than hiding, truth or Being that we find elsewhere in both Sartre and Heidegger,[7] will not only give further clarification to Sartre's understanding of authenticity but exhibit another dimension of it. In addition, while unraveling the *Notebooks'* more developed and detailed view of the original structure and project of authentic existence, I intend to show how this posthumously published analysis by Sartre corroborates the features I have attributed to Sartrean authenticity and supports my passing contention that, for Sartre, the for-itself can, through a passage to authentic living, escape the hell of inevitable "failure" that accompanies human reality's project (or pursuit) of Being—namely, the project of giving itself a foundation and becoming one with itself. During the progress of these intentions, I plan also to continue to test other of my cumulative answers to questions that have engaged me in earlier chapters. I shall try, finally, to fill any conspicuous gap in my preceding analysis and reconstruction of Sartre.

An introductory profile

One does not have to go far into the *Notebooks* to see some ready confirmation of the interpretation and differentiating marks I tried to bring to a head in the last two chapters. In a number of places I anticipated this confirmation by citing a few telling statements from that work. In the first 37 pages alone of the *Notebooks*, we find Sartre rather unsystematically making declarations about the key terms of our study—*bad faith, good faith,* and *authenticity*—and at least sketching the path to and marks of authenticity. As I have pointed out before, he speaks here of the necessity of a "conversion" because of the for-it-self's "natural attitude" of "flight and inauthenticity."[8] In marked contrast to the language of *Being and Nothingness,* he now talks about a human "nature" that begins in fleeing its freedom and pursuing Being.[9] This "pursuit of Being is hell," and, although the pursuit, as we have seen, can "never be suppressed,"[10] its perpetual failure to *found* or *be* itself may precipitate a reflective *conversion* to a *new* attitude. In a remarkably telling passage, which seems to vindicate in summary, yet more mature, form the core of what I have attributed to Sartre above, Sartre says:

> The appearance of the For-itself is properly speaking the irruption of History in the world. The *spontaneous* movement of the For-itself as a lack (on the plane of the *unreflective*) is to seek the In-itself-For-itself. *Reflection* originally springs up as an accessory to this as the creation of a *new* diaspora in the attempt at recuperation.[11]

And he goes on to add:

But even then, as we know, it misses itself. Here, therefore, the possibility of *pure reflection* arises as admission of this missing the mark and as taking a stand *in the face of it.*[12]

Then, just a few lines later, Sartre indicates that, though reflection is "first of all impure" and in bad faith, because it "does not want to see its own failure," it becomes "motivation for pure reflection" and "good faith."[13] And "this passage to pure reflection" provokes a "transformation"[14]—a conversion which he initially characterizes here as "recognition of myself as ecstatic For-itself"[15] (*la reconnaissance de moi-même comme Pour-soi ek-statique*[16]). What is this but the recognition and acceptance of my troubled freedom as mine, or the transformation and deliverance to authenticity and salvation which we have seen in his earlier writings? In these earliest pages, Sartre calls the passage from the *prereflective* consciousness to *reflection* "a free drama of the *person*"[17] and makes it clear that we are now dealing with *ethics*, not just the dialectic. "It makes sense," he says, "that reflection should have as its direct and essential goal the unreflective For-itself. Nothing is *important* for it except the For-itself. In the *ethical* reflection that accompanies this reflection, what is *important* is the *moral* being of what is reflected upon."[18] As Sartre will say later in the *Notebooks,* reflection is a project of suspending or pursuing its unreflective project.[19] Whether or not the for-itself reflectively accepts its contingency and its "calling itself into question" will, in effect, *decide* its mode of existing and "morality." It will either regain itself as for-itself (authenticity) or lose itself in the impossible "natural" project of trying to found itself (bad faith).

Thus, in these first few pages of the *Notebooks,* we find Sartre's anticipation and outline of his more detailed discussion of reflection, conversion, and morality. This represents not only a profile of his pervasive concern in the *Notebooks* for under-

standing the conditions of authentic existing, but a clear corroboration of what I have submitted in the preceding chapter
as the criterial features of Sartre's view of authenticity. But
much more needs to be said about this in what follows.

Conversion and the "unveiling" of authenticity

It is in the last hundred pages of *Notebooks for an Ethics* that
Sartre gives his most focused attention to the relationship
among conversion, authenticity, and reflection and, perhaps for
the first time in his philosophical writing, reformulates his analysis in terms of a new guiding concept—specifically, that of
"unveiling." "Authenticity," he tells us early in those pages, "lies
in unveiling being through the mode of non-being." "Originally," he adds, "authenticity consists in refusing any quest for
being, because I am always *nothing*."[20] And, in refusing being,
the authentic for-itself "*unveils* itself to itself both in the immediacy of its perpetual calling into question *(Erlebnis)* and in the
reflective description of its concrete understanding."[21] For Sartre, here, reflection becomes an "unveiling of freedom." Moreover, a reflective reprise—which assumes gratuity at the core
of the human project—is now said to give the human project
"authentic existence,"[22] and we arrive at the "type of intuition"
that *unveils* authentic existing: "it is me, [whom] nothing justifies, who justifies myself inwardly"; I am an "absolute contingency" which has only myself to justify myself by *assuming* myself.[23] The reflective assuming of myself as mine[24]—that is, of
my gratuity—constitutes a *conversion* which renounces the
"category of appropriation" and *unveils* the "unappropriable
aspect" of the "reflected-upon" *Erlebnis.*[25] (I shall say more
about this later.) The connection between authenticity, conversion, and unveiling in these pages is emphatic, repeated, and
pervasive. The "consciousness of our gratuitousness . . . is in-

dissolvably linked to the consciousness of Being as a fixed explosion"[26]; in grasping my freedom, in grasping myself as unjustifiable (in conversion), I unveil my freedom, unveil Being "in and through my project of *creating* Being."[27] But we must now seek elucidation and clarification of this connection, particularly as it involves the notion of "unveiling" or, as he sometimes says, "illuminating."[28]

As AN initial point in the elaboration, I want first to indicate a preliminary clarification and general emphasis which come out of Sartre's *Truth and Existence,* an essay that Sartre likely wrote concurrently with his *Notebooks* and in which he appears to reflect—even in disagreement—the influence of Heidegger's "On the Essence of Truth."[29] Here Sartre makes it clear that any human project "unveils"; that all unveiling "results from a project"[30]; and that at the center of all unveiling is freedom. "*All* freedom is unveiling,"[31] "all free behavior is revelatory" or "unveiling,"[32] he assures us, and unveiling "can have meaning only for a freedom."[33] This means that, though unveiling implies "something that is veiled,"[34] it is hardly mysterious. Any free behavior—practical, intellectual, affective—"unveils being and makes *truths* appear."[35] As Sartre tells us in the *Notebooks,*[36] "the illumination of Being begins from Non-Being"[37] ("It is only through a being which is not yet what it is that truth can come to *Being*"[38]), but unveiling behavior must be seen as activity. Even to let being appear as it is, "we have to go out and look for it."[39]

Although this point of emphasis from *Truth and Existence* relates primarily to Sartre's account of truth and invites additional clarifications, it allows us to see—what we have come to expect in Sartre—that freedom or the for-itself is at the heart of all "unveiling" of Being and that Sartre, generally speaking, uses unveiling of being interchangeably with "illuminating" and "revealing" being. What *is* is illuminated by what is not; this is "the structure of truth."[40] Although Being is already present in an "undifferentiated manner to consciousness,"[41] it is freedom or consciousness that is the "foundation of all revelation of being."[42] (In the *Notebooks*, he says: "I unveil *a* being against the background of undifferentiation."[43]) To put the matter in a somewhat different Sartrean way, it is consciousness that "lights up" all being and reveals everything as it is through its nihilating activity. To employ a figure other interpreters have used and Sartre himself invokes, consciousness lights up a "this" against an undifferentiated background which it must negate in order for "this" to be revealed—and to be differentiated—as it is. And, for Sartre, "it is impossible" that an upsurge of freedom not entail both an "unveiling comprehension of Being" and a "project of unveiling."[44] For, as he showed us explicitly in *Being and Nothingness*, all consciousness is *act*, and for consciousness to be consciousness, there must be something of which consciousness is a "revealing intuition." And, even allowing that "unveiling" implies the possibility of "not unveiling" or "not revealing," a contradiction does not follow; for, as Sartre says, it is through freedom or conscious being ("being of consciousness"[45]) that both unveiling and "the veil" "come to being."[46]

To be sure, questions justifiably arise about Sartre's use of "Being," his contrasting use of "being" with "Being" both here and (as we increasingly see) in *Notebooks for an Ethics*, and the similarities and dissimilarities between his uses of these terms and those of Heidegger.[47] Yet, in our effort to understand the relationship between unveiling and authenticity, we need not be deterred or distracted by his sudden dominant use of "unveiling." For we come readily to see that the free for-itself exists as unveiling being, and what it unveils, illuminates, discloses, reveals, is the being to which it alone gives meaning. This is vintage Sartre or—if you prefer—vintage *Being and Nothing-*

ness. But we must now return to the *Notebooks* and try to see more clearly the connection between unveiling and authenticity.

"Unveiling" and the "*Causa Sui*"

In trying to elucidate this connection and make clear the transformation and conversion to authenticity, Sartre himself contrasts the project of "unveiling" to "the project of being *Causa Sui.*"[48] For, as we have already anticipated in our profile above, and have reviewed in different ways in preceding chapters, authenticity demands a passage, a conversion, *from* the project "to-be-for-itself-in-itself," to attain identification or to appropriate being (or what Sartre also calls the project to be God), *to* a project of renouncing the quest for being or self-coincidence and assuming or affirming one's gratuitous freedom. It is in respect to the latter project—and process—that Sartre now links the concepts of *unveiling* and *authenticity.* Among other accomplishments, the unveiling of freedom and "creation"— the passage to authenticity—will unveil to us, according to Sartre, the myth of *Causa Sui,* the myth of the "creator God."[49]

"What lies *behind* the *Causa Sui* (in the psychoanalytic sense)" says Sartre, "is the project of the For-itself that feels itself to be *Nothing* and wills to give itself *Being.*" In the *Causa Sui,* the for-itself as nihilating consciousness, ascribes being to itself and "transforms itself" into an "In-itself-for-itself."[50] This is simply another way of saying what he has already said in *Being and Nothingness;* namely, that given the anguish of consciousness's awareness of itself as freedom, as nothing, consciousness seeks to run away from itself (Heidegger) as freedom and ground itself, to give itself a foundation without losing itself as freedom, to be the synthesis of in-itself and for-itself. But this is a "futile passion": their synthesis is ontologically impossible.

Here in the *Notebooks* Sartre puts it somewhat differently: as a for-itself aspiring to be an in-itself, human reality seeks an impossible synthesis. "The impossible idea, the synthesis, is a For-itself that is In-itself in creating itself For-itself or an In-itself that creates itself For-itself in its Being-in-itself."[51] "But Being cannot come from Existence; that is excluded"[52] ("Mais l'Être ne peut sortir de l'Existence, cela est exclu"[53]). He puts it yet another way: "The For-itself cannot found a For-itself, because this would be an unfounded foundation that would found a foundation as unfounded."[54] The futility of the project of *Causa Sui* (the project to be God) is reaffirmed. As Heidegger also has pointed out, all of human reality's attempts to make itself into its own foundation are condemned to failure.

In *unveiling*, on the other hand, the For-itself, as "pure presence to itself of *Nothing*," far from seeking identity or Being or its ground, and far from trying to justify itself, "exists only in as much as it reveals itself to itself as consciousness of this or that."[55] "Not tempted to recapture itself as Being," the For-itself becomes aware of itself as "destined to *manifest* Being." As the "pure clarity of Being," For-itself "saves" Being from Nothingness by, if you like, revealing it, by being the nothingness which being is *for*. Anticipating what he will say a little later in *Truth and Existence*, Sartre states: "the for-itself springs up ["surgit"] so that Being may become Truth"; "for-itself is not Being and Being is not the For-itself but Being is for—the For itself that is—for itself."[56] As Sartre says later, "through the welling up of the For-itself, a being is put in relation to the whole of Being."[57] This relation is neither one of appropriation nor one of identification.[58] Although in "unveiling" the for-itself nihilates Being from the "shadows of undifferentiatedness," it does not intend to be anything other than "that across which Being manifests itself"; it intends only to allow Being to appear within the world, "to put it into relation."[59] I simply "well up as a being placed in relation to Being."[60] Yet for-itself grasps itself, post conversion, as "irreducibility *in exile* in relation to Being."[61] In unveiling, the for-itself "creates" what is, in the sense of making it appear on the "foundation of freedom." That is to say, I, as for-itself, while creatively "assuming" myself and Being, "decide . . . on the meaning of Being" (I make there be "Being"), yet preserve Being's transcendence,[62] for Being is other than the For-itself. It is through action[63] that the For-itself "unveils" and without the For-itself Being would remain undifferentiated, unintelligible, without meaning.

Although we have not yet focused sufficiently on the relationship between unveiling, reflection, and authenticity, we may at least note in passing that, for Sartre, the "authentic consciousness grasps itself in its deepest structure as creative:" in its very upsurge (or "springing forth") "it makes there be a word:" without unveiling, consciousness cannot "see," and "to unveil is [as we have seen] to create what is."[64] On the other hand, *inauthentic* consciousness dreams to "create oneself," to be *self-caused* being, "to be prior to Being as a nothingness that flows into Being in producing it."[65] "God," then, turns out to be "inauthentic man," "thrown into the futile project of trying to found itself." For the notion of a *Causa Sui*, an uncaused cause, is the dream of a being that has grasped itself as having no foundation, as being contingent, but which then, a posteriori, attempts to *found* itself through the "very unveiling of its lack of foundation." This "absolute dream" of creation of oneself by oneself, this projection of inauthentic consciousness—as we saw in *Being and Nothingness*—is "not even conceivable," for, in order to create oneself, one first has *to be.*[66] "Nothingness," as he says later, "cannot produce Being,"[67] cannot be a creator.[68] *Causa Sui* is consciousness's inauthentic and impossible project of being its own foundation. Sartre is repeating here what he has said in *Being and Nothingness;* namely, it is a "project of bad faith."[69] Although this point is hardly new to Sartre's thinking or to our inquiry, here it stands in marked contrast to Sartre's "new" emphasis (in the *Notebooks*) on the for-itself's authentic unveiling—in contrast to inauthentic consciousness's natural disposition to appropriate—being. To be sure, "For-itself is an intention and its initial intention is to give itself a foundation,"[70] but this does not mean that it is condemned to assume itself as such. In fact, for-itself, as we have seen, can accept the fact of its contingency, the facticity of its foundationless or gratuitous being, and through this reflective unveiling convert to authenticity. To this we must now give more focal attention.

Reflection

I have already noted that Sartre speaks of "assuming" and "attaining" oneself through "reflection"[71] and "conversion,"[72] and that he also refers to reflection in terms of the "unveiling" of freedom.[73] Because the importance of "reflection," both to Sartre's analysis of authenticity and to my argument in the preceding chapter, cannot be overstated, I must now turn to parts of the detailed elaboration of reflection which the *Notebooks* afford.

To begin, we may simply take note of Sartre's own searching question and his remarkably concise answer. *Question:* "What therefore can the project of a reflection that refuses to look for Being [refuses the quest for being] be?" *Answer:* "It can only be a question of a radical decision for autonomy." And he adds quickly—repeating the line that I sketched in the profile above—that this decision of "pure reflection" brings a "new type" of unity of existence—a new "integrity" of living, if you like—that does not seek self-identity or self-coincidence, but rather "appears to itself in the form of . . . a question" and is thus "in accord" with itself[74] (is authentic).

Time and again in the *Notebooks,* Sartre insists that reflection "is not contemplative," "is not contemplation," but is a project and a "form of willing."[75] He repeats here the distinction he has maintained since *The Transcendence of the Ego;* namely, the distinction between "pure" or "purifying" *(purifiante)* reflection and "accessory" *(complice)* or "impure" reflection. As we have seen, the "spontaneous movement" of the for-itself as lack seeks pre-or unreflectively to become one with itself, to seek the In-itself-For-itself, the a priori but impossible "ideal of all consciousness."[76] Reflection "originally springs up" as *accomplice* or *accessory* to this alienating effort of the for-itself to recuperate or recover itself by congealing itself in the In-itself.[77] Reflection cannot appear first since it presupposes the appearance of what is reflected on, a transcendent, an *Erlebnis* (a "lived experience") that is "given always as having been there before . . . on the unreflective level."[78] Hence my initial project of self-identification, of rejoining Being, *precedes* reflection (it is the "very structure" of my existence). However, because of the inevitable failure of the for-itself's project to be In-itself, human reality is "solicited" to put itself on the level of reflection and "question the meaning" of its (failed) acts. (Is this not like Heidegger's "silent call of conscience" which reclaims us, given our absorption in the mundane and the commonplace?) But reflection is initially impure, for it continues consciousness's primitive bad faith and is "an accomplice" to my "alienation"[79] [sic] by participating non-thetically in consciousness's futile effort to make itself in-itself-for-itself. And—now offering a clarification which he has explicitly sought in these *Notebooks*— Sartre contends that it is this continued failure of impure, accessory reflection that precedes and motivates pure or "purifying" reflection.[80] To use Sartre's words in a slightly different context, "I exhaust myself in nourishing it and alienate myself in it."[81] Impure reflection is in *bad faith* (here) because it does not want to recognize its perpetual failure,[82] so continues in consciousness's "alienation." But the failure of the for-itself's efforts to be in-itself-for-itself, combined with the failure and bad faith of my complicity with this project (I realize that I am not any one of these "characters, features, or situations"), make up a bundle of solicitations which conduce to *purifying* reflection.[83] In fact, to use the words of Elkaïm-Sartre, *pure reflection* is the "conscious grasping of the fundamental failure of accomplice [impure or accessory] reflection."[84] And it is the "first step," a "waking up"[85] toward the project of conversion, for it "constitutes" another kind of existence. This other kind suppresses bad faith and ignorance[86] and, though following from an already constituted freedom, calls itself into question, takes itself—as unjustifiable, gratuitous freedom—for its end (I "*take it up* as mine"[87]), decides to break from its non-thetic bad faith[88] and accept its "diasporatic" being.[89]

To be sure, the preceding both confirms and further clarifies my analysis in the foregoing chapter. But before I turn again to the key notion of "conversion"—the decisive step needed, I have argued, for authentic existence in Sartre—I must offer at least a few additional words of elucidation concerning the role of "will" here. For, in preceding chapters, I have already tried to show that in Sartre's earliest writing a "willed" (radical) conversion is prerequisite to authentic living, and that in *Being and Nothingness* the *voluntary* (or "will") is often identified with reflection and/or reflective (versus unreflective) consciousness.[90] And I have already noted above that in the *Notebooks* Sartre states emphatically that reflection is never contemplation but a form of willing.

So at least parenthetically we must observe that for Sartre, in the *Notebooks*, authenticity—insofar as it requires *pure* (or purifying) reflection—concerns what I *will,* not what I *am.*[91] Sartre says, "authenticity would rather see the will as the calling into question at the heart of the existing being than as that rigid blade one would like to define as being."[92] And just a little later he adds: "the grasping of the authentic self is not of the type of being ("n'est pas du type de l'être"[93]); it is rather "a willing directed to a willing." And "pure authentic reflection is a willing of what I will"[94] (*un vouloir de ce que je veux*[95]); it constitutes "a refusal to define myself by what I am (Ego) but instead by what I will [*par ce que je veux*]"—"that is, by my very undertaking . . . as it turns its subjective face toward me."[96] This *reflective will* "wills" (*veut*) what is "reflected upon" (*la réfléchie)* but does not will it in the manner that accessory or impure reflection does, which fails to put into question the project reflected upon (*le project réfléchi).*[97] Rather, pure reflection or pure reflective willing—which, here also, is essential to conversion—*wills* to exist as a project of "calling itself into question by itself." It "places its project in question [*elle met en question le projet*] before willing it"; it examines it in order to decide whether, in becoming an object for itself, it will not destroy itself. In doing this, it changes its relation to Being. It becomes a project that agrees to lose itself (in respect to recovering itself as Being) in order to save itself (as consciousness always at a distance from itself); that refuses to look for being in order "to appear as summoned before itself," in order to exist as "free, autonomous choice." Conscious of itself as project, as wanting itself (*se voulant),* the reflective project "recaptures itself in the existential dimension of a *choice.*"[98] "For-itself always wills the end for itself" but is aware of itself as "willing this end."

Thus, because pure reflection wills (*veut*) its project of *autonomy* and gratuity, that gratuity, that "dimension of choice," can be *unveiled* and *recaptured* as "absolute" without ceasing to be gratuitous.[99] This makes evident the interconnection among

pure reflection, willing, unveiling, and—as we shall see—
conversion and authenticity. The for-itself appears (is unveiled)
in its "absolute unjustifiability." Through reflection it unveils
itself as freedom (as we have seen), *assumes*, or wills, this gratuitousness, and by so doing, "transforms" gratuitousness into
freedom, contingency into a passion. Although reflection, as a
project of reflecting on, *wills* being, wills the *reflected upon*, it
wills it "not as upholding the for-itself but as upheld by it,"[100] as
unveiled and continued by it. This transformation, marked by
consciousness's assuming of itself as gratuitous, of nihilating
itself as Ego, and willing and recapturing itself as "in question"
and autonomous, constitutes human reality's passage and conversion to a "new type"[101] of existence—namely, *authentic* existence. To this central notion of *conversion* I must now give further attention, for Sartre's discussion of it in the *Notebooks*
provides the elaboration needed to elucidate further the "unveiling" of authenticity through pure reflection, and to corroborate further the major differentiating marks I presented in the
preceding chapter.

Conversion

We have already seen that, in the *Notebooks*, impure reflection
is motivation for pure reflection, that the possibility of pure or
non-accessory reflection arises with consciousness's recognition of reflection's failure in the "impure" accessory project of
the for-itself to recover itself as in-itself-for-itself. Every attempt
on the part of reflection to cooperate in consciousness's "natural" effort to regain itself is doomed. The "noematic unifica-
tion" which it brings about ("in-itself-for-itself") is necessarily
separated by a "nothingness": I am *not*, for instance, *this* feeling
that I have, "for I am separated from it" by my non-thetic, non-
positional self-consciousness, and any attempt on my part to

nurture it, to identify with it, *alienates* me from it without my being able to become it.[102] In other words, because consciousness always has a non-thetic awareness (of) itself, any effort on the part of consciousness or accessory reflection to make itself something or to cooperate in the project *to be* is "self-alienating, is destined to failure and to the hell[103] of being conscious of its continued failure to become what it wills to be. And, as I stated above, the failure of this "natural attitude" and of accessory reflection's recuperative efforts can motivate a purifying reflection which affirms consciousness as consciousness—free, metastable, and without self-coincidence or identity. As Sartre has stated in *The War Diaries*, "this state of misery *can* be a reason for consciousness to return to an accurate view of itself and stop fleeing itself."[104] It is as if this "failure" and "misery" can initiate what Heidegger labels a "call of conscience" through which human reality acknowledges its "original sin" (or "guilt" for Heidegger) and calls itself home to the "essential" freedom that it is. The passage from complicity with the "natural," original, bad-faith attitude to pure, non-accessory reflection, must, says Sartre, "provoke a transformation."[105] The purifying, nonaccessory reflection, he maintains, *is* "conversion."[106]

I need not repeat all the details of *conversion* already provided—explicitly or implicitly—in my account above of Sartre's understanding of the role and meaning of reflection and will in authenticity's unveiling. But we may proceed to note that, in his outline of his "plan for an ontological ethics,"[107] he specifically refers to the "meaning of conversion" as the "rejection of alienation" and goes on to designate it as a "modification" of "one's project," of one's "original relation to oneself," of the way one exists one's existence. To be sure, we have already seen that human reality's (consciousness's) initial project is "fascinated" with Being, is pre-reflectively and "congenitally oriented" (Spiegelberg) toward being in-itself-for-itself, and that accessory or accomplice (impure) reflection (thetically) wills or decides to continue the (non-thetic) bad faith (or, as he often says here, "alienation") of consciousness's "natural" quest for a foundation, self-identification, and justification. But the point to see again, now, is that pure or non-accessory reflection breaks with this project, wills *not* to comply with it, but to accept and affirm itself as unjustifiable and without foundation. This affirmation becomes the "project of a reflection that refuses to look for being." In other words, this resolution is the break with self-alienation, the "radical decision for autonomy," the assuming of the project of authenticity.[108] In short, this constitutes consciousness's decisive, reflective act of *conversion* to a new way of "being oneself and for oneself"[109] in which, having recognized its "original sin,"[110] its running away from itself—its "guilt," as Heidegger would say—the for-itself thematically grasps the freedom that it is, takes up gratuity as its own, and embarks on a project of living in accord with, not alienated from, the nothingness (freedom) of its subjectivity. "Resolved," Karsten Harries would say—interpreting Heidegger—"we appropriate ourselves as we are in our freedom . . . and surrender all claims to something like a firm foundation."[111] To use Sartre's expression, in conversion human reality, initially predisposed to bad faith, now "unveils" itself to itself, takes up its mode of being as "diasporic being,"[112] consents to be human,[113] and takes on a new, nonappropriative[114] relation to itself, the world, its body, and other people.[115] Moreover, as we have seen, in conversion human reality, by renouncing the impossible and bad-faith project to be "god" (in-itself-for-itself), *unveils* the "unappropriable," existential dimension of human living, and decides, radically, to live "in accord with" itself; that is, consistently with its being an unstable, evanescent freedom on which all meaning and values depend. This elucidation gives flesh to Sartre's earliest reference to conversion in the *Notebooks* as "recognition of myself as ec-static for-itself,"[116] to which he adds that, through conversion, we grasp the freedom in us and "establish a new relation of the For-itself to its project."[117]

Thus, in focusing on "conversion," we see again what we saw in our account of Sartre's views on "unveiling" and "reflection"; namely, that conversion involves a *willed* renunciation of appropriation (which governs only human reality's relationship with things), a reflective refusal to define myself as a what, a thing, or an Ego (alienation) in favor of my acceptance of myself as gratuitous and unjustifiable freedom, and my radical decision to make the freedom to which I am condemned my life's project. Conversion constitutes a radical *choice* to affirm and live the ambiguity, gratuity, tension, non-coincidence, and interrogation of "detotalized" human reality. Though human reality pre-reflectively opts for being (in-itself), for thingness, and though, through impure reflection, it is disposed to continue its pursuit of being, in *conversion* it radically decides, through pure reflection, to break with this project in favor of the project of *autonomy*—the affirmation of freedom "that takes itself as its end"[118] and takes responsibility for itself. This rejection of alienation, this modification of one's bad faith project—what in *Being and Nothingness* he calls "an abrupt metamorphosis of [one's] initial project"[119]—constitutes for Sartre, consciousness's radical conversion from the natural attitude to a "new '*authentic*' way" of existing.[120] To join this with our analyses above, we may now say that the pure reflection that unveils my freedom and reclaims it as mine (conversion) unveils authentic existence to me and *delivers* me from bad faith. Conversion—to revisit the language of the preceding chapters—leads me to my "genuine self-recovery" and (yes, even Sartre uses the word!) to "salvation."[121]

In passing, one may note that, in spite of Sartre's tendency, at times, to distance himself from Heidegger, Sartre's analysis of conversion is not—and I have already suggested this here and there—entirely unlike Heidegger's views on "resoluteness" in relation to authenticity. Realizing our freedom, our "responsibility," and our "guilt" (there appears to be a closeness if not an interchangeability between these two latter terms in Heidegger)—in other words, the inadequacy of authorship or self-constitution—conscience for Heidegger calls us back to who we are (zurückgeholt) and demands resoluteness—that is, Dasein's (human reality's) affirmation of itself in its entirety, even in its failure and guilt. In fact, for Heidegger resoluteness is, as Harries points out, "inseparable from an acknowledgment of guilt."[122] The role of pure reflection for Sartre in human reality's conversion to authenticity is reminiscent of the role of Heidegger's "resolve" or "resoluteness" as Dasein's authentic response to the "silent call of conscience" (to authenticity). As resoluteness in Heidegger appears to be an affirmation of "an openness to the clearing in Being," a resolve to be amenable to the continued self-questioning of one's being, and a decision to be open "to the groundlessness of our existence,"[123] so "purifying reflection" in conversion, for Sartre, is a resolve, decision, will, on the part of human reality to be open to its own freedom and groundlessness, and to assume and affirm itself as "in question," gratuitous and yet totally responsible for (completely the author of) its way of being. Just as in Heidegger "resoluteness" represents a particular—and, I assume, reflective—decision to accept one's guilt, one's lack (of which Dasein is the author), one's "being-towards-death" (Being and Time), and involves the willing of "one's ever guilty self,"[124] so purifying reflection in Sartre has been shown to be the (willed) resolve to accept oneself as the free and responsible being that one "essentially" is (lack) and to renounce the "natural" pursuit of being or ground. Although Sartre does not speak the language of "guilt" and "being-toward-death," he clearly shares with Heidegger the view that a resolute ontological "self"-acceptance within the facticity of the human condition—be it called "resoluteness" or "reflective conversion"—is a necessary step in the human being's passage to authenticity. Sartre's "pure reflection" or purifying will, like Heidegger's "resoluteness" and perhaps Kierkegaard's "purity of heart," may be said—to use Heidegger's words—to "harbor in itself . . . *the possible existential modality of its own authenticity.*"[125] In each case, one might say, a resolute conversion, away from domination by the "natural" and the "impurities of 'everydayness,' " becomes a necessary condition for authenticity.

Of course, speaking for Heidegger, Karsten Harries does not intend to bring Sartre and Heidegger close together on this issue. In "Authenticity," for instance, he indicts what he takes to be Sartre's attempt to ground authenticity and value on an "abstract freedom."[126] And he maintains that we can exist authentically, in Heidegger's sense, "only as concrete individuals able to make inevitably particular decisions."[127] Sartre's sense, he claims, of freedom and responsibility lacks both concreteness and a measure: how then authenticity and morality?

Here is not the place for me to try to show Harries's misunderstanding of Sartre in this context. But in the section that follows, I shall perhaps answer Harries indirectly as I deal anew with the question of whether Sartre's authenticity has a moral or ethical dimension. For the interim, I simply remind the reader of Sartre's insistence that "to the extent that I have, in attaining myself through *conversion,* refused the abstract in order to will the *concrete* . . . I *value* it in that it makes this project a *concrete* and particular existence."[128] In the *Notebooks* and elsewhere,[129] one thing is sure: Sartre does not intend his freedom to be abstract. Rather, freedom—always situated—becomes a primary value, always practiced in "concrete circumstances," and this valorization is the *sine qua non* of authenticity. To this general issue I now turn.

Is authenticity "moral"?

Thus far, the details and analysis of Sartre's *Notebooks for an Ethics* that I have provided in this chapter not only corroborate but, as I already have suggested, significantly elucidate the passage to Sartrean authenticity and some of the features of that authenticity that I tried to specify in the two previous chapters. Sartre's account of reflection, will, and conversion in the *Notebooks*, as well as his idiosyncratic emphasis here on the concept of "unveiling," bring out connections and refinements that were both omitted in and in turn invited by my account in the foregoing chapters. Moreover, his extensive notes and brilliant, though often unsystematic, analysis provide even clearer grounds for the manner in which I have viewed the transformation to Sartrean authenticity and have distinguished that authenticity from even a reconstructed, "redeemed" sense of good faith. The for-itself's "unveiling" and reflective assuming or "grasping" of its gratuitous, ontological freedom is a refined statement of the willed "assumptive conversion" of the *War Diaries;* of the willed "radical conversion" from "natural" bad faith to genuine "self-recovery" and freedom in *Being and Nothingness;* and of the pure, reflective passage from "factual" freedom to "freedom as valued" that we saw in Jeanson's "approved" interpretation in *Sartre and the Problem of Morality.* Human reality's reflective (and radical) placing of itself into question, its grasping of gratuitous consciousness as "almost inessential unveiling . . . in the face of Being,"[130] signals in the *Notebooks,* as in each of these earlier works, what Jeanson calls the "point of departure"[131] for authentic consciousness and authentic existing.

But, though we have seen much to confirm pure reflection and conversion as differentiating marks of the "taking hold" of authenticity, I have, to this point in the present chapter, offered virtually no explicit details from the *Notebooks* that would confirm my attribution of "moral" or "ethical" to the "new attitude" and new "way of being oneself"[132] that conversion to authenticity brings about. (The reader will recall my earlier contention that conversion for Sartre involves the taking on of a new *moral* attitude that accepts and affirms the freedom and responsibility to which one is condemned.) Thus, before pointing out some anomalies and confusions in Sartre's use of *bad faith, inauthenticity,* and *alienation* in these *Notebooks,* I want to attend first to the issue of whether the *Notebooks* vindicate my ascription of moral or ethical to authenticity, and in turn to whether my fundamental thesis in the preceding chapters can be justified further by what he says here. This point of focus is especially appropriate in the light of the strong likelihood that the *Notebooks* are Sartre's aborted outline and notes for the work on ethics that he promised at the end of *Being and Nothingness.*

The first point to note is that the "non-accessory" (or "non-accomplice") reflection that marks "conversion" in these *Notebooks* is, as we have seen, "purifying." And this purification involves—and here he is consistent with his analysis in *Being and Nothingness*[133]—deliverance from the "corruption" of reflective consciousness's domination by the pursuit of being; from the hellish failure of being for-itself to recover itself as Being-in-itself. Although authenticity refuses the pursuit of being, it cannot, by way of conversion—we must note again—suppress that quest.[134] As Sartre has said, "The project is not absolutely suppressed by pure reflection any more than the natural attitude is suppressed in the phenomenological ἐποχή [epoché]."[135] To put it another way, there is no *absolute* moral conversion.[136] And it should be observed, as Joseph Fell has pointed out, that the deliverance or salvation is not *from* the ambiguity, or freedom, or tension, of human reality, but *to* it.[137] It is not, in Heidegger's language, a "resolve to be resolved," a deliverance *from* an unbearable freedom. To use Sartre's own language once more, the purifying reflection of authentic consciousness "maintains the tension" "at the heart of . . . authenticity";[138] it proposes to live the "new tension,"[139] to affirm and value its own non-coincidence. Conversion to authenticity appears to be consciousness's willed resolve to accept and *value* itself as gratuitous freedom—in other words, to be freedom's (human reality's) liberating or saving itself from the "corruption" (bad faith) of consciousness by freeing itself from all the values that its quest for identity and self-coincidence (the "spirit of seriousness"[140]) has produced.[141] Freedom's converted project of "taking itself as an end,"[142] of valorizing itself, of affirming itself as autonomous—or as the only value—and of maintaining itself at a distance, appears to be precisely the project to which, on the last page of *Being and Nothingness*, Sartre refers to as carrying us to "the ethical plane."[143] (Structurally, as I have already suggested, this is similar to Heidegger's "resolve" to valorize our "being-towards-death.") There seems to be no question that the *purification* initiated by conversion (more specifically, by purifying reflection) has in the *Notebooks* an ethical, if not theological, dimension. For, if conversion is, as we have seen, the "rejection of alienation," and if alienation is "original sin,"[144] then clearly the purification that takes place involves, at a minimum, a personal value transformation—a life reorientation of what we value, a redirection of our attitude toward our ontological freedom (toward ourselves) and, in turn, toward being, toward others, and toward the "world" (the meaning of which I have created). This is likely what Simone de Beauvoir has in mind when, using Sartre's ontological framework, she says, "Ethics is the triumph of freedom over facticity."[145] But let us look at additional evidence in regard to the ethical.

In one of his earliest references to reflection in the *Notebooks*, Sartre speaks first of a reflection that has the "unreflective for-itself" as its "direct and essential good," but then speaks—perhaps misleadingly—of an "*ethical* [italics mine] reflection that accompanies this reflection," for which the "*moral* [italics mine] being of what is reflected upon" is "*important.*"[146] Putting aside the issue of why Sartre speaks of an ethical reflection *accompanying* an impure (I assume) reflection,[147] it yet seems clear that he views the pure reflection that converts as moral in its intent. It is a matter, he says, of "willing the Good (in the unreflected upon) in order to be ethical."[148] And he goes on to assure us both that all ethics is "situated" (by the human being) and that "there would be no ethics if man was not a question in his being," that is, "if existence did not precede essence."[149]

Of interest, too, is not only—as we have seen—that Sartre here rejects the possibility of an "*absolute* moral conversion" but, more importantly, that in a number of passages he refers to conversion as "moral"[150] and insists, further, that "one cannot be converted alone"; "in other words" (he says), "ethics is not possible unless" others are "ethical."[151] And, specifically, he refers, though in a different context, to "Ethics" as "liberating the for-itself from alienation."[152] For, in "conversion," in grasping, assuming, affirming, our gratuity, freedom, finitude, I—in the absence of God and in our suspension of the pursuit of being (or of the "spirit of seriousness")—give up my claims to transcendent values and instead make freedom—freedom-in-a-situation—my highest value[153] and the source of all of my other (secondary) values. "If God does not exist," Sartre says, "we have to decide by ourselves [even] on the meaning of Being."[154] In affirming the (concrete) freedom that human reality is, I affirm a faithfulness to "myself" and human reality and adopt a way of being consistent with, not alien to, human reality—my own or the Other's. The pure reflection by which I suspend (not suppress!) my project of being and convert to an authentic mode of autonomous existing is a "waking up"[155] to my "pure autonomy"[156] and involves my placing the "world's significations" in parentheses in favor of my own value "creations,"[157] my own creativity. (Again, Sartre's appeal to Husserl's "purifying" practice of the *epoché* comes to mind.[158] And, in transforming my contingency into autonomy, in assuming myself—as we observed—as *accident* and without foundation, I not only acknowledge myself as the contingent source of all my values, all my meanings, and my world, but "make there be a world" and "take on all at once the *responsibility* for [myself] and for the universe."[159] My willed acceptance of my freedom in conversion—as we saw—"unveils" my freedom as creator of all my meanings—even the meaning of Being[160]—for which I take full responsibility.[161] In fact, as we saw in my earlier section on "unveiling," when I reflectively affirm, "unveil," assume my freedom, I justify it,[162] recognize it as "absolute" in the sense of its being the only source of meaning and values, indeed of all "creations." As the creator and justifier of values, human freedom (human reality or being for-itself) must thus take responsibility for all of its values and meanings. To invoke the language of his early *War Diaries* (which I examined in Chapter 5 on "Authenticity"), when I "adopt reality as [my] own," when "my freedom becomes mine," I claim responsibility, I take responsibility for my *being-in-situation* whatever that situation may be, and I am "without excuse."[163] As Sartre puts it, it is not just a matter "of *recognizing* that one has no excuse but also of *willing* it."[164] Or, as we saw abundantly in *Being and Nothingness,* my awakening to my freedom is at the same time an awakening to my responsibility. My "taking on" the facticity or contingency of my freedom is, simultaneously, a taking on of the facticity or contingency of my responsibility. (Freedom for Sartre—as for Heidegger—implies responsibility, existential as well as ontological.) Moreover, my condemnation to my being responsible for all my choices and actions leaves me, after purifying reflection, responsible for (that is to say, the "incontestable author" of) my "new" attitude, and for my relation to the freedom of others and to the "world" (which "I made to be"), as well as to the freedom which I *am*.[165] There seems to be no question that Sartre in the *Notebooks*, no less than in the *War Diaries* or his problematic "Existentialism Is a Humanism," regards this conversion to the *authentic* consciousness and attitude as an entry into the moral and ethical life. Authenticity cannot function at a purely ontological, factual, or descriptive level alone. In the *Notebooks*, freedom "triumphs" over facticity, to repeat de Beauvoir's words. And my reflective choice of my unjustified freedom as *mine* implies—at least "existentially," as Tom Flynn would say[166]—my valuing of the freedom of others. For it would be hardly rational—or "experientially" (my word) coherent— for me to accept freedom as my highest value and recognize the acceptance and willing of it as a moral imperative or "good," without recognizing it as the Other's "good" and choosing to affirm or will freedom for the Other as the would-be chooser of the same highest value (freedom). If the willing of my concrete freedom is what I ought to do *because* it is "consistent" with human reality as freedom ("existentially consistent" or coherent) and human freedom is the source (or "foundation") of all my values and meaning, then I should will the Other's freedom—and his willing of freedom as his end and primary value—for the same reasons.[167] As Sartre says later in the *Notebooks*, "the being of the Other is *my affair*."[168]

Sartre would appear to be still at ease with the ethical dimension he suggests in "Existentialism Is a Humanism" and to which he refers as the "plane of morality":

> When I recognize, as entirely authentic, that man is a being whose existence precedes his essence, and that he is a free being who cannot . . . but will his freedom, at the same time I realize that I cannot *not* will the *freedom of others.*[169]

We may note again that for Sartre here it would be inconsistent for human freedom, as the source of all values and meanings, to will *unfreedom*. And already we find a basis for Sartre's version of a "city [or "kingdom"] of ends," which he develops in his *Notebooks*[170]—that is, a basis for a "human realm" and classless society in which everyone recognizes and wills herself or himself and the Other as freedom and "end," and, reciprocally, accepts the legitimacy of each other's free ends.[171] But let us go on to what Sartre says on the same page of "Existentialism Is a Humanism":

> [And] in the name of the will to freedom which is implied in freedom itself, I can *form judgments* upon those who seek to . . . hide from this total freedom ["cowards"] . . . [or] try to show that their existence is necessary ["scum" or *salauds*]. . . . But neither cowards nor scum can be identified except on the plane of strict *authenticity.*[172]

To be sure, as I have already noted, the first part of this sentiment is echoed in Sartre's later assertion in the *Notebooks*—offered in a different context—that "morality is not the fusion of consciousness into a single subject but the *acceptance* of the detotalized Totality and the *decision* within this acknowledged inequality to take each consciousness in its *concrete* singularity as its concrete end."[173] And throughout the *Notebooks* one gains the strong impression that, after reflection, to treat any other freedom as less than a concrete end or living freedom, to be destructive in any way of another human freedom as absolute end,[174] to treat the other as a means to an end—or even as a "lesser freedom"—is to do violence to that freedom and to behave *inauthentically.*[175]

But it is clear that, even in his *Notebooks,* Sartre is stingy in his use and analysis of the words *ethical* and moral. David Pellauer is right, I think, when he says in his "Introduction" that Sartre here never discusses "what he means by an ethics" *(une morale),* at least not in any typical Anglo-American metaphilosophical sense.[176] Certainly our detailed study and argument in the preceding chapters have not reflected, through their corroborating references to Sartre's early works, any confrontation by Sartre with this issue. But Pellauer—who (modestly) disowns any claim to being an authority on Sartre[177]—is also right in maintaining that readers must distinguish between two questions in Sartre's reflections: (1) the ontological question concerning the very possibility of an ethics given Sartre's ontology, and (2) the question of whether there are in Sartre's (early) philosophy any specific normative principles or criteria by which to judge the morality or immorality of particular actions.[178]

In our attempt to find the differentiating characteristics of authenticity, in both the previous and the present chapters, we have viewed enough evidence to conclude that for Sartre ethics is possible, given his ontology in general and the possibility of radical conversion in particular. I say this, of course, in spite of Sartre's statement in *Being and Nothingness* that "we cannot possibly derive imperatives from ontology's indicatives."[179] And although in these *Notebooks* he refers to "ethics" in certain places as an "abstract fact"[180] and as "not having any real content,"[181] it is clear that Sartre proceeds on the assumption that ethics does have norms or content and that human reality's willed affirmation of its freedom does provide a basis for "forming" judgments. Moreover, he states explicitly, for instance, that the *ethical* "suspension" or "epoché" (ἐποχή) "must not remove any nuance of human life" and that "any ethics that *mutilates life* is suspect."[182] And although he tells us that ethics' "respect for freedom" "leaves undetermined the relation we ought to have with the content of this freedom,"[183] he makes it clear in the *Notebooks* that the creative, willed assumption, in conversion, of my unjustifiable freedom—freedom's *willing* of freedom as its only end—makes freedom the highest and primary value and provides a norm according to which any attempt to objectify, identify, or appropriate freedom—one's own or the Other's—can be judged to be inauthentic, "alienating," and even immoral. Against Harries and others who fault Sartre's "freedom" for being abstract and empty, one can see that Sartre's "willing" of freedom (in authenticity) does—when fleshed out—provide a general "measure" by which one can "respond appropriately" to human situations. It is not the case for Sartre, as Harries implies, that "all things matter equally" and that Sartre's view of freedom yields no criterion that will "preserve an understanding of responsibility."[184] In fact, Sartre's developing ethics of freedom suggests a Kantian—but, I should argue, existential—moral imperative that, more that Kant's, can provide measure and guidance for free action in concrete situations. In a "city of ends," in which we are summoned to promote freedom—my freedom and the Other's—in concrete circumstances, each of us is responsible for the freedom of the Other and what that concretely implies.

So, again, I want to suggest that, although the terms are sometimes different and the details of the "conversion" more complete, Sartre seems, in the *Notebooks*, to be moving gradually past *The War Diaries* and *Being and Nothingness*, and to be developing—with a certain noticeable consistency—what he has said less carefully in "Existentialism Is a Humanism." In the latter, in particular, though he acknowledges that "the content of morality is variable," he admits that "a certain form of this morality is universal."[185] And as though—in response to the question he posed at the end of *Being and Nothingness*—he were anticipating his *Notebooks for an Ethics*, he declares:

> I can pronounce a *moral* judgment. For I declare that freedom, *in respect of concrete circumstances,* can have no other end and aim but itself; and when once a man has seen that values depend upon himself . . . he can *will only one thing,* and that is freedom as the foundation of all values.[186]

Further, appealing to an "attitude of strict consistency" as the mark of "good faith" (note that he does not use *authenticity* here), he adds:

> That does not mean that he wills it in the abstract: it simply means that the actions of men [sic!] of *good faith* [note!] have, as their ultimate significance, the quest of freedom itself as such. . . . We will freedom for freedom's sake in and through particular circumstances.[187]

As we have seen, freedom here already replaces "God" as the fundamental value, and Sartre clearly sees it as belonging to the "moral" realm.[188]

And, to move conversely again for a moment, one might say that the *Notebooks* reinforce "Existentialism Is a Humanism's" insistence on the implications of willing my freedom as mine or of grasping my end as mine—of valorizing my freedom—for my approach to the freedom and "end" of the Other. Quite early in the *Notebooks,* he tells us that "in pure reflection there is already a summons to transform the Other into a pure, free subjectivity."[189] "The other's end," Sartre says, "can appear to me as an end only in and through the indication of my adopting that end."[190] And in grasping another's end, my freedom, Sartre says later, has a "pre-ontological comprehension" of the Other's freedom; and the "only *authentic* form of willing here consists in wanting the [Other's] end to be realized by the Other [freedom].[191] For in recognizing, grasping, willing, adopting, freedom as "my" end during *purifying reflection*, I cannot—if I am to remain logically and existentially consistent—but will and value the Other's freedom and end, and posit, affirm, and value freedom as her highest and primary value. It is individual human reality as freedom that gives ends their value, so when I posit the Other's end as "my end," I do so not because it is "unconditioned" (to do so in this way would be in the "spirit of seriousness") but because the Other "posited it as . . . end." I preserve the *autonomy* of end and value "for them in relation to me." "I want [and 'adopt'] this end only as the other wants it" and only "because the other wants it."[192] In this manner, I alienate neither my nor the Other's will or freedom.

We appear to have here not only an outline of the way to overcome the ontological conflict that frustrates any possibility of authentic intersubjective relations in *Being and Nothingness*, but additional grounds for an "Ought-to-be"[193] and a further basis for promoting a "city of ends" in which human freedoms (human beings) can relate to each other *authentically*. This is done, as we have seen, by each for-itself's, each freedom's, will-ing and adopting each Other's freedom and end (in concrete circumstances), rather than viewing each Other as an objectify-ing and menacing Other. In other words, the "new attitude" of authenticity in the *Notebooks* seems to "unveil" the possibility of an ethical community that breaks down the "predominance of the Other" and the "priority of the objective" which charac-terize humankind's "primitive alienation"[194] or "original fault."[195] Unlike *Being and Nothingness*, in which the described "concrete relations with others" were all pre-conversion rela-tions, the *Notebooks* prefigures a moral "ought" in respect to the willing of one's own freedom and the freedom and ends of the Other through what Sartre calls a "deeper recognition and comprehension of freedoms."[196] Each person *ought* to will and promote the freedom of every subject through "conversion" and what Sartre calls "comprehension"[197]—an empathetic understanding of and openness to the freedom of the Other. Genuine intersubjectivity, generosity, and love are now among human possibilities and "goods." Thus, "pure reflection" or the purifying will of conversion, by recognizing and affirming freedom as the primary value and unique source of all values, "outlines" a general criterion by which "good" and "bad" may be distinguished and an "ethical" city of ends can come into being.

Of course, one must not, in suggesting a basis for making moral distinctions in the post-conversion authentic life, insinuate an a priori or absolute moral principle into Sartre's thought; for that, to be sure, would violate his overall position and commit him to a form of the "spirit of seriousness" which he so strongly opposes in the *Notebooks*[198] and his other formative works. "It is the spirit of seriousness," he says, "that takes value as a *being* [*étant*] which must, however, be wanted and willed. Another form of *inauthenticity*."[199] And, if we are to follow de Beauvoir's analysis, it is precisely because a perverted or evil will is possible (though self-destructive) that the words "to will oneself free," or the idea of virtue for that matter, have any meaning.[200]

But one need not have resolved definitely either of the two issues, delineated above, related to ethics in Sartre to conclude here with a number of points. Among these are the following:

1. That the conversion in the *Notebooks* from the "natural attitude" and "accomplice" reflection to "pure reflection" and purified authentic consciousness—performed by a reflective taking hold of ourselves as free and autonomous—constitutes specifically what Sartre in *The War Diaries* recognizes as the affirmation of "true fidelity to ourselves"[201] and labels "authenticity."

2. That, despite Sartre's sparse references to the meaning and conditions of morality/ethics in the *Notebooks*, he says enough about each to allow us to infer that, for him, "moral" is adjectival in respect to conversion,[202] and that the "authentic plane of existence" to which pure reflection converts us, qualifies, for Sartre, as moral at the individual level and ethical at the subject-subject, freedom-freedom, or community/social level.

3. That the conversion to authenticity, involving as it does a suspension of one's orientation toward self-objectification and the world[203] and an acceptance and affirmation of "oneself" as gratuitous, spontaneous freedom, meets Sartre's "essential characteristic of morality" mentioned in the *Notebooks*—namely, "spontaneity"[204] or, more precisely, the "valorization" (Jeanson) of my freedom.

4. That, more than any other work of Sartre to which I have appealed in this study, *Notebooks for an Ethics* identifies the authentic consciousness with the new moral attitude, which—to invoke Jeanson's words again—refers us back for its genesis to "the singular act of an individual *conversion*"[205] and is the "point of departure" for authenticity.[206]

5. That the *Notebooks'* new emphasis on "unveiling" *reinforces* our earlier attribution of "moral" or "ethical" to authenticity by showing both that freedom's "unveiling" uncovers what human reality, in flight from itself, has "naturally" and pre-reflectively "veiled"; and also that, by deciding for freedom and "autonomy," human reality transforms itself as factual or ontological freedom into freedom-as-valued; that is, into what Jeanson has called "moral agency."

6. That the "unveiling" performed by pure reflection (in the *Notebooks*) offers a "deliverance" from the "buffeted" consciousness and flight from freedom and responsibility

(of which Sartre speaks in *The War Diaries*) to consciousness's recognition that human freedom is the sole source of values and is totally responsible for all of its choices—including its mode of relating to itself, others, the "situation," and the "world." "Only in this way," Sartre says, "can the *new* come into the world."[207]

In short, the conversion through "purifying reflection" from corrupted consciousness to lucid recognition and acceptance of freedom constitutes for Sartre in the *Notebooks*, as it did in a more skeletal form in both *The War Diaries* and "Existentialism Is a Humanism," the "moralization" of human consciousness; that is, the advent of authenticity and individual morality. This passage to authenticity marks, as we have seen, human reality's genuine salvation and deliverance from its "original fall" into the world—that is, from its kinship with things, from domination by the "facticities" of the human situation. It does this through its resolve and will to make freedom (and responsibility) its only value and to live consistently with the freedom (and responsibility) that human reality *is*.[208] To borrow an expression from Simone de Beauvoir,[209] morality for Sartre—as for de Beauvoir, who builds her ethics on Sartre's ontological foundation—involves "adhesion to the self" where the "self" is to be understood as freedom (human reality). And this kind of existential or practical "adhesion" to itself as freedom is, I continue to maintain, the core of what Sartre means by authenticity—the "new [moral] way of being to oneself and for oneself" ("Nouvelle manière ... d'être à soi-même et pour soi-même,"[210] which Sartre refers to also as freedom's new "accord with" itself,[211] or as one's new "contractual agreement with oneself."[212] It is the "true fidelity to ourselves" of which he speaks in *The War Diaries*.[213] Functioning in this way, authentic choosing, reflective conversion, thus brings unity—Sartre says, "*ethical* unity"[214]—"self-integration," and proper measure to human reality.[215] For, among other considerations, this accord with myself as freedom (human reality) is accord with the Other, also, as a freedom (human reality).

Thus, despite their inadequacies and, certainly, indefiniteness at crucial points, Sartre's "notes" in the *Notebooks*— especially when bolstered by "Existentialism Is a Humanism" and reliable "readings" of Sartre by Jeanson and de Beauvoir and (to a lesser extent) Elkaïm-Sartre—strongly support my ascription of the moral and ethical to Sartre's understanding of authenticity. Indeed, the *Notebooks* appear to "establish" moral obligation and the morality of authenticity for Sartre.

Yet I cannot proceed in good conscience without pointing out at least a few recalcitrant passages which appear to frustrate my thesis concerning the marks by which authenticity can be differentiated from my redeemed sense of good faith in Sartre, and inauthenticity from both bad faith and (presumably) alienation. In my judgment, as I have already suggested, Sartre at times plainly confounds and confuses these notions by either misspeaking or using interchangeably terms that his emerging philosophical system has rather carefully distinguished. Let us take note of a few of these instances.

Some terminological confusions

In spite of his focus in the *Notebooks* on authenticity, and his general insistence on the necessity of reflection for the category of authenticity or inauthenticity, Sartre, very early in the *Notebooks*, for example, appears badly to confuse these categories with what he has previously presented as the *non-*or *pre-*reflective categories of good and bad faith. As early as on page 12, he tells us, as we have seen, that "impure reflection . . . is originally bad faith" and "pure reflection is good faith." If, in fact, bad faith is, as Sartre has so often affirmed, pre-reflective or non-reflective—that is, not a "consciousness directed upon consciousness"[216]—and if reflection is a necessary and differentiating feature of authenticity, then Sartre's way of (mis)-speaking here seriously confounds the two sets of categories which he—I have argued—intends to differentiate. And even a few pages earlier, he sets the stage for some confusion. In now admitting that there is a human "nature" and affirming the need for conversion because of our "natural attitude," he states that human reality (freedom or consciousness) "begins with flight and inauthenticity."[217] But if the *willed*, reflective conversion is *from* our "natural attitude" to authenticity, must we not say that inauthenticity—as the weight of Sartre's analysis strongly suggests—is the result of human reality's reflective choice to continue his or her "natural," non-reflective *bad faith*? Sartre's reference to "nature" as inauthenticity[218] and not bad faith not only frustrates my analysis but also—at the very outset of the *Notebooks for an Ethics*—confounds the project and line of argument that Sartre appears to have in mind for this important sequel to *Being and Nothingness*. And the differentiation I am attributing to Sartre is further confused and challenged by Sartre's choice of works in Appendix I of the *Notebooks*. Here also, as I have noted earlier, Sartre refers to the "initial project" or human reality's "original choice" of herself (flight) as "inauthenticity." To this "very structure of human existence" as "flight" he here, rather bafflingly, gives the name *inauthenticity*—not bad faith—but then goes on to acknowledge that human freedom first realizes itself on an "unreflective level" and that "salvation" (authenticity) will depend on whether *reflection* (note!) refuses to go along with this initial project (authentic) or "takes it up" (inauthentic).[219] Just a few lines later, he correctly, I believe, refers to accessory reflection's "prolongation of [primitive] bad faith." So, in an otherwise discerning summary statement of the human being's basic existential predicament as chooser, Sartre seems either sloppy, careless, or plainly confused about his own maturing analysis of the basic existential "attitudes." And I suspect that this misspeaking by Sartre in the *Notebooks,* on which Arlette Elkaïm-Sartre relies so heavily, is the source of Elkaïm-Sartre's tendency at times to conflate the human being's bad-faith project and "natural attitude" with inauthenticity. "The original project", she says, "is fascination with Being"—the "Being-in-itself-for-itself of inauthenticity."[220]

The problem of philosophical interpretation of Sartre is exacerbated in the *Notebooks* by Sartre's tendency also to speak of "alienation" as if it were alternately bad faith or inauthenticity or both. To be sure, Sartre can talk of "alienation" as the "social aspect of reification,"[221] and as grasping oneself "as Other starting from Other"[222]; or say that "man alienates himself in defining himself"[223]; or speak of the Ego as "the subjective type of alienation"; or contend that "freedom destroys one form of alienation with another form."[224] And to be sure he tells us that by "alienation" he means "a certain type of relations that man has with himself, with others, and with the world, where he posits the *ontological priority of the Other.*"[225] Moreover, as we have seen, Sartre refers to alienation here as "original sin."[226] But it is important to note again that Sartre speaks of "conversion"—the purifying will (or reflection) to overcome one's "natural attitude" and grasp one's gratuitous freedom—as "the rejection of alienation"[227] and "refusal" of the natural "quest for being."[228] It is clear that, in this context of "conversion," Sartre is equating alienation with what he generally refers to as our original non-reflective project of "bad faith,"[229] which can be "transcended" through reflective conversion. In fact, in one supporting passage that I invoked earlier in my present chapter, he appears to refer to "the failure of the for-itself's attempt to be in-itself-for-itself" (that is, of its original project) as the "very structure of alienation"[230] (*la structure même de l'aliénation*[231]). But in parentheses he speaks (confusingly) of my having "to uphold [it] in bad faith with my own complicity" (*soutenir de mauvaise foi avec ma propre complicité*).[232] On the one hand, Sartre seems to identify alienation, or our "original form of alienation"[233] with our "original pursuit of being, our primitive bad faith, our futile *bad faith* pursuit of for-itself-in-itself, our "original sin," and even our "Hell."[234] On the other hand, even in these short illustrated passages, he appears also to identify alienation with the failure or futility of *accessory* (or "accomplice," or "impure") reflection's complicity with our original bad faith. If, of course, he means the latter, he is conflating "alienation" with his dominant use of "inauthenticity," for according to his *dominant* usage, only authenticity and inauthenticity—not good faith and bad faith—can be categories of "will" or "reflection."[235] And, for Sartre, inauthenticity, not (it would seem) bad faith, is a function of the "springing up" of impure reflection as an "accomplice" (or as "accessory" to) consciousness's *spontaneous, alienating* (bad-faith) effort to recuperate and congeal itself in Being (in the In-itself). But if alienation equals bad faith, and if for Sartre bad faith precedes the reflective consciousness, then how can impure reflection—even if it is accessory or "accomplice" to original bad faith—be said to be "originally *bad faith*"?[236] (In *Being and Nothingness*, Sartre has told us that at the pre-reflective level freedom does not exist as will.) And how can Sartre offer, while remaining self-consistent, some of the contentions I quoted at the outset of this section—for example, "Freedom destroys one form of alienation with another"[237]—or speak about the Ego as "the subjective type of alienation"?[238] It would seem reasonable to assume that freedom's intentional project of destroying one form of alienation and replacing it with another, or consciousness's self-alienating construction of an Ego, would involve consciousness's "operating" on and directing itself "upon consciousness"; that is to say, would *require* reflection.[239] For we may remember that, for Sartre in *Being and Nothingness,* reflection is "a *second* effort by the for-itself to found itself; that is, *to be for-itself what it is.*"[240]

To be sure, Sartre discusses many forms of "alienation" in the *Notebooks,* and I have not begun to do justice to his probing and often methodical analysis of a number of them (such as the "alienation" involved in "the original relation of the Other to me"[241] and "reciprocal alienation"[242]). But a careful, extensive consideration of Sartre's analysis of alienation was not among my announced aims for this book. Instead, my intention in the related discussions above has been the secondary and more modest one of showing—as I suggested earlier—that Sartre sometimes seems to confound the core "existential attitudes" and concepts of this study (bad faith/inauthenticity; good faith/ authenticity); and that, in the *Notebooks* in particular, he seems to confuse the meaning of inauthenticity with both "bad faith" and "alienation."

But even if my illustrations hold and serve to challenge the neatness of my own differentiating thesis, it does not follow that the *Notebooks for an Ethics* call seriously into question my argument and conclusions in the preceding chapters. If anything, as I've tried to show systematically throughout this chapter, *Notebooks for an Ethics* both clarifies and corroborates the Sartrean feature I have attributed to authenticity in the present book. Although Sartre appears either to misspeak or to be conceptually sloppy at certain points, the weight of the *Notebooks* speaks unmistakeably to his maturing view of authenticity as a "new way" of being oneself which requires a willed purifying *reflection* and *conversion*—a reflective, "radical modification"[243] of one's fundamental project—and takes on an *ethical* dimension in which human freedom "unveils," assumes, grasps itself as spontaneous and as *morally* (not just ontologically or factually) responsible for its (free) choices and acts. The three marks by which I earlier distinguished Sartrean authenticity—reflection (or will), conversion, and morality—are clearly visible. Despite Sartre's apparent slips in language, conversion to authentic existing is again shown to represent "deliverance" from human reality's (freedom's) "natural" pre-reflective and "exhausting" disposition to flee its freedom in pursuit of being. As de Beauvoir, following Sartre, puts it, conversion to authenticity is a conversion of "my flight into will" and thus a relinquishing of my "servitude" to the "serious."[244] In other words, the *Notebooks* demonstrate that this "new" authentic consciousness and way of existing constitute a radical escape and salvation from the self-alienating bad faith of one's corrupted original natural attitude and primitive project of flight. It represents, one might say, freedom's genuine self-recovering of itself as freedom. In short, more than in any other single work I have discussed, Sartre here succeeds in showing how the reflective passage to authenticity involves being-for-itself's valorization of itself as freedom, constitutes the "moralization" of the human being (Jeanson), and allows what in *Being and Nothingness* he anticipates as an "ethics of deliverance and salvation."[245] Although Sartre may have confused the language of bad faith and inauthenticity, and that of the relation of our "natural" attitude and impure reflection to the project of In-itself-For-itself, the *Notebooks* are unambiguous in contending that authenticity—as salvation—is a "new beginning" which "neutralizes" the "hell" of our original bad-faith project of trying to flee from our awesome freedom in order to attain *being*.

Suggestions for the sake of clarity and coherence

But, in passing, I wish to suggest a distinction which, I submit, Sartre fails to make, but which may eliminate at least part of the confusion surrounding his terminology in regard to his own basic existential attitudes. More specifically, I believe a distinction needs to be made between what *is* bad faith (or good faith or inauthenticity) in the sense of being identical with it, and what is *in* bad faith (or *in* good faith or *in* a "state" of inauthenticity). In the latter case, one might prefer to say that the "is" is used predicatively but not, as in the former, to designate identity. When Sartre, early in the *Notebooks,* referred to "impure reflection" as "originally bad faith" (*originellement mauvaise foi*[246]) and to "pure reflection" as "good faith"[247] (*la réflexion pure est bonne foi*[248]), he might better have said that impure reflection is *in* bad faith and pure reflection is *in* good faith, or that bad faith may be predicated of *impure* reflection and good faith of *pure* reflection. That would not have eliminated all of Sartre's confusion in this regard, but it would have done away with the appearance that Sartre *identifies* impure reflection as (makes it identical with) bad faith, which, at least on initial observation, seems inadmissible to Sartre's system, on his own premises. And despite Sartre's insistence on a distinction between a spontaneous, non-reflective consciousness and a willed, reflective one,[249] and his overall tendency to view bad and good faith in terms of the former and authenticity/inauthenticity in terms of the latter, this *predication* or *attribution* of bad or good faith, for example, to reflection can be supported by his discussion of *will* both in *Being and Nothingness* and in *Notebooks for an Ethics.* In the former, as we saw earlier, Sartre maintains that even "in the form of the reflective consciousness" the will can constitute *in bad faith* "false psychic objects as motives."[250] (Of course, he has already told us that reflection is in bad faith insofar as it constitutes itself as "*the object* which I make-to-be-me."[251]) The "very will" of the person who has chosen "inferiority," for example, is "*in* bad faith," he tells us, for it "flees the recognition of the true ends chosen by the spontaneous consciousness."[252] To be noted is that, in these *Being and Nothingness* references, Sartre does not say that the will—in this case, the will presumably as *impure* reflection—*is* bad faith, but rather that it is *in* bad faith. This way of speaking supports the distinction that I think needs to be made in and by Sartre. The will is "posited as a reflective decision" in regard to "certain ends"[253]; and when the "voluntary deliberation" decides "to offset or hide" our inferiority, it is *in* bad faith. This voluntary, reflective decision made *in* bad faith, Sartre may then more consistently say, leads to an "alienated" freedom and to inauthenticity; that is, to a reflectively inauthentic way of "existing [one's] existence."[254] And with this clarification he can go on to show—as he has tried to show in the *Notebooks*—how accessory (or impure) reflection can emerge "from the pre-reflective"—"an already constituted freedom"—and how "pure reflection *emerges from* impure reflection."[255]

In the *Notebooks* also, as we have seen, Sartre says emphatically that reflection is a "form of willing," and, as a form of willing, it "can issue from" the non-reflective ("natural") project of bad faith. And, presumably in bad faith, this form of "realized" freedom can continue to flee from itself as freedom (will inauthenticity) rather than "recover" itself and be in "accord with itself" (*accord avec soi*[256]) as freedom (authenticity).[257] To be sure, in the *Notebooks* Sartre states unambiguously that it is authenticity, or inauthenticity, that "has to do with what I will."[258] But it seems to me that Sartre here—following *Being and Nothingness*—allows one to say, albeit nervously, that the impure will, or reflection that wills the project of inauthenticity (that continues our "natural" bad-faith project of becoming *something*), is in bad faith "because it does not want to see its own failure."[259] By participating in the impurity of the *unreflective*, Sartre seems to want to say, even reflection—specifically, *impure* reflection—can be in bad faith, for it reflectively prolongs the primitive (non-thetic) project of bad faith, the consequence of which is *inauthentic* existence.[260]

Of course, even if this distinction can be maintained, it does not justify or excuse Sartre's reference to impure reflection as bad faith (rather than *in* it)—or, for that matter, to pure reflection as good faith. Nor does it excuse the inadvertence with which Sartre seems to intermingle or conflate these terms. Certainly, Sartre's reference to the "new *'authentic'* way of being oneself" as transcending "the dialectic of sincerity and bad faith"[261] suggests strongly that Sartre views authenticity as at another "plane of freedom" or existence from bad or good faith—specifically, at the reflective and moral level. Yet that does not vitiate my contention that predicating "bad faith" of impure reflection (that is, saying that impure reflection is *in* rather than *is* bad faith) eliminates at least part of the confusion that results from Sartre's *identification* in the *Notebooks,* of impure reflection with bad faith. Nor does it weaken my view that this refinement makes Sartre's basis for associating reflection with bad faith or good faith more feasible. Certainly, in spite of what appear to be contrary emphases by Sartre in the *Notebooks* and elsewhere, the attribution of the *predicate* of bad faith to impure reflection is compatible with both my reconstruction of Sartrean bad faith and, in turn, my detailed argument regarding the cynicism of bad faith, which I offered in earlier chapters of this book. For bad faith, in spite of Sartre's emphasis, need not—at least on my reconstruction—be restricted to the pre-reflective, as it is in respect to the "natural" attitude or pursuit of being. The structure or mechanism of bad faith, as I have interpreted it, may also be shared by consciousness "operating" on consciousness when that consciousness tries to hide or escape its "*de trop*-ness" and thus prolong its quest for coincidence. We must remember what Sartre says in *Being and Nothingness*—namely, that "if bad faith is possible, it is because it is an immediate, permanent risk to *every* project of the human being; it is because consciousness conceals in its being a permanent risk of bad faith."[262] Of course one might object that to allow this move is only to confound further Sartre's notions of bad faith and inauthenticity and their relation to reflection. But to this objection one might respond—even granting my preceding analysis and differentiation—that impure reflection's *choice* of an inauthentic consciousness and inauthentic way of existing (consciousness's choice to continue in its "natural" bad faith) is itself a reflection that is *in* bad faith, for it self-deceptively (and self-inconsistently) prolongs, as a mode of existing, freedom's non-thetic, "original" *flight* from the freedom that it *is,* without acknowledging the continuous failure of that project.

I want to make one last point before leaving this specific suggestion and topic. In short, I believe that, in spite of what is generally taken to be Sartre's intentions, both Sartre and Sartrean scholarship would read and fare better if a distinction were drawn more sharply between the original bad faith of the human being's original pre-reflective project or "natural attitude" of attaining self-coincidence or in-itself-for-itself (what I have earlier called "ontological" bad faith), and the bad faith of more specific "acts," "choices," "beliefs," "behaviors," and "ways" of living (which would include what I have called "epistemological" bad faith). To put the matter another way, there would be less confusion in understanding Sartre's position regarding basic existential "attitudes" if Sartre and his interpreters had distinguished more carefully between what Sartre calls the "immediate" (or "original" or "natural") attitude (or "primitive project")[263] of bad faith—presumably bad faith's "coming into the world"[264]—and the "phenomena" or instances of the bad-faith consciousness (for example, the coquette, homosexual, or waiter) which he analyzes and illustrates so meticulously in Chapter 2, Part I, of *Being and Nothingness.*[265] To be sure, our "natural attitude" or "original project" and our particular acts of bad faith share the same *Weltanschauung*[266] of bad faith—specifically, flight from freedom and quest for identity—whether it be fleeing from the angst of our awareness of our spontaneous freedom, or selectively bypassing the facticity of critical evidence in order to define ourselves as, for instance, one of our "possibles." It is nevertheless important to be able to speak of acts, choices, or deeds of bad faith without identifying them with the bad faith of our original project of "flight" from the freedom we "are"—what in Appendix 1 of the *Notebooks* he refers to as "the bad faith found non-thetically within the primitive project."[267] That is to say, even though Sartre contends, for example, that the bad faith of a will and its ends can be understood only within the perspective of for-itself's pre-reflective "fundamental choice" or "fundamental project,"[268] we must be careful not to take bad faith as it is *applied* to a particular reflection or will as identical to the original bad faith of our primitive project of being. The need for his distinction—which I can suggest here only in passing—provides further space for allowing us to say, without inconsistency, that *reflection* for Sartre may be affirmed to be in bad faith. Just because, for Sartre, an impure will or accessory reflection, by continuing the bad faith of our original project, *initiates* inauthentic consciousness and inauthentic living, it hardly follows that only inauthenticity and never bad faith can be predicated of it. To be sure, the *purifying* reflective will (for Sartre) effects the conversion from bad faith to the authentic consciousness, and the reflective impure will to continue our "original" bad faith leads to inauthenticity. But the acknowledgment of that connection between modes of reflections and ensuing modes of authenticity/inauthenticity does not necessarily preclude the ascription of bad faith to the reflection that effects inauthenticity. Sartre's own views and the musings of some of his interpreters would,

I suspect, seem less confused if this point or qualification (assuming it is correct) were articulated and emphasized.

After the *Notebooks:* Is our differentiation still viable?

One question remains prior to our concluding the inquiry of this culminating chapter. Granted that *Notebooks for an Ethics* corroborates and elucidates the characteristics I have attributed to authenticity in the preceding chapters, and granted that Sartre's uncompleted work on ethics adds new insights and dimensions to his understanding of human reality's basic existential attitudes, are we able to retain the distinction between authenticity and the salvaged ontological sense of good faith which I have offered in the preceding chapters? My allusions and indirect (though positive) answers are not quite enough. I need now to make a few more direct concluding observations.

First, I must state what the reader has likely surmised—namely, that in *Notebooks for an Ethics* Sartre makes only scarce reference to "good faith" and, when he does, he appears, problematically, to use it interchangeably with authenticity. Unfortunately, he offers no followup to the sparse and problem-ridden discussion of good faith in *Being and Nothingness* but simply allows it to stand in direct contrast to both bad faith and inauthenticity. In short, his appeal to good faith in the *Notebooks* does more—as we have seen—to confound than to enlighten, though his contention that "only bad faith can be at the origin of good faith"[269] appears to confirm his earlier contention in *Being and Nothingness* that bad faith "slides to the very origin of the project of good faith."[270]

Yet, although Sartre's references to good faith in the *Notebooks* remain minimal, stifled, and problematic—and peculiarly confused at times with authenticity—it seems clear that the overriding analysis of the *Notebooks* at least allows the distinction between my reconstructed Sartrean sense of good faith and the recurrent—indeed, pervasive—sense of authenticity which I have drawn in the previous chapters. Despite Sartre's tendency at times to conflate good faith with authenticity, bad faith with inauthenticity, it is unambiguous that the focus in the *Notebooks* is on authenticity and that authenticity, not good faith, constitutes a "deliverance" from the pre-reflective "natural attitude" of bad faith on which *Being and Nothingness*'s pre-conversion ontology (*une ontologie d'avant la conversion*) focused.[271] I am only repeating myself badly when I remind the reader that Sartre tells us explicitly that authenticity transcends "the dialectic of sincerity and bad faith." And we might also remember that, very early in the *Notebooks*, he has told us that "reflection suppresses bad faith and ignorance."[272] But this does not, of course, logically imply that authenticity in the *Notebooks* also transcends good faith, especially given what I alleged above to be the Sartre's misidentification in the *Notebooks* of pure reflection with good faith. And one must allow for the possibility that, even in his lapses in precise language, Sartre wants to include pure reflection as good faith (when it "wills" *in* good faith) *within* the more comprehensive post-conversion category of authenticity. Or, put more simply, he wants to collapse good faith into authenticity. Yet, even given these allowances, I reaffirm my point that the overall emphasis and structure of Sartre's argument permit a conception of "good faith" in which the good faith consciousness recognizes and accepts the spontaneity, non-coincidence, and self-interrogation of consciousness, while resisting the temptation of bad faith's ideal of *being* or *oneness with itself* (self-coincidence) or—epistemologically viewed—"believing what one believes." And, certainly, given the distinction I have made between the pre-reflective, primitive, original project of bad faith and bad faith as predicated of a will or choice or reflection, for example, I can continue to maintain that, while authenticity for Sartre is reflective and willed, bad and good faith are generally viewed by Sartre as pre-reflective "immediate attitudes" or "determinations of being."[273] (This does not preclude—given another of my distinctions above—the possibility of a reflection or a will *being in* good or bad faith). My point is also supported indirectly—but certainly not established— in the *Notebooks* by Sartre's acknowledgment that freedom first "realizes itself" at a *pre-reflective* level[274] and is naturally disposed to bad faith (I have corrected this from Sartre's, I contend, mistaken use here of "inauthenticity"), but that a reflective project can "issue" from it and transform it into an *authentic* consciousness.[275] In fact—as I have already shown— insofar as "I exist as choice," and pure and impure reflection (and, in turn, authenticity and inauthenticity) "take their source from the non-thetic consciousness that freedom has of itself," Sartre makes it clear that the reflective modes of consciousness or existing—such as authenticity or inauthenticity— presuppose the appearance of the "unreflective plane" or the "reflected upon"[276] to which, generally speaking, I have relegated *good* as well as bad faith for Sartre.

Yet I must acknowledge that one is hard pressed to find in the *Notebooks direct* evidence that explicitly and unequivocally substantiates and upholds the distinction I have drawn between authenticity and good faith. I am left, rather, to go with what is unsaid and with the force of his overall position. For reasons that should be blatantly clear by now, there is, of course—even without the differentiation I have offered—no "radical conversion" from good faith to authenticity as there is from (pre-reflective) bad faith to (reflective) authenticity. There would be no reason for it. So, on his own grounds, Sartre apparently sees no need to analyze "good faith" in a work in which he is attempting both to show the possibility and the motivation for "recovery" from the "hell" of pursuing Being and to analyze the passage from "natural" bad faith to authenticity. As a consequence, we are left to conclude that, while the ontological analysis in the *Notebooks* confirms and clarifies the categories and fundamental existential attitudes of bad faith, authenticity, and inauthenticity, it does little to illuminate (or "unveil," if you like) the "immediate attitude"[277] of good faith which Sartre discusses so briefly in *Being and Nothingness* and which I have tried to salvage in an earlier chapter.

Nor, however, do the *Notebooks* preclude it. Although Sartre misspeaks—as I have pointed out—in one of his major references to good faith in the *Notebooks,* he clearly refers to good faith in a positive sense—specifically, as "pure reflection"—and contrasts it sharply with bad faith as "impure reflection." That is to say, *Notebooks for an Ethics* allows a constructive, salutary sense of good faith that is in keeping with my positive line of reconstructing it on Sartrean terms. Although, to be sure, Sartre appears occasionally, in this work, to collapse good faith into his concept of authenticity—sometimes even using the two interchangeably[278]—and to acknowledge an "immediate," unreflective attitude of *bad faith* only, his detailed analysis of reflection and conversion would seem to permit consciousness's non-reflective good-faith acceptance of its own "self-distance" or "calling itself itself into question." And his analysis suggests also a "waking up" by consciousness prior to pure reflection's *willed* decision to take up this project of freedom as an autonomous, therefore authentic, mode of existing.[279]

Finally, whether my point—namely, that in Sartre there can be a constructive sense of good faith that does not identify it with authenticity—is right or wrong, Sartre's "unveiling" of authenticity in *Notebooks for an Ethics* makes abundantly clear, as we concluded in the preceding chapter, that for Sartre it is possible to deliver oneself from the tormenting ontological "hell" of consciousness's *original (bad faith)* project of attaining in-itself, self-coincidence, identity—that is to say, from the project to be *Causa Sui* or "God." In spite of some recalcitrant and misleading passages in Sartre's writings, it is a *misreading* of Sartre to conclude, as too many interpreters do, that Sartre's philosophy condemns us irreversibly to bad faith and hell.[280] Authentic existing, as I have said before, is the way out of bad faith and Sartrean hell. *Notebooks for an Ethics* makes that unequivocal. Although, for Sartre, authenticity may not give us the security and foundation for which we may be looking, it gives us an exit from the torment that comes from the futile attempt to *secure* ourselves in being, things, objects, and the world. We may not be able to suppress our tendency to want this grounding, but we can free ourselves from the hell of *pursuing* it.

Notes

Introduction

1. Jean-Paul Sartre, *L'être et le néant* (Paris: Éditions Gallimard, 1943), 68–70.
2. Ibid., 70.
3. Ibid.
4. Jean-Paul Sartre, *Notebooks for an Ethics,* trans. David Pellauer (Chicago: University of Chicago Press, 1992), 482.
5. Ibid., 478.
6. Ibid., 103.

Chapter 1

1. Jean-Paul Sartre, *Being and Nothingness,* trans. Hazel E. Barnes (New York: Philosophical Library, 1956), 63.
2. Ibid., li.
3. Herbert Spiegelberg, *The Phenomenological Movement* (The Hague: Martinus Nijhoff, 1960), vol. 2, 488, italics mine.
4. Sartre, *Being and Nothingness,* lxi. Here I use Spiegelberg's, rather than Hazel Barnes's, translation of *naît portée sur* (*L'être et le néant,* 28).
5. Spiegelberg, *Phenomenological Movement,* 469.
6. Sartre, *Being and Nothingness,* lx, lxii.
7. Ibid., 63, 58.
8. Ibid., 70.
9. Ibid., lxv.
10. Ibid., 74.
11. Ibid., 95.
12. Ibid., 74.
13. Ibid., lvi.
14. Ibid., lii.

15. Ibid., liii.

16. Ibid., 74.

17. Ibid., 43.

18. Ibid., 25.

19. Ibid., 39.

20. Ibid., 43.

21. Ibid.

22. Ibid., 45.

23. I shall develop this concept sufficiently here to make my contentions clear. But I shall reserve for two subsequent chapters a more detailed and intense analysis of Sartre's notion of bad faith.

Note also that, against the suggestion of Walter Kaufmann, I stay with the more literal translation of *mauvaise foi*. I do so because I think that Kaufmann's "self-deception" carries with it, in everyday discourse, the suggestion of an "unconscious" or "subconscious" element at work. Sartre's *mauvaise foi,* depending as it does on the pre-reflective cogito, explicitly precludes this element (see, e.g., *Being and Nothingness,* 52). In addition, the translation "self-deception" makes for difficulty of translation in key sections of *Being and Nothingness.* Consider, for example, the title of Section III: "The 'Faith' of Bad 'Faith.' " In my judgment, this section would lose some of its punch, some of the power of its contentions, if it spoke of "the" *'faith'* of *self-deception.''* It is not accidental that Sartre spoke of *la foi de mauvaise foi.*

24. Sartre, *Being and Nothingness,* 48.

25. Ibid., 48, 49.

26. Ibid., lii.

27. Ibid., 53.

28. Ibid., 70.

29. Ibid., 56.

30. Ibid., 56, 57.

31. Ibid., 57.

32. Ibid., 67.

33. Ibid., 58.

34. Ibid.

35. Ibid., 62.

36. Ibid., 59.

37. Ibid., 65.

38. Ibid., 62–65.

39. Ibid., 65, 66.

40. Ibid., 66, italics mine.

41. Because I have quoted only part of Sartre's full statement, I have found it necessary to change the punctuation mark here.

42. Ibid., 67.

43. Ibid.

44. Ibid., 58.

45. Ibid., 58–59.

46. Ibid., 67.

47. Ibid., lxii.

48. Ibid., 86.

49. Ibid., 63.

50. Ibid., 68, italics mine.

51. Ibid., 70.

52. I refer specifically to Xavier Monasterio, who made this point in his unpublished response to me "On Bad Faith and Sincerity: A Vindication of Sartre," presented at the 1988 meetings of the Sartre Society of North America, held at Duquesne University.

53. Ronald E. Santoni, "Sartre on 'Sincerity': 'Bad Faith' or Equivocation?" *The Personalist* (Spring 1972): 150–160.

54. Among others, I think of the comments and questions of Joseph Catalano, Phyllis Morris, Xavier Monasterio, and A. D. M. Walker. Though not all published, they became important issues for discussion at professional meetings and for my reconsideration of some of my contentions.

55. A. D. M. Walker, "Sartre, Santoni, and Sincerity," *The Personalist* (January 1977): 88–92.

56. In my paper on sincerity cited above, I do specifically say that Sartre "seems either to ignore or exploit" the ambiguity of which I accuse him.

57. Sartre, *Being and Nothingness*, 64.

58. See, in particular, Walker, "Sartre, Santoni, and Sincerity," p. 89.

59. Ibid.

60. Compare, for example, Santoni, "Sartre on 'Sincerity,'" pp. 153–154 to pp. 155–158.

61. Sartre, *Being and Nothingness*, 62.

62. E.g., Santoni, "Sartre on 'Sincerity,'" 156, 157.

63. Here and in what follows, I am reliant on Walker's formulation of his argument, in Walker, "Sartre, Santoni, and Sincerity," pp. 90–92.

64. Ibid., 90.

Chapter 2

1. Jean-Paul Sartre, *Being and Nothingness*, trans. Hazel E. Barnes (New York: Philosophical Library, 1956), 47.

2. Ibid., 48, italics mine.

3. Ibid.

4. Ibid.

5. For Sartre, it is to be remembered, all consciousness is consciousness (of) consciousness: consciousness is non-thetically aware of itself.

6. Ibid., 49.

7. Jean-Paul Sartre, *L'être et le néant* (Paris: Éditions Gallimard, 1943), 87, translation mine.

8. Sartre, *Being and Nothingness*, 49.

9. Ibid., lii.

10. Marjorie Grene, in her noteworthy book *Sartre* (New Viewpoints, 1973), takes issue with Sartre's self-referential view of consciousness. For a discussion of this, see Ronald E. Santoni, "Marjorie Grene's *Sartre*," *International Philosophical Quarterly* (December 1975).

11. Sartre, *Being and Nothingness*, 43.

12. Ibid., 49.

13. Ibid.

14. Sartre, *L'être et le néant*, 88 ("qui n'existe que dans et par sa propre distinction").

15. Sartre, *Being and Nothingness*, 50.

16. Ibid., italics mine. The French word *aspect* might also be translated "appearance." But, in the present context, a looser translation, "way," might be better suited. See Sartre, *L'être et le néant*, 88, or *Being and Nothingness*, 50.

17. Ibid., 48.

18. Of course, the difference between the *unitary* structure of the former and the ontological *duality* of the latter remains.

19. Ibid.

20. On the following page, Sartre says clearly (regarding bad faith): "I must know the truth very exactly *in order* to conceal it more carefully."

21. Ibid., 67ff.

22. Ibid., 68.

23. See, for example, Lee Brown and Alan Hausman, "Mechanism, Intentionality, and the Unconscious: A Comparison of Sartre and Freud," in *The Philosophy of Jean-Paul Sartre*, ed. Paul A. Schilpp, Library of Living Philosophers Series, (LaSalle: Open Court, 1981), 539–581. It is not within the purposes of my immediate project to deal with this disagreement here.

24. Of course, a number of interpreters and critics have disputed Sartre's claim. See, e.g., Ivan Soll, "Sartre's Rejection of The Freudian Unconscious," in *Philosophy of Sartre*, ed. Schilpp, 582–604.

25. Sartre, *Being and Nothingness*, 55; cf. also 47.

26. Ibid., 56.

27. Ibid., 57.

28. Ibid., 55.

29. Ibid., 57.

30. Ibid., 56.

31. Ibid.

32. Ibid., 49.

33. I borrow this telling expression in this context from Joseph S. Catalano, *A Commentary on Jean-Paul Sartre's "Being and Nothingness"* (New York: Harper & Row, 1974), 85, 86. I commend this little book as a significant addition to Sartrean scholarship. For my more

extended response to this book, see my review of it in *International Philosophical Quarterly* (December 1975).

34. Sartre, *Being and Nothingness*, lxv; exact words 58, italics mine.

35. Ibid., 95.

36. Ibid., 25, cf. also 439.

37. Ibid., 78.

38. Ibid., 58.

39. Ibid., 439–440.

40. Ibid., 67.

41. Ibid., 58, italics mine. In a relevant supportive statement, Sartre says, "If I were sad or cowardly in the way in which this inkwell is an inkwell, the possibility of bad faith could not even be conceived" (Ibid., 66).

42. Ibid.

43. Sartre himself, in a statement that at this point seems problematic, says, "There exists an affinity of types of behavior in bad faith which explicitly reject this kind of explanation [by means of the unconscious] because their essence implies that they can appear only in the translucency of consciousness" (Ibid., 54).

44. Ibid., 67–70.

45. I have some difficulty with Hazel Barnes's translation of *évidence* as "certainty" (Sartre, *L'être et le néant*, 108, "si l'évidence est la possession intuitive de l'object"). Yet, given the context and Sartre's later discussion of knowledge (e.g., *Being and Nothingness*, 216–218), I accept it as adequate. Note, however, that Barnes translates the same word on the next page as "evidence"—specifically, "l'évidence non-persuasive."

46. Ibid., 67.

47. Sartre says (*L'être et le néant*, 109): "elle n'ignore pas, dit elle, que la foi est décision." I am baffled as to why Barnes translates this "it is not ignorant . . . that" instead of "it does not ignore . . . that." See *Being and Nothingness*, 68.

48. Ibid., italics for "barely" mine.

49. Ibid., 48.

50. Ibid., 68. Sartre, *L'être et le néant*, , 108.

51. Sartre, *Being and Nothingness*, 68, italics mine.

52. Ibid., 69.

53. I borrow this term from Catalano, *Commentary*, 88. I acknowledge some insights of his here.

54. Sartre, *Being and Nothingness*, 69.

55. *L'être et le néant*, 110.

56. I deliberately steer clear, here, of an extended discussion of good faith. The issue of its meaning and possibility also involves problems but is a topic for a separate chapter. I shall deal in detail with this concept in the second half of the book.

57. Sartre, *Being and Nothingness*, 68.

58. "Je ne pourrai me dissimuler que je crois pour ne pas croire et que je ne crois pas *pour* croire." Sartre, *L'être et le néant*, 110, translation mine.

59. Sartre, *Being and Nothingness*, 49.

60. Sartre, *L'être et le néant*, 111.

61. I acknowledge following Sartre closely on these pages (*Being and Nothingness*, 69–70, italics mine).

62. Ibid., 69.

63. Ibid., 78.

64. Ibid., 75.

65. Ibid., lii.

66. Ibid., 70.

67. Ibid., 67.

68. Ibid.

69. We must recall that, early in his analysis of bad faith, Sartre offers this double property as a condition for the possibility of the *métastable* concept of bad faith.

70. Ibid.

71. One may remember that this was one of Sartre's own worries about lying to oneself.

72. Ibid., 48.

73. Ibid., 67, 70.

74. Ibid., 48.

75. Sartre, *L'être et le néant*, 111, "préparation savante."

76. Sartre, *Being and Nothingness*, 49.

77. This refers, of course, to the fact that for Sartre human reality is a being which is not what it is and is what it is not; that nothingness therefore lies at the heart of human reality.

78. One must not forget that, in the early part of his treatment of bad faith, Sartre has told us that the " 'evanescence' of bad faith . . . vacillates continually between good faith and cynicism" (Ibid., 50). This perhaps suggests the importance of not *identifying* "cynicism" with the "cynical lie." Among other differences, the former is clearly the broader concept.

Chapter 3

1. Jean-Paul Sartre, *Being and Nothingness*, trans. Hazel E. Barnes (New York: Philosophical Library, 1956), 70.

2. Ibid., 67, added italics mine.

3. Ibid., 48.

4. Ibid., 68. I have reversed the order of the sentences here for emphasis. I do not believe that it has altered Sartre's meaning.

5. Ibid., 49; Jean-Paul Sartre, *L'être et le néant* (Paris: Éditions Gallimard, 1943), 88.

6. Sartre, *Being and Nothingness*, 50.

7. "L'idéal du menteur serait donc une conscience cynique, affirmant en soi la verité, la niant dans ses paroles et niant pour lui-même cette négation" (Sartre, *L'être et le néant*, 86). I realize that I part slightly but significantly from Hazel Barnes in my translation here.

8. Sartre, *Being and Nothingness*, 48.

9. Ibid. Words in square brackets have been changed from Barnes's translation.

10. Sartre, *L'être et le néant*, 86, italics mine.

11. Ibid.

12. Ibid.

13. Sartre, *Being and Nothingness*, 48.

14. Joseph S. Catalano, *A Commentary on Jean-Paul Sartre's "Being and Nothingness"* (New York: Harper & Row, 1974), 79. I express appreciation for his insights in this regard.

15. Sartre, *Being and Nothingness,* 47.

16. Ibid., 48.

17. I deal with this question, as an essential aspect of Sartre's treatment of bad faith, in the preceding chapter.

18. Sartre, *L'être et le néant,* 87.

19. Sartre, *Being and Nothingness,* 49.

20. I have tried to make this differentiation clear in the preceding chapter.

21. For my present purposes, I make no distinction between bad faith and self-deception in Sartre. Both of these expressions have been translated from *Mauvaise foi,* but we must understand that bad faith usually involves self-deception for Sartre. I prefer the more literal translation "bad faith," because—among other reasons—it allows a more faithful and consistent translation of "La Foi de la Mauvaise Foi" as "The 'Faith' of Bad Faith," rather than as "The 'Faith' of Self-Deception," in the crucial section of Sartre's analysis that goes by that title. In short, it preserves Sartre's clear emphasis and intent here.

22. Ibid., 68.

23. Ibid., 49; Sartre, *L'être et le néant,* 87.

24. See, in particular, the parts of the preceding chapter entitled "Faith, Belief, and 'Nonpersuasive' Evidence" and "A Modified Sense. . . ."

25. Ibid., 108.

26. Sartre, *Being and Nothingness,* 68.

27. Sartre, *L'être et le néant,* 109.

28. Ibid., 110.

29. Ibid., 111.

30. Ibid.

31. Sartre, *Being and Nothingness,* 69.

32. Ibid., 75.

33. Sartre, *L'être et le néant,* 108; *Being and Nothingness,* 68. Although some of the analysis here repeats references and some material that I have used in the preceding chapter, it is presented in a different context, with the quite different intent of showing the cynical aspects of the patterns or mechanism of bad faith.

34. It is important to note that the Barnes translation has omitted a whole clause from the French: "c'est à dire qui parviennent à se masquer la jouissance que leur procure l'acte sexuelle" (Sartre, *L'être et le néant*, 93). I have been baffled by this omission for the passage is importantly relevant, not redundant, to this context. But Hazel Barnes has assured me, in personal correspondence, that this represents a serious editorial error for which there has been a published correction. I gratefully accept her assurance.

35. Sartre, *Being and Nothingness*, 54.

36. Sartre, *L'être et le néant*, 93, translation mine.

37. Sartre, *Being and Nothingness*, 54. My use of this example should *not* be taken to imply my agreement with Sartre's bad-faith analysis of the "frigid woman." I use it only to show, on Sartre's own ground, the deficiency of his claims that bad faith is not cynical.

38. See Ibid., 55–56; also my discussion in the preceding chapter.

39. Ibid., 68.

40. Sartre, *L'être et le néant*, 109.

41. I shall deal in detail with this issue in subsequent chapters.

42. Ibid., 87.

43. Sartre, *Being and Nothingness*, 48.

44. Ibid., 49.

45. See preceding chapter, especially the third major section.

46. I realize, of course, that many would question my use of "resolution" or "resolve" in the context of bad faith on the grounds that these words suggest *reflection*, and bad faith is *not* reflective. I shall deal with this issue in detail in subsequent chapters.

47. Sartre, *L'être et le néant*, 86.

48. Sartre, *Being and Nothingness*, 48.

49. I use this figure in the preceding chapter.

50. I refer, of course, to Sartre's example of the coquette in the section called "The Patterns of Bad Faith," pp. 55–67.

51. Although the meaning of the word ("objet"; *L'être et le néant*, 86) is not entirely clear in this context—either in the original French or in the English translation (*Being and Nothingness*, 48)—it is sufficiently clear to say, as we have, that in the "cynical consciousness" of

the ideal lie, the "flaunted intention" also becomes an intentional object of the liar's negation.

52. Ibid.

Chapter 4

1. Jean-Paul Sartre, *Being and Nothingness*, trans. Hazel Barnes (New York: Philosophical Library, 1956), 70, italics mine.

2. I am referring to section III of Sartre's Chapter 2 on "Bad Faith." In my judgment, as I have said elsewhere, this section is the most important part of Sartre's analysis of bad faith.

3. Ibid., 69.

4. Earlier parts of my study of Sartre's analysis of bad faith include, among others, Ronald E. Santoni, "Sartre on 'Sincerity': 'Bad Faith' or Equivocation?" *The Personalist* (Spring 1972); "Bad Faith and 'Lying to Oneself,'" *Philosophy and Phenomenological Research* (March 1978); "Sartre on Sincerity: A Reconsideration," *Philosophy Today* (Summer 1985); "The Cynicism of Sartre's 'Bad Faith,' " *International Philosophical Quarterly* (March 1990), much of which—in reworked and revised form—I am incorporating into the early chapters of the present book.

5. Robert V. Stone, "Sartre on Bad Faith and Authenticity," in *The Philosophy of Jean-Paul Sartre*, ed. Paul A. Schilpp, Library of Living Philosophers Series (LaSalle: Open Court, 1981), 246–256.

6. See, especially, Joseph S. Catalano, "On the Possibility of Good Faith," *Man and World* 13 (1980): 207–228, and "Authenticity: A Sartrean Perspective," *The Philosophical Forum* 22 (Winter 1990). He read a condensed version of this paper, in a symposium with Phyllis Morris and me, at the meetings of the Society for Phenomenology and Existential Philosophy, held at Duquesne University, October 1989.

7. See, e.g., Catalano, "On the Possibility of Good Faith," 224. I plan to deal with this issue at greater length later.

8. I refer, of course, to Chapter 2 of *Being and Nothingness*. My detailed examination and reconstruction of Sartre's analysis of bad faith (or self-deception) appears in Chapter 2 of this book.

9. Sartre, *Being and Nothingness*, 58.

10. Sartre, *Being and Nothingness*, 67. I have tried to show the bases for Sartre's contention in "Sartre on 'Sincerity': 'Bad Faith'? or Equivocation?" and in "Sartre on Sincerity: A Reconsideration." For full documentation, see footnote 4 of this chapter. See also Chapter 1 of this book, in which I incorporate the arguments of both of these articles.

11. Ibid., 68, 70.

12. Ibid., 69, italics mine.

13. Ibid., 68, italics mine.

14. Jean-Paul Sartre, *L'être et le néant* (Paris: Éditions Gallimard, 1943), 109.

15. Ibid., italics mine.

16. Sartre, *Being and Nothingness*, 68.

17. Ibid.

18. Ibid., 69; Sartre, *L'être et le néant*, 109; "la foi du charbonnier" is also translatable as "implicit faith."

19. Sartre, *Being and Nothingness*, 69.

20. Ibid., 78.

21. Ibid., 67.

22. I develop these themes in greater detail in relation to *bad faith* in my earlier chapters "Bad Faith and Lying to Oneself" and "The Cynicism of Sartre's 'Bad Faith.' "

23. Sartre, *L'être et le néant*, 110, translation mine; "l'être de la conscience est d'exister par soi, donc de se faire être et par là de se surmonter."

24. Ibid., translation mine.

25. Sartre, *Being and Nothingness*, 69.

26. Catalano, "On the Possibility of Good Faith," 211.

27. Sartre, *Being and Nothingness*, 69.

28. Ibid., 70.

29. Ibid., 69.

30. Ibid., 70.

31. Ibid., 66.

32. Ibid., 69.

33. Ibid., 68.

34. Sartre, *L'être et le néant*, 110.

35. Sartre, *Being and Nothingness,* 68.

36. Ibid., 69, 70.

37. Ibid., 77.

38. Ibid., 70.

39. Catalano, "On the Possibility of Good Faith," 213.

40. Sartre, *Being and Nothingness,* 68.

41. Ibid., 67.

42. Ibid., 66, italics mine. For a detailed analysis of Sartre's treatment of sincerity, see my Chapter 1.

43. Ibid., 68.

44. Ibid., 70, italics mine.

45. Jean-Paul Sartre, *Cahiers pour une morale* (Paris: Éditions Gallimard, 1983), 42 ("La poursuite de l'Être c'est l'enfer"). See also the excellent, recently published English translation, *Notebooks for an Ethics,* trans. David Pellauer (Chicago: University of Chicago Press, 1992), 37; also 472. I am, initially, attempting deliberately to confront and reconstruct Sartre's basic concepts of bad faith, good faith, and authenticity without detailed examination of the *Cahiers (Notebooks).* Only in the last chapter will I test my analysis of these concepts in Sartre's formative writings against the details of his somewhat later and maturing contentions in the *Notebooks.* The reader is asked to note that most of this book, the present chapter included, was written prior to the publication of Pellauer's translation in late 1992.

46. Ibid., 472.

47. Catalano, "On the Possibility of Good Faith," 211.

48. This follows a suggestion of Catalano in "On the Possibility of Good Faith."

49. Sartre, *Being and Nothingness,* 68.

50. Catalano, "On the Possibility of Good Faith," 216.

51. Sartre, *Being and Nothingness,* 70.

52. Ibid., 68.

53. This may well turn out to be a variation of what Sartre in the *Notebooks* calls the "*a priori* ideal of all consciousness"; Sartre, *Notebooks,* 518. See also chapter 7 ahead.

54. Sartre, *Being and Nothingness,* 62.

55. Ibid., 70.

56. Ibid., 69.

57. Ibid., 67–68.

58. Ibid., 70.

59. Catalano, "On the Possibility of Good Faith," 212, italics mine. It is of interest to note that, in an article by Catalano published after my preparation of this chapter, Catalano reformulates this point more carefully. He says, "The characteristic of good faith is that it recognizes, either implicitly or explicitly, *that the ideal of faith is in bad faith*." "Successfully Lying to Oneself," *Philosophy and Phenomenological Research* 4 (June 1990): 686.

60. Sartre, *Being and Nothingness*, 66, 67.

61. Ibid., 90.

62. Ibid., 69.

63. Sartre uses this specific expression. See, e.g., Ibid., 68.

64. Again, this is very much in line with Catalano's suggestion and interpretation. But later in this section I shall point out more emphatically where I disagree with Catalano.

65. Catalano, "On the Possibility of Good Faith," 216; italicizing of "its" is mine. Catalano repeats many of these points in "Successfully Lying to Oneself," *Philosophy and Phenomenological Research* (June 1990): 673–693, an article to which I had access only *after* the initial writing of this chapter. His writing of the latter article was prompted—as he graciously acknowledges—by my presentation of my paper "Bad Faith and Cynicism: A Challenge to Sartre," to which he was respondent at the Eastern Division Meetings of The American Philosophical Association, December 1988.

66. For the sake of emphasis, I am adding this short quotation from Catalano's most recent article, "Successfully Lying to Oneself," 684–693. His essential contentions, in this regard, are analyzed in greater detail in his earlier "On the Possibility of Good Faith,"

67. Sartre, *Being and Nothingness*, 69.

68. Catalano, "On the Possibility of Good Faith," 217.

69. Ibid., 212.

70. Ibid., 211.

71. Sartre, *Being and Nothingness*, 90.

72. Sartre, *Notebooks for an Ethics*, 518.

73. Sartre, *Being and Nothingness*, 70.

74. Catalano, "On the Possibility of Good Faith," 216–217.

75. Sartre, *Being and Nothingness*, 70.

76. Jean-Paul Sartre, *The War Diaries*, trans. Q. Hoare (New York: Pantheon, 1984), 112.

77. Sartre, *Being and Nothingness*, 440.

78. Ibid., 620.

79. Ibid., 440.

80. Ibid., 451.

81. "L'homme authentique ne peut pas par la conversion supprimer la poursuite de l'Être car il n'y aurait plus rien," Sartre, *Cahiers pour une morale*, 42; *Notebooks for an Ethics*, 37. I shall attend later to the distinction between "good faith" and "authenticity." But, in passing, I must point out again, in part to reinforce my present contention, that on this same page of the *Cahiers*, Sartre refers to the incessant "pursuit of Being" as "hell" ("La poursuite de l'Être c'est l'enfers").

82. Sartre, *Being and Nothingness*, 626.

83. Ibid., 68.

84. Sartre, *L'être et le néant*, 108.

85. Sartre, *Being and Nothingness*, 68.

86. Ibid., 70.

87. Ibid., italics mine.

88. Ibid., 627.

89. Ibid., 483.

90. Ibid., 553.

91. Ibid., 556.

92. Ibid., 626.

93. Ibid., 580.

94. Sartre, *The War Diaries*, 307.

95. Sartre, *Being and Nothingness*, 464, italics mine.

96. Ibid., 556.

97. For an illustration of such an interpretation, see e.g., Thomas C. Anderson, *The Foundation and Structure of Sartrean Ethics* (Lawrence: The Regents Press of Kansas, 1979), 44.

98. See, e.g., "Sartre on 'Sincerity': Bad Faith? or Equivocation?"

99. I have argued this on a number of panels and symposia of The American Philosophical Association and related organizations. In this connection, it is of relevance to take note of Sartre's contention, while discussing the "spirit of seriousness," that "we are already on the *moral* plane but concurrently on that of bad faith" (Sartre, *Being and Nothingness*, 626, italics mine).

100. Catalano, "On the Possibility of Good Faith," 225. We may note, early, that Sartre makes connections between authenticity and morality in *The War Diaries*. See e.g., 94, 110–112. See also, e.g., *Being and Nothingness*, 564. It is of interest to note that Sartre refers here to the language of "authentic" and "unauthentic" [sic!] projects (Heidegger) as "tainted with an *ethical* concern" (italics mine).

Chapter 5

1. See, for example, Jean-Paul Sartre, *Being and Nothingness*, trans. Hazel Barnes (New York: Philosophical Library, 1956), 70, 80–81, 412, 531, 534.

2. Compare, e.g., footnote on ibid., 70, with 290, 531, 627.

3. E.g., ibid., 290.

4. Let it be clear, as I stated in the preceding chapter, that I am attempting to develop this concept, at the present stage, without resort to the details of *Cahiers pour une morale* (*Notebooks for an Ethics*).

5. Jean-Paul Sartre, *The War Diaries*, trans. Q. Hoare (New York: Pantheon, 1984), 51, 61–62. Originally published as *Les Carnets de la drôle de guerre: novembre 1939–mars 1940* (Paris: Éditions Gallimard, 1983). These "diaries," though published posthumously, were written by Sartre in 1939–1940, while he was a prisoner of war. I must note that as many as nine of the presumed fourteen notebooks are viewed as lost and thus unpublished. At the time of my writing, the mystery of their whereabouts continues—but with greater intensity during the tenth (1990) anniversary of Sartre's death. See, e.g., "Sartre Introuvable: À la recherche des carnets perdus," *Lire* 175 (Avril 1990): 35–44.

6. Ibid.

7. Sartre, *War Diaries*, 53–54.

8. Ibid., 110.

9. Ibid.

10. Ibid., 111.

11. Ibid.

12. Ibid., 112, italics mine.

13. Ibid., 258.

14. Ibid., 112, italics mine.

15. Ibid.

16. Ibid., 112–113. Unless otherwise noted, all quotations in this present paragraph are from *The War Diaries*, 113.

17. Sartre, *Being and Nothingness*, 553.

18. Ibid., 555.

19. Sartre, *War Diaries*, 134.

20. Ibid., 114.

21. See also ibid., 95, 96.

22. Ibid., 297.

23. Ibid., 54.

24. Ibid., 96.

25. Ibid., 94.

26. Ibid., 219.

27. Ibid., 61.

28. Ibid., 221.

29. Ibid., 219.

30. Ibid., 54.

31. Ibid., 219.

32. Ibid., 220.

33. Ibid., 221.

34. Ibid.

35. Ibid., 51.

36. Sartre, *Being and Nothingness*, 70.

37. Ibid., 412, 627.

38. Sartre, *War Diaries*, 113.

39. Sartre, *Being and Nothingness*, 412.

40. Joseph Catalano, "On the Possibility of Good Faith," *Man and World* 13 (1980): 214.

41. Sartre, *Being and Nothingness,* 440.

42. Sartre, *War Diaries,* 327.

43. Sartre, *Being and Nothingness,* 580.

44. Ibid., 627-628.

45. Ibid., 564.

46. Ibid., 531.

47. Jean-Paul Sartre, *Notebooks for an Ethics,* trans. David Pellauer (Chicago: University of Chicago Press, 1983), 4.

48. Ibid., 474.

49. Jean-Paul Sartre, *Anti-Semite and Jew* (New York: Schocken Books, 1948, First Black Cat Edition, 1962). I am assuming that Sartre wrote *Anti-Semite and Jew* in 1945–1946.

50. Ibid., 90.

51. Ibid., 60, italics mine.

52. Ibid., 32.

53. Ibid., 136.

54. Ibid., 91.

55. Ibid., 27, 53.

56. Ibid., 54.

57. Ibid., 91, 92.

58. Ibid., 106–107, 137.

59. Ibid., 109.

60. Ibid., 103, 133–134.

61. Ibid., 135.

62. Sartre, *War Diaries,* 297, 298.

63. Ibid., 128. Also Sartre, *Being and Nothingness,* 555.

64. Sartre, *Anti-Semite and Jew,* 135, italics mine.

65. Sartre, *Being and Nothingness,* 487, 488.

66. Ibid.

67. Sartre, *War Diaries,* 114; *Being and Nothingness,* 555.

68. Sartre, *War Diaries,* 134.

69. Sartre, *Anti-Semite and Jew,* 60.

70. Sartre, *War Diaries,* 297.

71. Sartre, *Being and Nothingness,* 554.

72. Sartre, *Anti-Semite and Jew,* 60.

73. Sartre, *Being and Nothingness*, 487.

74. Ibid., 524.

75. One of the best books available on this topic is Thomas Busch, *The Power of Consciousness and the Force of Circumstances in Sartre's Philosophy* (Bloomington: Indiana University Press, 1990), to which I refer here. Although it appeared after my completion of the initial draft of this book, I shall have occasion to refer to it more extensively toward the conclusion of my next chapter. See my review of Busch's book in the *Journal of the British Society of Phenomenology*, forthcoming. I am indebted to Busch here for some important insights and references on this topic.

76. Jean-Paul Sartre, "The Itinerary of a Thought," in *Between Existentialism and Marxism* (New York: Pantheon Books, 1974), 33.

77. Jean-Paul Sartre, *Sartre by Himself*, trans. Richard Seaver (New York: Urizen Books, 1978), 58.

78. Sartre, *War Diaries*, 54, italics mine.

79. Sartre, *Anti-Semite and Jew*, 60, 90.

80. See ibid., 60; *War Diaries*, 53.

81. Sartre, *Being and Nothingness*, 439.

82. Sartre, *War Diaries*, 53.

83. Jean-Paul Sartre, *Critique of Dialectical Reason*, vol. 1, trans. Alan Sheridan-Smith (London: New Left Books, 1976; Vergo, 1982). Originally published in French as *Critique de la raison dialectique* (Paris: Éditions Gallimard, 1960).

84. For a discussion of authenticity that focuses on this issue, see Joseph Catalano, "Sartre: On Action and Value," *Man and World* (1988): 417–431. See also Thomas Flynn, *Sartre and Marxist Existentialism* (Chicago: University of Chicago Press, 1984), for an excellent analysis of "collective responsibility" in Sartre. In this connection, see my feature-review of Flynn's book in *International Philosophical Quarterly* (September 1986): 183–187.

85. Sartre, *Being and Nothingness*, 489.

86. Joseph S. Catalano, "Authenticity: A Sartrean Perspective," type-script version of full paper, 16–17. See note 6, Chapter 4.

87. I develop this Sartrean distinction, which I attribute to Sartre,

in—among other places—my review-article, "Sartre and Morality: Jeanson's 'Classic' Revisited," *International Philosophical Quarterly* (September 1981): 333–342; esp. pp. 335–338. More recently, David Detmer has offered a similar distinction, using the same terms as I, in *Freedom and Value* (LaSalle: Open Court Publishing, 1987).

88. Sartre, *War Diaries*, 54.

89. Catalano, "Authenticity: A Sartrean Perspective", 32.

90. Sartre, *Being and Nothingness*, 627.

91. Sartre, *War Diaries*, 113.

92. Sartre, *Anti-Semite and Jew*, 27, 54.

93. Sartre, *War Diaries*, 112.

94. Francis Jeanson, *Sartre and the Problem of Morality*, trans. with an introduction by Robert V. Stone (Bloomington: Indiana University Press, 1980), xxxix. A more complete expression of this evaluation is as follows: "You have so perfectly followed the development of my thought that you have to pass beyond the position I had taken in my books at the moment I was passing it myself, and to raise with regard to the relation between morality and history, the universal and the concrete transcendence, the very questions I was asking myself at that same time. . . . Thus I have no hesitation in recommending your work to the public." For my detailed study of Jeanson's study, see my "Sartre and Morality: Jeanson's 'Classic' Revisited." Hereafter referred to as *Sartre*.

95. Ibid., e.g., 116, 146, 189, 192–193, 218, etc.

96. Ibid., 130, 193.

97. Ibid., 130.

98. Ibid., 209.

99. Ibid., 209, 218.

100. For my articulation of these two different senses of "freedom," see, again, my "Sartre and Morality: Jeanson's 'Classic' Revisited." See note 87.

101. Sartre, *War Diaries*, 112.

102. Jeanson, *Sartre*, 209.

103. Ibid., 194, 198, italics mine.

104. Ibid., 208.

105. Ibid., 219, italics mine.

106. Ibid., 221.

107. Ibid., 218.

108. Ibid., 208–209.

109. Ibid., 201.

110. Ibid., 218.

111. Sartre, *War Diaries*, 221.

112. Sartre, *Being and Nothingness*, 70, 412. In subsequent chapters, I shall try to show, however briefly, that this analysis is also consistent with Sartre's views on the topic in *Notebooks for an Ethics*.

113. It seems clear from the context (see *Being and Nothingness*, 70 n. 9) that the corruption referred to is, for Sartre, bad faith.

114. Jeanson, *Sartre*, 135.

115. I introduce my reservations about Jeanson's attribution of "bad faith" to "factual freedom" in "Sartre and Morality: Jeanson's 'Classic' Revisited." See, again, note 87.

116. Jeanson, *Sartre*, 219.

117. Ibid., 208, 209.

Chapter 6

1. Among other places, see, for example, Joseph Catalano, "On the Possibility of Good Faith," *Man and World* 13 (1980): 212ff, 222, 224, etc. In this regard I am not persuaded that Sartre himself is completely consistent in his use of these terms. In *Anti-Semite and Jew*, in "Existentialism Is a Humanism," and in his conclusion to *Being and Nothingness*, he sometimes appears to use the two terms interchangeably, in violation of his own more technical analyses. And, since the writing of this chapter I have found evidence of this conflation also in *Notebooks for an Ethics* and *Truth and Existence*, which I shall illustrate later.

2. Jean-Paul Sartre, *Being and Nothingness*, trans. Hazel Barnes (New York: Philosophical Library, 1956), 70.

3. Ibid., 70, 412. This point gains considerable support from *Cahiers pour une morale*, written in 1947 but only published (posthumously) in 1983, where Sartre gives much attention to the importance of "conversion" for authenticity. In the preceding chapters, I have de-

liberately chosen not to focus on these *Notebooks*. But now, after the completion of Chapter 6, I intend, in this connection, to do an intensive study of the *Notebooks* in my final chapter.

4. Sartre, *Being and Nothingness*, 70.

5. Ibid., 556.

6. Ibid., 68.

7. Ibid., 70, 412. It must be pointed out—both for the sake of fairness and to anticipate what is to come—that Sartre later refers to our "natural attitude" also as both "inauthenticity" and "alienation" rather than "bad faith." See, e.g., Jean-Paul Sartre, *Notebooks for an Ethics*, trans. David Pellauer (Chicago: University of Chicago Press, 1992), 6: "One begins with flight and inauthenticity"; or 470: "The meaning of conversion: rejection of alienation." Sartre's occasional misuse, or at least inconsistent use, of key terms makes efforts at analytic differentiation all the more difficult and baffling. I deal with this in greater detail in my subsequent chapter.

8. In this regard, it is of interest to note that my general point is confirmed by Sartre's contentions in *Cahiers pour une morale* (Paris: Éditions Gallimard, 1983). Consider, e.g., "the fact, even, that *Being and Nothingness* is a pre-conversion ontology supposes that a conversion is necessary, and, as a consequence, that there is a natural attitude" (13, translation mine). After the initial completion of the present chapter, I may now add that, in his 1992 translation of the *Notebooks for an Ethics*, Pellauer translates this in the following way: "The very fact that *Being and Nothingness* is an ontology before conversion takes for granted that a conversion is necessary and that, as a consequence, there is a natural attitude" (6). In this general regard, it is of interest to note Simone de Beauvoir's confirming point that "*Being and Nothingness* is in large part a description of the serious man and his universe," *The Ethics of Ambiguity* (Secaucus: Citadel Press, 1948), 46. I again acknowledge that I have attempted thus far to develop Sartre's concepts of good faith, bad faith, and authenticity from the early Sartre without a detailed examination of his posthumously published *Cahiers pour une morale (Notebooks for an Ethics)*.

9. Sartre, *Cahiers*, 492.

10. Ibid.

11. Sartre, *Being and Nothingness*, 163.

12. Ibid.

13. I borrow from Catalano's articulation of his own point here.

14. Ibid., 443.

15. Catalano, "On the Possibility of Good Faith," 220.

16. Sartre, *Being and Nothingness*, 443, 444.

17. Ibid., 474.

18. Ibid., 473.

19. Ibid., 471.

20. See, e.g., Catalano, "On the Possibility of Good Faith," 218, 225; "Authenticity: A Sartrean Perspective," unpublished manuscript, 13. Since initially writing the present chapter, I have discovered that this piece has appeared in *The Philosophical Forum* 22 (Winter 1990). But all references here are to the original prepublished manuscript.

21. Catalano feels that he is drawing out, perhaps more sharply than Sartre, the distinction Sartre is making in *Being and Nothingness*, 150–170, in particular. See his "Authenticity: A Sartrean Perspective," and note his n. 4.

22. Jean-Paul Sartre, *The Transcendence of the Ego* (New York: Noonday Press, 1957), 44–45.

23. I am indebted, for this point, to Phyllis Sutton Morris, who offers her customarily careful (though in this case, incomplete) outline of the structures of consciousness for Sartre in, e.g., "Sartre on the Self-Deceiver's Translucent Consciousness," *The Journal of the British Society for Phenomenology* 23, no. 2 (May 1992): 107–110 especially.

24. Sartre, *Being and Nothingness*, li.

25. Ibid., liii.

26. Ibid., 47–70.

27. Ibid., 49, italics mine.

28. Ibid.

29. Ibid., 471.

30. Ibid., 451.

31. Ibid.

32. Ibid., 471.

33. Ibid.

34. Catalano, "Authenticity," 7. See 6–7 for Catalano's summary of the types of consciousness in Sartre.

35. Sartre, *Being and Nothingness*, 150.

36. Ibid., 154, italics mine.

37. Ibid., 160; *L'être et le néant*, 207, translation mine. "La signification de la réflexion est donc son être-pour. En particulier, le réflexif est le réfléchi se néantisant *pour* se récupérer."

38. Sartre, *Being and Nothingness*, 154.

39. Translation mine. David Pellauer, in his translation of *Cahiers*, which appeared after my writing of this chapter, offers a slightly different rendition: "The origin of reflection is an effort by the For-itself to recuperate itself in order to arrive at a For-itself that would be Itself," 5. This point is virtually repeated on p. 472, although here he uses "regain" instead of "recuperate."

40. Ibid., 451, italics mine.

41. Ibid., 475, italics mine.

42. Ibid., 471.

43. Ibid., 472.

44. Ibid., 473.

45. Ibid., italics mine.

46. Ibid., italics mine.

47. Ibid., 474.

48. Ibid., 475.

49. Ibid., 459.

50. Ibid., 472.

51. Except when I have indicated otherwise, I have taken the quotations in this paragraph from Catalano, "On the Possibility," 220, 221, and, more recently, from Catalano, "Successfully Lying to Oneself," *Philosophy and Phenomenological Research*, vol. L, no. 4, June 1990, 689.

52. Sartre, *Being and Nothingness*, 451.

53. Ibid., 476.

54. Ibid., 475, italics mine.

55. Ibid., 474.

56. E.g., ibid., 70, 412.

57. Ibid., 464.

58. Ibid., italics mine.

59. Ibid., 451.

60. Sartre, *Transcendence*, 44.

61. See, e.g., Sartre, *Being and Nothingness*, 480, for Sartre's identification of "fundamental project" with one's "total being-in-the-world."

62. After the completion of this chapter, I recognize that Sartre, in *Notebooks for an Ethics*, has sometimes referred to "pure reflection" as "good faith" (e.g., 12). But I believe that Sartre has misspoken here. I shall give detailed attention to these *Notebooks*—as they concern my present argument—in my subsequent, culminating chapter.

63. Sartre, *Being and Nothingness*, 460.

64. Sartre, *Cahiers*, 42.

65. This view of authenticity as recognizing and living consistently with the freedom and responsibility to which one is abandoned comes close to being the view he attributes to "good faith" in "Existentialism Is a Humanism," in *Existentialism from Dostoevsky to Sartre*, expanded edition, ed. W. Kaufmann (New York: New American Library, 1975), 366. This again shows a tendency, even on the part of Sartre, to conflate authenticity and good faith.

66. Sartre, *Being and Nothingness*, e.g., 70 n., 412 n.

67. Ibid., 49.

68. Ibid., 479.

69. Sartre, as I intend to show in greater detail later, repeats that theme and language in *Notebooks for an Ethics*. See, e.g., 473–474, 478–480.

70. Sartre, *Being and Nothingness*, 70.

71. Francis Jeanson, *Sartre and the Problem of Morality*, trans. Robert V. Stone (Bloomington: Indiana University Press, 1980, e.g., 191); also Jean-Paul Sartre, *The War Diaries*, trans. Q. Hoare (New York: Pantheon, 1984), 113.

72. Sartre, *Being and Nothingness*, 290.

73. In the Pellauer translation of *Notebooks for an Ethics*, the word *regain* is used instead of *recover* (472).

74. Sartre, *Cahiers*, 489.

75. Ibid., 490.

76. Ibid.

77. Sartre, *Being and Nothingness*, 471.

78. E.g., ibid., 49.

79. For some writers, self-deception is—as I've mentioned earlier—the preferred interpretation of *mauvaise foi* in Sartre. See, for example, Walter Kaufman's translation of Sartre's "Bad Faith" in *Existentialism from Dostoevsky to Sartre*, 299–328. The *minimum* I should wish to contend is that bad faith frequently takes the form of self-deception.

80. Sartre, *Being and Nothingness*, 55–67.

81. E.g., ibid., 54–57.

82. See, in particular, Ronald E. Santoni, "Bad Faith and 'Lying to Oneself' " and "The Cynicism of Sartre's 'Bad Faith.' " In revised form, they now constitute the substance of two earlier chapters in the present book.

83. In this regard, it is of interest to note that, in his latest article on bad faith, "Successfully Lying to Oneself: A Sartrean Perspective," Joseph Catalano, while contending that "there is a practical identity of bad faith with self-deception," suggests the possibility "that some forms of bad faith are not self-deceptions" (674). And, in a footnote in this article, as well as elsewhere, he maintains that self-deception represents a "strong," not a "weak," general sense of bad faith (686, n. 12).

84. Sartre, *L'être et le néant*, 108.

85. In "The Cynicism of Sartre's 'Bad Faith,' " (see preceding Chapter 3), I try to offer a detailed account of how bad faith in Sartre is *cynical* both in the ordinary usage sense and in Sartre's idiosyncratic sense of "cynical."

86. Sartre, *L'être et le néant*, 111.

87. Sartre, *Being and Nothingness*, 49, italics mine.

88. Ibid., 68.

89. Sartre, *L'être et le néant*, 109.

90. When, in the next chapter, I test my claims against Sartre's con-

tentions in *Notebooks for an Ethics*, I shall make this point more strongly.

91. Sartre, *Being and Nothingness*, 471.

92. Sartre, *L'être et le néant*, 550.

93. Catalano, "Successfully Lying to Oneself," 680; see also 689. Catalano's points may certainly be corroborated by an appeal to Sartre's text; see, e.g., *Being and Nothingness*, 67.

94. Sartre, *Cahiers*, 490, translation mine. In the English edition, Pellauer translates it "a new 'authentic' way of being oneself and for oneself" (*Notebooks for an Ethics*, 474).

95. Sartre, *Being and Nothingness*, e.g., 412; 70, 627.

96. Ibid., 531.

97. Ibid., 564.

98. Ibid., 464.

99. Sartre, *War Diaries*, 113.

100. Sartre, *Being and Nothingness*, 626, italics mine.

101. Ibid.

102. Quotations and other ideas in this paragraph come from Catalano, "On the Possibility of Good Faith," 225. See also, e.g., Catalano, "Authenticity: A Sartrean Perspective", 14.

103. Sartre, *Being and Nothingness*, 553.

104. See my "feature-review" of Thomas Flynn's *Sartre and Marxist Existentialism*, in which I elaborate on these "imputability" and "accountability" senses of "responsibility," pp. 185–187, especially.

105. This distinction resembles Jeanson's distinction between "factual freedom" and "freedom as valued," and my own distinction between ontological freedom and existential or practical freedom in Sartre (see note 87 in the preceding chapter).

106. Catalano, "Authenticity," 14.

107. Catalano, "On the Possibility of Good Faith," 225.

108. Sartre, *War Diaries*, 113, 114, 327; *L'être et le néant*, 295.

109. Sartre, *Being and Nothingness*, 553.

110. Sartre, *War Diaries*, 95.

111. Ibid., 114.

112. I acknowledge that, in *Anti-Semite and Jew*, for instance, when

referring to the "inauthentic Jew," Sartre suggests that inauthenticity implies "no moral blame" (93). But, as I have pointed out in an earlier part of my study, this qualification is rooted in the "bad-faith" situation in which the anti-Semite has placed the Jew.

113. Sartre, "Existentialism," 364–365.

114. In addition to the above examples (Sartre in *Being and Nothingness* and *Anti-Semite and Jew* and Catalano in the cited article), I submit that Linda Bell, in a recent book entitled *The Ethics of Authenticity* (Tuscaloosa: University of Alabama Press, 1989), shows this same kind of inconsistency. And, at times, in my judgment, she confounds the terms *inauthenticity, bad faith,* and *alienation* (see e.g., 45). Part of the problem relates to Sartre's own discussion in *Cahiers* (see, e.g., 486, 487) and to what I have already pointed out in footnote 7: a confused use of terms on, e.g., *Notebooks,* 6, 468, 470, 559. In this connection, it is of interest to note that, whereas in *Being and Nothingness* Sartre views "bad faith" as "original sin," in the *Notebooks for an Ethics* he refers to "alienation as original sin" (471). In spite of my questions about Bell's interpretations, I commend her book to the attention of readers.

115. Sartre, *Being and Nothingness,* 626.

116. I remind the reader again that I develop this point in detail in my earlier chapter "The Cynicism of Sartre's 'Bad Faith.'" See earlier footnote references to it for details.

117. Sartre, *L'être et le néant,* 111.

118. Sartre, *Anti-Semite and Jew,* 99.

119. As I shall doubtless show in my next chapter, even in the first pages of the *Notebooks for an Ethics,* Sartre makes links between bad faith and morality.

120. Jeanson, *Sartre,* 209.

121. Sartre, *War Diaries,* 94, italics mine.

122. Jean-Paul Sartre, *The Transcendence of the Ego,* trans. Forrest Williams and R. Kirkpatrick (New York: Noonday Press, 1957).

123. Thomas W. Busch, *The Power of Consciousness and the Force of Circumstances in Sartre's Philosophy* (Bloomington: Indiana University Press, 1990). Hereafter referred to as Busch, *Power of Consciousness.*

124. Sartre, *Transcendence*, 98.

125. Ibid., 82.

126. Ibid., 98, 99.

127. Ibid., 100–102.

128. Ibid., 81, italics mine.

129. Busch, *Power of Consciousness*, 30, italics mine.

130. Sartre, *Transcendence*, 102.

131. Ibid., 101, italics mine.

132. Ibid.

133. Busch, *Power of Consciousness*, 10–11. I express my gratitude to Thomas Busch whose book has provided me with important clues to some of my interconnective points here. In particular, I acknowledge the influence of the first 40 pages of Busch's book, especially 8–11, 15–17, 32–33. I consider it a felicitous coincidence that I came upon Busch's book for review just as I was bringing the first, more skeletal, draft of the present manuscript to a conclusion. The reader may also note that David Detmer, in a well-received work entitled *Freedom as Value* (1986), also makes the identification between the "purifying reflection" of *The Transcendence of the Ego* and Husserl's "phenomenological reduction" (120, e.g.).

134. Sartre actually refers to this process as an instance of "epoché" in *The Transcendence of the Ego*, 103. In my study of *Notebooks for an Ethics*, in preparation for writing the next chapter, I have found that Sartre again makes this specific connection between "pure reflection," "natural attitude," and the epoché (357–360).

135. Busch, *Power of Consciousness*.

136. Ibid., 11.

137. Sartre, *Being and Nothingness*, 412.

138. Sartre, *Transcendence*, 106, italics mine.

139. Busch, *Power of Consciousness*, 14, 16, 17, e.g.

140. Busch quotes this, on p. 15, as coming from "Phenomenology as a Rigorous Science," in *Phenomenology and the Crisis of Philosophy*, ed. Q. Lauer (New York: Harper, 1965), 78.

141. These quoted words are taken from Husserl, *The Crisis of European Sciences and Transcendental Phenomenology*, trans. David Carr

(Evanston: Northwestern University Press, 1970), 137, and cited by Busch, *Power of Consciousness*, 16.

142. Sartre, *War Diaries*, 113.

143. Busch, *Power of Consciousness*, 16.

144. Sartre, *War Diaries*, 113.

145. Sartre, *Notebooks*, 475.

146. Sartre, *Cahiers*, 492.

147. Sartre, *Being and Nothingness*, 556.

148. Sartre, *Cahiers*, 13. One may recall my having pointed out that Sartre here refers to *Being and Nothingness* as "une ontologie d'avant la conversion," "an ontology before conversion." See also Pellauer translation, *Notebooks*, 6.

149. Ibid., 474.

150. Sartre, *War Diaries*.

151. Sartre, *Notebooks*, 480; *Cahiers*, 497.

Chapter 7

1. Jean-Paul Sartre, *Cahiers pour une morale* (Paris: Éditions Gallimard, 1983); *Notebooks for an Ethics*, trans. David Pellauer (Chicago: University of Chicago Press, 1992).

2. It is important for the reader to recognize that the English translation of Sartre's posthumously published work appeared only in late 1992, *after* I had completed the initial versions of all of the preceding chapters of the present work.

3. See, e.g., Pellauer's Introduction to his excellent translation of *Notebooks for an Ethics*, vii–x.

4. Sartre, *Notebooks*, xix.

5. Sartre also referred to this type of ethics, which he later disparaged as "writer's ethics," as "idealist ethics." See Ronald Aronson, "Introduction," in *Truth and Existence*, trans. Adrian van den Hoven (Chicago: London: University of Chicago Press, 1992), xxxii, and M. Contat and M. Rybalka, *The Writing of Jean-Paul Sartre* (Evanston: Northwestern University Press, 1974), 228–229. In the former work, Sartre also uses the word "abstract" to characterize this approach (see, e.g., 58). But I must point out that, even in the *Notebooks*, Sartre says clearly

that "there is no abstract ethics"; that "there is only an ethics in a situation and therefore it is concrete"; and "ethics is therefore disinterested when it is abstract" (*Notebooks*, 17). Late in the *Notebooks* he also indicates that "in attaining myself through conversion, I have refused the abstract in order to will the concrete" (507).

6. Sartre, *Notebooks*; see note 1 of this chapter.

7. The most sustained discussion by Sartre of the "unveiling" of truth and Being is to be found in another posthumously published work, *Verité et Existence* (Paris: Éditions Gallimard, 1989), a work written concurrently with, or just after, the *Cahiers*. Translated by Adrian van den Hoven and edited (with introduction) by Ronald Aronson, it has been published recently (1992) by the University of Chicago Press. More than any other of Sartre's writings, it shows the influence of Heidegger's thinking on Sartre in respect to this matter of "unveiling" Being and truth. In particular, Heidegger's notion of "letting Being be" is echoed here. See *Truth and Existence*, e.g., 4, 30, 61. It is likely that Sartre had Heidegger's *On the Essence of Truth* in mind while writing this work and that Sartre is here responding to it.

8. Sartre, *Notebooks*, 6. It is important to note, for reasons we have already discussed, that Sartre has either misspoken here or has (erroneously) identified inauthenticity with bad faith. I shall discuss this matter further at a later time.

9. Ibid.

10. Ibid., 37.

11. Ibid., 11, italics mine. My italics are intended to emphasize some key aspects of my past attribution to Sartre.

12. Ibid., italics mine. The reader will recognize that, in the preceding chapter, I already invoked Sartre's contention that "the origin of reflection is an effort by the For-itself to recuperate itself in order to arrive at a for-itself that would be itself" (ibid., 5).

13. Ibid., 12. In the light of what I have contended in the last three chapters, it is again questionable whether Sartre has spoken correctly here. "Authenticity" would seem to fit this more consistently than good faith.

14. Ibid.

15. Ibid., 10.

16. Sartre, *Cahiers*, 17.

17. Sartre, *Notebooks*, 5, italics mine.

18. Ibid. Italicizing here of *ethical* and *moral* is mine.

19. Ibid., 479.

20. Ibid., 474–475.

21. Ibid., 478, italics mine.

22. Ibid., 481.

23. Ibid., 482.

24. This self-assumption or self-affirmation, as a necessary condition for authenticity, appears also in Heidegger, but, as I shall try to show briefly later, the self-affirmation in Heidegger is of one's "guilt" and "mortality."

25. Ibid., 479.

26. Ibid., 493–494.

27. Ibid., 508.

28. Although "illuminating" or "illumination" is used in the *Notebooks*, Sartre uses it with greater frequency in *Truth and Existence*, 12, 18, 20.

29. Arlette Elkaïm Sartre confirms this in her edited publication of *Truth and Existence*, 84 n. 6. And in his introduction to this English publication, Ronald Aronson makes the same claim (xxv ff.).

30. Ibid., 16.

31. Ibid., 60.

32. Ibid., 17.

33. Ibid., 16.

34. Ibid., 13.

35. Ibid., 17.

36. Sartre, *Notebooks*, 474. As I have pointed out above, Sartre here says that authenticity consists in "unveiling being through the mode of nonbeing."

37. Sartre, *Truth and Existence*, 20.

38. Ibid., 18.

39. Ibid., 13.

40. Ibid., 18.

41. Ibid., 14.

42. Ibid., 15, 16.

43. Sartre, *Notebooks*, 485.

44. Sartre, *Truth and Existence*, 16.

45. Sartre, *Being and Nothingness*.

46. Sartre, *Truth and Existence*, 16.

47. In this regard, it is of interest to note that Joseph Fell, in *Heidegger and Sartre* (New York: Columbia University Press, 1979), 168, sees Heidegger's "turn" in relationship to Sartre as consisting in " 'seeing' through nothing to Being, in comprehending nothing as 'the veil of Being.' "

48. Sartre, *Notebooks*, 482.

49. Ibid., 515.

50. Ibid., 482–483.

51. Ibid., 100.

52. Ibid., 483.

53. Sartre, *Cahiers*, 499.

54. Sartre, *Notebooks*, 441.

55. Ibid., 484.

56. Ibid.

57. Ibid., 535.

58. Ibid., 478, 484, 495.

59. Ibid., 484, 495–496.

60. Ibid., 498.

61. Ibid., 484.

62. Ibid., 485, 486.

63. Ibid., 480, 514.

64. Ibid., 514–515.

65. Ibid., 521.

66. Ibid., 520–521.

67. Ibid., 535.

68. Ibid., 528.

69. Ibid., 474. As I have noted earlier, Sartre appears at times in the *Notebook* to use *bad faith* and *inauthenticity* interchangeably. (See also note 8.) For reasons I have already offered, which subsequent discus-

sion will confirm, I believe that this is a careless and misleading confusion in Sartre's own terms. I shall deal explicitly with this issue in the concluding part of this chapter.

70. Ibid., 533.

71. Ibid., 499.

72. Ibid., 507.

73. Ibid., 482.

74. Ibid., 478–479.

75. Ibid., 478–479, 484, 559.

76. Ibid., 518.

77. Ibid., 11, 5; Sartre, *Truth and Existence*, 83. In this regard, Arlette Elkaïm-Sartre helps to make my point in her first expansive note on *Truth and Existence* (83).

78. Sartre, *Notebooks*, 559.

79. Ibid., 359.

80. Ibid., 472, 559, 11.

81. Ibid., 473.

82. Ibid., 12. One has reason to pause (again) when one notes this contention by Sartre. Here is another instance in which Sartre appears to allow bad faith to be reflective. If my above analysis holds, I suspect that Sartre has misspoken here. I shall have considerably more to say about this later in the chapter.

83. Ibid., 473. Again, this has a ring to it of Heidegger's essential self calling herself home again: authenticity's call or conscience's call for Dasein to come back to itself.

84. Sartre, *Truth and Existence*, 83.

85. Sartre, *Notebooks*, 350.

86. Ibid., 4.

87. Ibid., 492.

88. Ibid., 473, 559–560; Sartre, *Truth and Existence*, 83.

89. Sartre, *Notebooks*, 479; Sartre, *Truth and Existence*, 83.

90. Sartre, *Being and Nothingness*, 443, 451.

91. Sartre, *Notebooks*, 479.

92. Ibid., 477. Although I am going along with this translation, I believe that Pellauer is here taking liberties in his translation of the

following: "l'authenticité verra plutôt la volonté comme une mise en question au coeur de l'existant que comme cette lame rigide qu'on se plaît à définir" (*Cahiers*, 494).

93. Ibid., 496.

94. Sartre, *Notebooks*, 479–480.

95. Sartre, *Cahiers*, 496.

96. Sartre, *Notebooks*, 479.

97. Sartre, *Cahiers*, 496; Sartre, *Notebooks*, 480.

98. Sartre, *Notebooks*, 480.

99. Ibid., 480–481; Sartre, *Cahiers*, 496–497.

100. Sartre, *Notebooks*, 481–482; "non en tant que soutenant le Pour-soi, mais en tant que soutenant par lui" (Sartre, *Cahiers*, 499).

101. Sartre, *Notebooks*, 478.

102. Ibid., 473.

103. Ibid., 37, 472.

104. Jean-Paul Sartre, *The War Diaries*, trans. Q. Hoare (New York: Pantheon, 1984), 112.

105. Sartre, *Notebooks*, 12.

106. Ibid., 470.

107. Ibid., 470ff.

108. Ibid., 478–479.

109. Ibid., 472.

110. Ibid., 471.

111. Karsten Harries, "Authenticity, Poetry, God," unpublished typescript, 1994, 8; forthcoming in a *Festschrift* in honor of William J. Richardson, S.J. I express gratitude to Harries for making this article available to me before publication and at the time of my revising this chapter. And I express thanks for the insights into Heidegger which he has shared with me over the years. I am also indebted to him for prodding me to reexamine Sartre in the light of some of Heidegger's relevant contentions.

112. Sartre, *Notebooks*, 479.

113. Ibid., 482.

114. Assuming the correctness of Karsten Harries's interpretation of Heidegger, one may infer that Heidegger does not share Sartre's em-

phasis on the "non-appropriativeness" of the authentic attitude. Harries not only characterizes Heidegger's "understanding of authenticity" as "self-possession" but also refers to Heidegger's authenticity as, for example, "appropriating our mortality," "appropriating our own being," "appropriating ourselves as we are," and as a "resolute appropriation and affirmation of our essential mortality" (Harries, "Authenticity, Poetry, God," 23; 9, 7, 8.

115. Sartre, *Notebooks*, 12.

116. Ibid., 10.

117. Ibid., 508.

118. Ibid., 559–560.

119. Jean-Paul Sartre, *Being and Nothingness*, trans. Hazel Barnes (New York: Philosophical Library, 1956), 464.

120. Sartre, *Notebooks*, 474.

121. E.g., Sartre, *Being and Nothingness*, 70, 412, 627; *Notebooks*, 491, 559.

122. Harries, "Authenticity, Poetry, God," 13.

123. Ibid., 10, 13.

124. Ibid., 12. In a new, justifiably spirited book, *Demythologizing Heidegger*, which radically challenges and "disrupts" Heidegger's "myth of Being" with the "myth of justice," John Caputo says, similarly, that for Heidegger "the very Being of Dasein is to live under this guilt/ responsibility," and quotes Heidegger's claim that the "task for Dasein" is to "*be* guilty *authentically*—'guilty' in the way that it is" (from *Being and Time*, trans. Edward Robinson and John MacQuarrie (New York: Harper and Row, 1962), 333; *Gesamtausgabe*, in Martin Heidegger, *Sein und Zeit* (Frankfurt: Klosterman, 1977), 381. The opposite of guilt (*schuldig*) in *Being and Time*, he adds, "is the unbearable lightness of irresponsibility, unshouldered Being" (*un-schuldig*), flight from responsibility. Resoluteness "meets death face to face." This "anticipation of death," by "burning out the impurities of everydayness and the 'they,' " strips "Dasein down to ownmost essence, its essential *haecceitas* [its singular essence]"; *Demythologizing Heidegger* (Bloomington and Indianapolis: Indiana University Press, 1993), 3, 76, 77, 78, 79, respectively. In my judgment, Caputo's book is "must" reading for all

students and scholars of Heidegger. While demythologizing Heidegger, it presents "another Heidegger, a Heidegger against Heidegger" (ibid., 92). It challenges Heidegger exactly where he needs to be challenged: on the relationship (in his philosophy) of Being and the "call of conscience" to moral action and to the "call of the [suffering of] others."

Listen, for a moment, to Caputo's dramatic challenge: "On my demythologized reading, there is no other voice: there is nothing to hear. One hears only the echo of the shifting, withdrawing ground.... There is only 'there is' and ... the confession of the multiple senses of Being" (ibid., 98). "The mythical call of Being [in Heidegger] drowns out the 'call of the other,' " he adds.

For Sartre—especially in his later works—the "call" is much clearer, though many would question the grounds for that call, especially given his approach in *Being and Nothingness*. Harries, for example, feels that the grounding for responsibility to others is lacking in *both* Sartre and Heidegger. Harries and Caputo—in spite of their differences—appear joined in the view that the "call of conscience"— especially as formulated in *Being and Time*—"gives no specific ontic directions" (Caputo, *Demythologizing Heidegger*, 99, 76; see also Harries, "Authenticity," e.g., 13–14). As Caputo puts it, "passing under the eyes of death" may give "resoluteness its urgency" (p. 80), but it does not afford direction or criteria as to what is "appropriately" (Harries) responsible action. Caputo and Harries seem to share in the question: How can we respond and be responsible if we do not know what to do? (Caputo, *Demythologizing Heidegger*, 76; also 80; Harries, "Authenticity," 14). That is the challenge often posed to Sartre also.

125. This quotation is taken from a much longer passage in Martin Heidegger, *Sein und Zeit*, 7th Ed., (Tubingen: Niemeyer, 1953), p. 305. Trans. J. McQuarrie and E. Robinson, *Being and Time* (New York: Harper and Row, 1962), 305. Quoted by Harries, ibid., 12. I also owe the suggested connection between Sartre and Kierkegaard here to Harries's suggestion of a similar connection between Heidegger and Kierkegaard—specifically, between Kierkegaard's "purity of heart" and Heidegger's "willing one's guilty self."

126. Ibid., 13.

127. Ibid., 31.

128. Sartre, *Notebooks*, 507, italics mine.

129. See, for example, Jean-Paul Sartre, "Existentialism Is a Humanism," in *Existentialism from Dostoevsky to Sartre*, expanded edition, ed. W. Kaufmann (New York: New American Library, 1975), 365–366: "I declare that freedom, *in respect of concrete circumstances*, can have no other end and aim but itself" (italics mine).

130. Sartre, *Notebooks*, 497.

131. Francis Jeanson, *Sartre and the Problem of Morality* trans. Robert V. Stone (Bloomington: Indiana University Press, 1980), 218.

132. Sartre, *Notebooks*, 474.

133. See, again, Sartre, *Being and Nothingness*, 70, 412.

134. Sartre, *Notebooks*, 37, 473.

135. Ibid., 473.

136. Ibid., 9, italics mine.

137. Fell, *Heidegger and Sartre*, 152.

138. Sartre, *Notebooks*, 476–477.

139. Ibid., 477.

140. Ibid., 506.

141. I acknowledge the influence here of Fell's analysis of Sartre's position in *Being and Nothingness*; see, e.g., Fell, *Heidegger and Sartre*, 140–151.

142. Sartre, *Notebooks*, 559–560.

143. I must note here, in advance of additional evidence, that the last line in Sartre's uncompleted Appendix 1 of the *Notebooks* contains the following similar reference: "This is why, although it would be much more advantageous to live on a plane of freedom that takes itself for its end, most people have a difficulty" (560). But one should remember that this appendix was most likely written two years *before* the main body of the *Notebooks* and just two years *after* the completion of *Being and Nothingness*.

144. Ibid., 471.

145. Simone de Beauvoir, *The Ethics of Ambiguity*, trans. B. Frechtman (Secaucus: The Citadel Press, © Philosophical Library, 1948), 44.

146. Sartre, *Notebooks*, 5.

147. Later, on the same page, he speaks, as I have shown, of pure reflection as *emerging* from impure reflection.

148. Ibid.

149. Ibid., 17, 33.

150. Ibid., 9, 89, italics mine.

151. Ibid., 9.

152. Ibid., 486.

153. In a book that just came to my attention after my writing and second revision of this chapter (March 1994), Thomas C. Anderson addresses the issue of why, for Sartre, I *ought* to accept and affirm human freedom as my primary and highest value. His interpretation, though in line with mine, gives more detailed attention to this important issue. Though I shall here quote only a summary of his position, I recommend his discussion of both this issue and the question of why one ought, also, to will the freedom of others. Here is his summary statement regarding the former: "Sartre argues that, since human freedom alone can supply an absolute foundation and thus a full-fledged justification for its own and everything else's being, the logical thing for humans to do is to choose to accept their freedom and to confer value and meaning on it," Thomas C. Anderson, *Sartre's Two Ethics* (Chicago and LaSalle: Open Court, 1993), 61. See also the subsection, "Reasons for Willing the Freedom of Others," ibid., 68–77. The latter, too, is in line with my interpretation but—with justification—gives more consideration to the meaning of Sartre's appeal to "consistency." It merits close examination, as does Anderson's book in general.

154. Sartre, *Notebooks*, 486.

155. Ibid., 359.

156. Ibid., 482.

157. Ibid., 359, 360.

158. See, e.g., ibid., 358, 89, and the concluding part of my preceding chapter.

159. Ibid., 493.

160. Ibid., 485.

161. Ibid., 515.

162. Ibid., 482.

163. Sartre, *War Diaries*, 95–96, 113.

164. Ibid., 113.

165. Sartre, *Notebooks*, e.g., 12, 470.

166. Thomas Flynn, *Sartre and Marxist Existentialism* (Chicago: University of Chicago Press, 1984). I allude to his reference to "existential consistency." I hope to say more later about this matter of consistency in Sartre. But, for the time being, although I wish to acknowledge that Tom Flynn's notion of existential consistency appears to give greater content to Sartre's claim to make freedom (one's own and the freedom of others) one's primary value, I must point out that the concept of existential consistency presupposes *logical* consistency as well as (to sound like Thomas Anderson) a prior commitment to the latter as a value (Anderson, *Sartre's Two Ethics*, 64). Though important, this concept and distinction are in need of further exploration and clarification.

167. It is of interest to note that Thomas Anderson, in his recently published book (1993), already cited, raises important questions about this line of argument. "This conclusion," he says, "can result only if there is a necessary connection between my proposing that each person's freedom should be *his* or *her* supreme value, and my choosing his or her freedom as a value for *me*" (Anderson, *Sartre's Two Ethics*, 70). His examination of the bases for making this connection deserves the reader's consideration.

168. Sartre, *Notebooks*, 506.

169. Jean-Paul Sartre, "Existentialism Is a Humanism," 366, italics mine.

170. Sartre, *Notebooks*, e.g., 10, 170, 500.

171. Ibid., 290.

172. Sartre, "Existentialism Is a Humanism," 366, italics and resetting mine.

173. Sartre, *Notebooks*, 88–89, italics mine.

174. Ibid., 161.

175. E.g., ibid., 277–280. See my discussion of this specific topic in Ronald E. Santoni "On the Existential Meaning of Violence," *Dialogue and Humanism* 4 (1993): 139–150.

176. Sartre, *Notebooks,* ix.

177. Ibid., xx.

178. Ibid., xiii. Simone de Beauvoir also takes up these issues in *The Ethics of Ambiguity* (Secaucus, N.J.: Citadel Press, 1948), 15–18ff.

179. Sartre, *Being and Nothingness,* 625.

180. Sartre, *Notebooks,* 103.

181. Ibid., 103.

182. Ibid., 89, italics mine.

183. Ibid., 103.

184. See Harries, "Authenticity," 13–14. The words quoted and claims to which I'm responding are in this article. Harries argues that for Sartre—as for Heidegger in important places—freedom is in need of criteria, grounds, "some authoritative measure to guide actions" and "integrate life." Eventually, Harries argues that the "Godhead" ("Authenticity," 29, 31) serves this function in Heidegger—a position that would, of course, be totally unacceptable to Sartre, for it would exhibit the "spirit of seriousness." One wonders if even Sartre's ethics of freedom can finally escape the "spirit of seriousness" (e.g., Sartre, *Being and Nothingness,* 626; *Notebooks,* 480). One wonders also whether, in the end, Heidegger would accept as "integrating center" the godhead which Harries assigns to him (29).

In regard to Harries's criticism, one may recall my earlier note that John Caputo similarly indicts the "call of conscience" in Heidegger's *Being and Time* for its emptiness in respect to "responsibility" to others, and for its lack of direction (Caputo, *Demythologizing Heidegger,* 76, 99, e.g.). See also Caputo's article "Heidegger's Scandal," in *The Heidegger Case,* ed. T. Rockmore and J. Margolis (Philadelphia: Temple University Press, 1992), which becomes Chapter 7 of *Demythologizing Heidegger.*

185. Sartre, "Existentialism Is a Humanism," 366. Simone de Beauvoir, who appears clearly to have read Sartre's *Notebooks* by 1948, seems to echo this: "By turning toward this freedom we . . . discover a principle of action whose range will be universal" (*Ethics of Ambiguity,* 23).

186. Sartre, "Existentialism Is a Humanism," 365–366, italics mine.

It is of interest to note, again, that there appears to be a parallel between Sartre's willing of freedom as "one thing" in authenticity and Kierkegaard's "purity of heart" as "to will one thing," just as—if Harries is right—there is a parallel between Heidegger's singular willing of one's guilty self (authenticity or purity of heart) and Kierkegaard's "purity of heart"; see, e.g., Harries, "Authenticity," 12, 29.

187. Sartre, "Existentialism Is a Humanism," 366, italics mine.

188. Ibid., 364.

189. Sartre, *Notebooks*, 11.

190. Ibid., 277.

191. Ibid., 277, 279, italics mine. For the sake of consistency and, I believe, Sartre's intention, I capitalize "Other" here in spite of the translation.

192. Ibid., 279.

193. Ibid., 278.

194. Ibid., 413.

195. Ibid., 11.

196. Ibid., 414.

197. Ibid., e.g., 277–284.

198. Ibid., e.g., 5, 60, 493.

199. Ibid., 279, italics mine.

200. de Beauvoir, *Ethics*, 32–33.

201. Sartre, *War Diaries*, 51.

202. In this regard, Arlette Elkaïm-Sartre appears to be correct when, in her "Notes" on *Truth and Existence*, she refers to the passage from *impure* to *pure* reflection as "moral conversion" (84).

203. The reader may recall that, as early as in *The Transcendence of the Ego*, Sartre sees the Ego as functioning "to mask from consciousness its very spontaneity" (100).

204. Sartre, *Notebooks*, 3–4.

205. Jeanson, *Sartre*, 194, 198, italics mine.

206. Ibid., 218.

207. Sartre, *Notebooks*, 493.

208. Sartre, *Being and Nothingness*, 444.

209. de Beauvoir, *Ethics of Ambiguity*, 33.

210. Sartre, *Cahiers,* 490.

211. Sartre, *Notebooks,* 478.

212. Ibid., 479.

213. Sartre, *War Diaries,* 51.

214. Sartre, *Notebooks,* 479.

215. In this regard, it is of interest to note (again) that the resolve to adopt freedom as mine, the will to live in accord with the freedom that one is—to *valorize* it existentially—provides for Sartre, as does "resoluteness" for Heidegger, an answer to what Harries, for one, labels authenticity's "call" for unity and "self-integration." Harries's suggestion that Sartre's "abstract freedom" does not allow (or deserve to be called) a "moral sense" ("Authenticity," 13), though not entirely without merit, rests, I believe, on an overinterpretation of the "abstractness" Harries attributes to Sartre's freedom. Sartre's notion of a spontaneous (uncaused) ontological freedom in *Being and Nothingness* does not—either there or in his later works—preclude or exclude all grounds for making responsible decisions and for "measuring" at the level of our existential and practical exercise of that freedom. But more needs to be said about this in other works. For the time being, the reader may note that Sartre's view of human reality as freedom, even in the forties, was not of a disembodied or pure consciousness, or of an abstract, unsituated freedom, completely independent of facticity or givens. (I say this notwithstanding passages in *Being and Nothingness* that clearly suggest it.) The reader may also note (again) that, in "Existentialism Is a Humanism," Sartre says specifically that "We will freedom for freedom's sake in and through particular circumstances" (366). And in the *Notebooks* he links the "authentic man of action" with "such and such particular circumstances" (507); tells us that "in attaining myself through conversion I have refused the abstract in order to will the concrete" (507); and assures us that "there is only an ethics in a situation and therefore it is concrete" (17). Moreover, as I tried to show in Chapter VI, the dialectical nature of the relation between freedom and facticities, freedom and the situation, freedom and circumstances, freedom and "nature," increases significantly during the progress of Sartre's writings. Certainly by the time of *Notebooks*

for an Ethics, freedom is "concrete" for Sartre, and Sartre indicts "abstract" morality (as we have seen).

216. Sartre, *The Transcendence of the Ego,* 44.

217. Sartre, *Notebooks,* 6.

218. Ibid., 5–6.

219. Ibid., 559.

220. Sartre, *Truth and Existence,* 84, sic!

221. Sartre, *Notebooks,* 468.

222. Ibid., 472.

223. Ibid., 356.

224. Ibid., 469.

225. Ibid., 382, italics mine.

226. Ibid., 471.

227. Ibid., 470.

228. Ibid., 475.

229. E.g., ibid., 474.

230. Ibid., 473.

231. Sartre, *Cahiers,* 489.

232. Ibid., translation mine. Pellauer translates this as "to uphold through the bad faith my complicity" (Sartre, *Notebooks,* 473).

233. Sartre, *Notebooks,* 474.

234. Ibid., 472, 559, 37.

235. See, e.g., ibid., 470–479. It is important to note, however, that in *Being and Nothingness* and elsewhere Sartre also speaks of certain forms of reflection as being "in bad faith" (e.g., *Being and Nothingness,* 161; "This reflection [making the reflected on appear as an object for the reflective] is in bad faith."

236. Sartre, *Notebooks,* 12. In *Being and Nothingness,* Sartre seems to speak to this point by saying that "reflection" is in bad faith insofar as it constitutes itself as "the revelation of *the object* which I *make-to-be-me*" (161). Although this is helpful in understanding Sartre, it does not eliminate the problem I am developing here. If anything, it appears to anticipate the problem related to Sartre's applying "bad faith" to "reflection."

237. Sartre, *Notebooks,* 469.

238. Ibid., 469. In a related (but not directly relevant) passage, Sartre says the following: "consciousness looks for its Me among things, without finding it there" (513).

239. Sartre, *The Transcendence of the Ego*, 44.

240. Sartre, *Being and Nothingness*, 153. Italicizing of *second* is mine. But, again, let me acknowledge that Sartre in *Being and Nothingness* also allows that reflection is sometimes in bad faith (161). And he conveys the distinct impression that impure reflection is in bad faith (160–161). I shall say more about this later in this chapter.

241. Sartre, *Notebooks*, 370.

242. Ibid., 380.

243. Sartre, *Being and Nothingness*, 474.

244. de Beauvoir, *Ethics*, 26.

245. Sartre, *Being and Nothingness*, 412, 627.

246. Sartre, *Cahiers*, 18.

247. Sartre, *Notebooks*, 12.

248. Sartre, *Cahiers*, 18.

249. E.g., Sartre, *Being and Nothingness*, 473.

250. Ibid., 473, italics mine.

251. Ibid., 161.

252. Ibid., 473.

253. Ibid., 443.

254. Sartre, *Notebooks*, 474.

255. Ibid., 5.

256. Sartre, *Cahiers*, 495.

257. Sartre, *Notebooks*, 478–479.

258. Ibid., 479.

259. Ibid., 12; cf. *Being and Nothingness*, 473.

260. Sartre, *Notebooks*, 12, 559.

261. Ibid., 474.

262. Sartre, *Being and Nothingness*, 70, italics mine.

263. Note, for example, that Sartre speaks of "bad faith" as "faith" that "*includes in its original project* its own negation" (ibid., 68, italics mine). Sartre, as we saw earlier, speaks of this original project as a "spontaneous determination of our being" (ibid., 68), a "type of being

in the world" which "tends to perpetuate itself" and from which it is difficult "to wake oneself up" (ibid.). This is why, for Sartre, it is so easy to continue to act in bad faith, and why also a "radical conversion" through reflection is necessary. (*Notebooks*, e.g., 359).

264. Sartre, *Being and Nothingness*, 68.

265. See Chapters 2 and 3, especially, of the present book for my consideration and reconstruction of Sartre's analysis.

266. Sartre, *Being and Nothingness*, 68.

267. Sartre, *Notebooks*, 560.

268. Sartre, *Being and Nothingness*, 473.

269. Sartre, *Notebooks*, 12.

270. Sartre, *Being and Nothingness*, 70.

271. Sartre, *Notebooks*, 6; *Cahiers*, 13.

272. Sartre, *Notebooks*, 4.

273. Sartre, *Being and Nothingness*, 70, 68.

274. Sartre, *Notebooks*, 559.

275. Ibid., 478–479, 472.

276. Ibid., 559.

277. Sartre, *Being and Nothingness*, 70.

278. E.g., Sartre, *Notebooks*, 12.

279. Ibid., 359, 479. I have already pointed out that Sartre also uses this notion of consciousness' "waking [itself] up" in *Being and Nothingness* (68, for example).

280. See, e.g., ibid., 472, 499, 559–560.

Index